I0812853

POSTCARD HISTORY SERIES

San Luis Obispo and Cal Poly

in Vintage Postcards

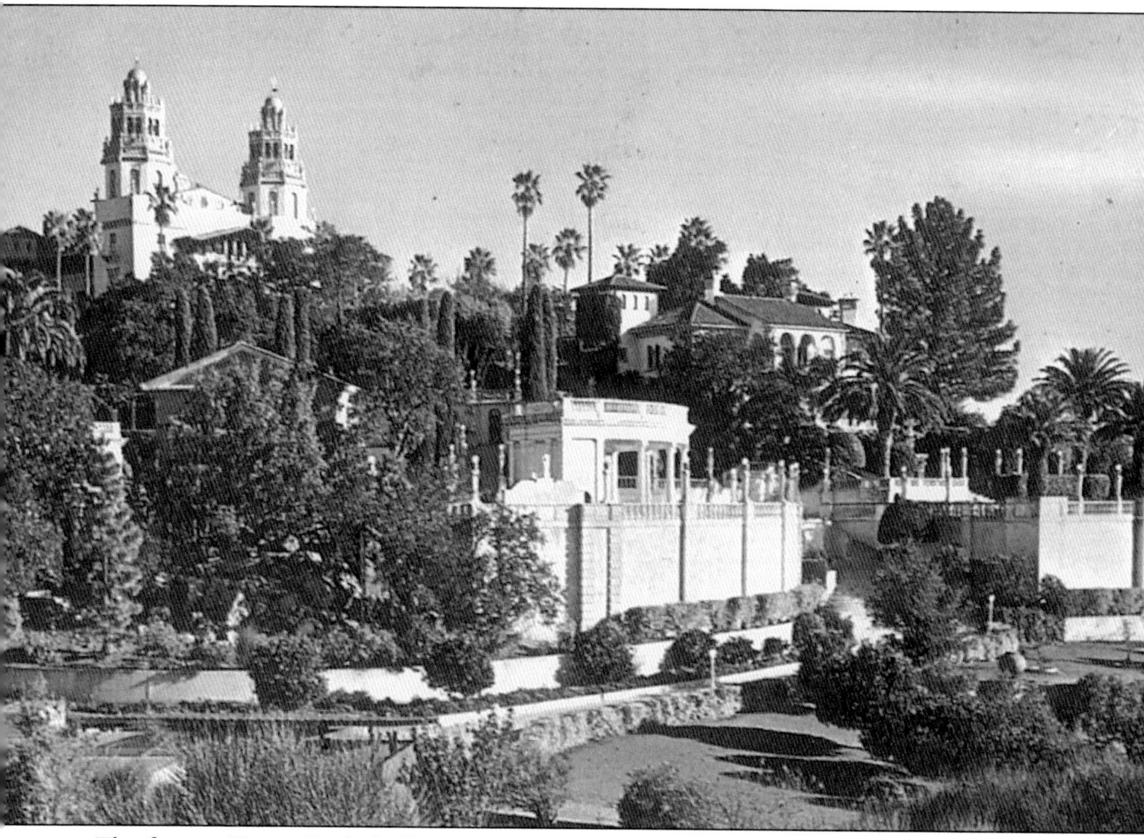

The famous Hearst Castle in San Simeon was built from 1922 to 1927 under the direction of the world famous architect Julia Morgan. William Randolph Hearst had wanted to construct a lavish and monumental estate along with his 130-room mansion, which he was quite successful in doing. The fantastic gardens became the home of more than exotic plants and flowers. Three guest houses are located within their boundaries, which today contain in their own right an extensive amount of artwork that compliments the holding in the main house. The bell towers of the mansion, which stand out above the tree line, contain two bedrooms, both filled with unbelievable luxuries. The Hearst Castle is now one of the California State Historical Monuments and can be easily accessed from Pacific Coast Highway 1. It attracts hundreds of thousands of visitors each year.

POSTCARD HISTORY SERIES

San Luis Obispo and Cal Poly

in Vintage Postcards

Thomas Maxwell-Long

ARCADIA
PUBLISHING

ISBN 978-0-7385-0811-5

Published by Arcadia Publishing
Charleston, South Carolina

Printed in the United States of America

Library of Congress Catalog Card Number: 00-111087

For all general information contact Arcadia Publishing at:
Telephone 843-853-2070
Fax 843-853-0044
E-Mail sales@arcadiapublishing.com
For customer service and orders:
Toll-Free 1-888-313-2665

Visit us on the Internet at www.arcadiapublishing.com

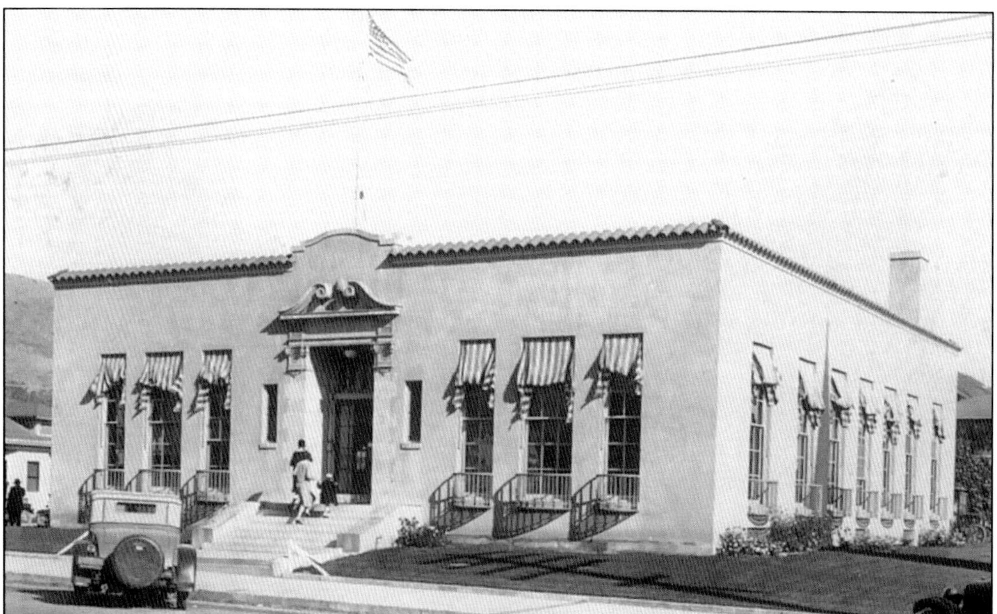

Pictured is the "New Post Office" built after World War I in downtown San Luis Obispo.

Contents

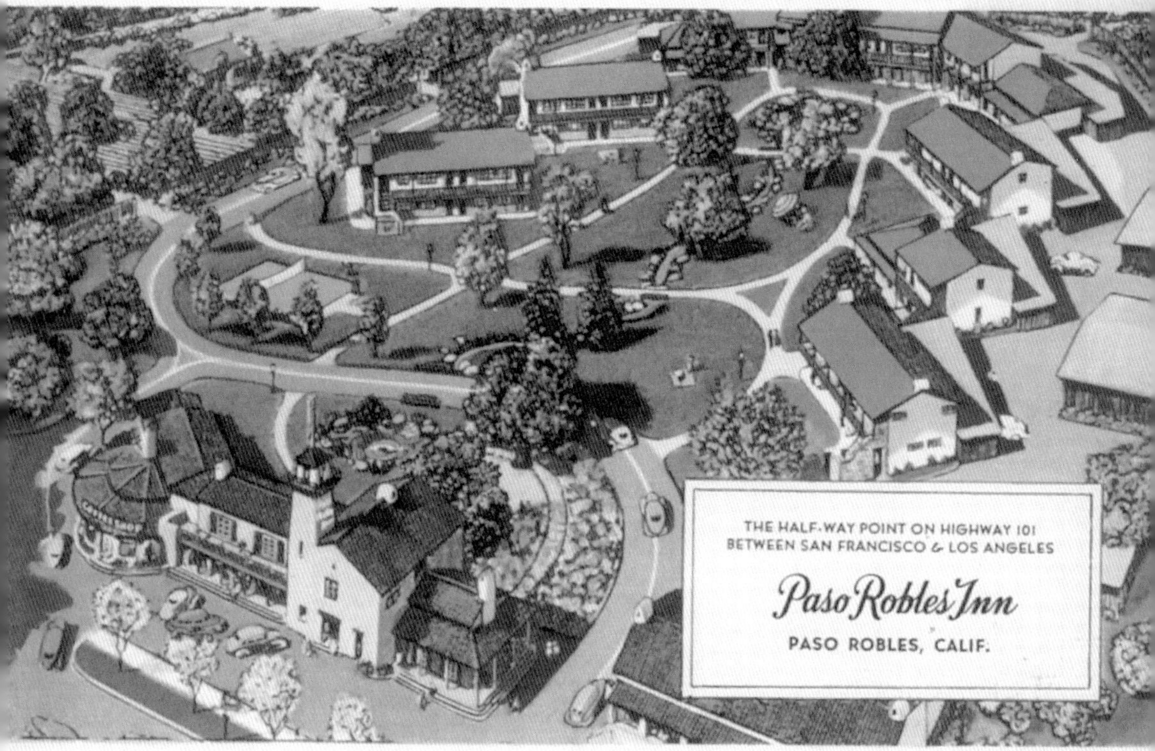

The magnificent Paso Robles Inn, whose history began back in 1857 with James and Daniel Blackburn. At the turn of the century a hot springs bath was added, which was claimed along with the rest of the Paso Robles Inn by a tragic fire in 1940. This postcard commemorates the rebuilt Paso Robles Inn, which was under construction for two years, and re-opened for business in 1942. As the postcard notes, the Inn is located at the half-way point between Los Angeles and San Francisco.

ACKNOWLEDGMENTS

I would like to offer special thanks to Lloyd Jones for his generosity in letting me use his (Aston) family's postcards. Also, great thanks to Max Bakke for allowing me to incorporate some of his collection into this book, and for the hours of historical perspectives on San Luis Obispo, which have proven to be of even greater value. Additionally, I would like to thank Gordon M. Bakken for helping me put together the time needed to assemble this book, as well as his unmatched, expert historical advice, which made the entire process much smoother for me. Lastly, I would like to express my deepest gratitude to my wife, Roberta, for having such great patience throughout this entire project.

INTRODUCTION

San Luis Obispo is located nearly equidistant between San Francisco and Los Angeles along the California Coastline. The flora-covered mountains, rolling hills, and sweeping valleys make this land one of the most beautiful points on the West Coast. According to archaeological evidence, man began to occupy this region and tap its abundant natural resources around 1400 BCE. These first inhabitants of the Mid-California Chaparral country were the Chumash and Salinan Indians.

Nearly 3,000 years went by before these California Indians would encounter European explorers in search of adventure and riches in the New World. Only 50 years after Christopher Columbus departed Spain in search of a new route for trade with India, another explorer of the Spanish monarchy encountered what is today San Luis Obispo.

In the winter of 1542, Captain Juan Rodriguez Cabrillo navigated two ships into Morro Bay. This Portuguese sailor and his crew, under the flag of Spain, became the first Europeans to see the Central Coast of California. By the mid-18th century San Luis Obispo had been the object of nearly a half-dozen explorations by various white men. In 1769, serious settlement in California by the Spanish began.

The year 1769 marks the genesis of Spanish occupation of California. Under the auspices of its first governor, Gaspar de Portola, this western land began to be scouted and surveyed, in search of riches and natural resources that could add to the wealth of the Spanish Crown. In 1772, Father Junipero Serra established the Mission San Luis Obispo de Tolosa—California's fifth mission—along a stream, and so began the official settlement of the land as San Luis Obispo.

In 1822 Mexico achieved full independence from Spain, and California became part of that new nation. The victory of the United States in the Mexican-American War in 1848 brought California along with other great stretches of western land under the champion's flag. November 13th of the following year, the California Republic adopted a constitution and on September 9, 1850, California was admitted to the Union as a state, with San Luis Obispo as one of the original 27 counties.

These fantastic postcards cover the transition that San Luis Obispo made from being a 19th-century community to a city at the dawn of the 20th century. In no small part of this growth process was the emergence of the Progressive Era's "scientifically designed" California Polytechnic School, which today is the California Polytechnic State University, or simply Cal Poly. This was the foundation period of contemporary San Luis Obispo. The arrival of the railroad, the development of the Union Oil of California's (Unocal) oil fields, and the tremendous agricultural and dairy industries all fed the development of San Luis Obispo. The first ten years of the 20th century cemented the wealth of SLO, as it became a center of trade in central California.

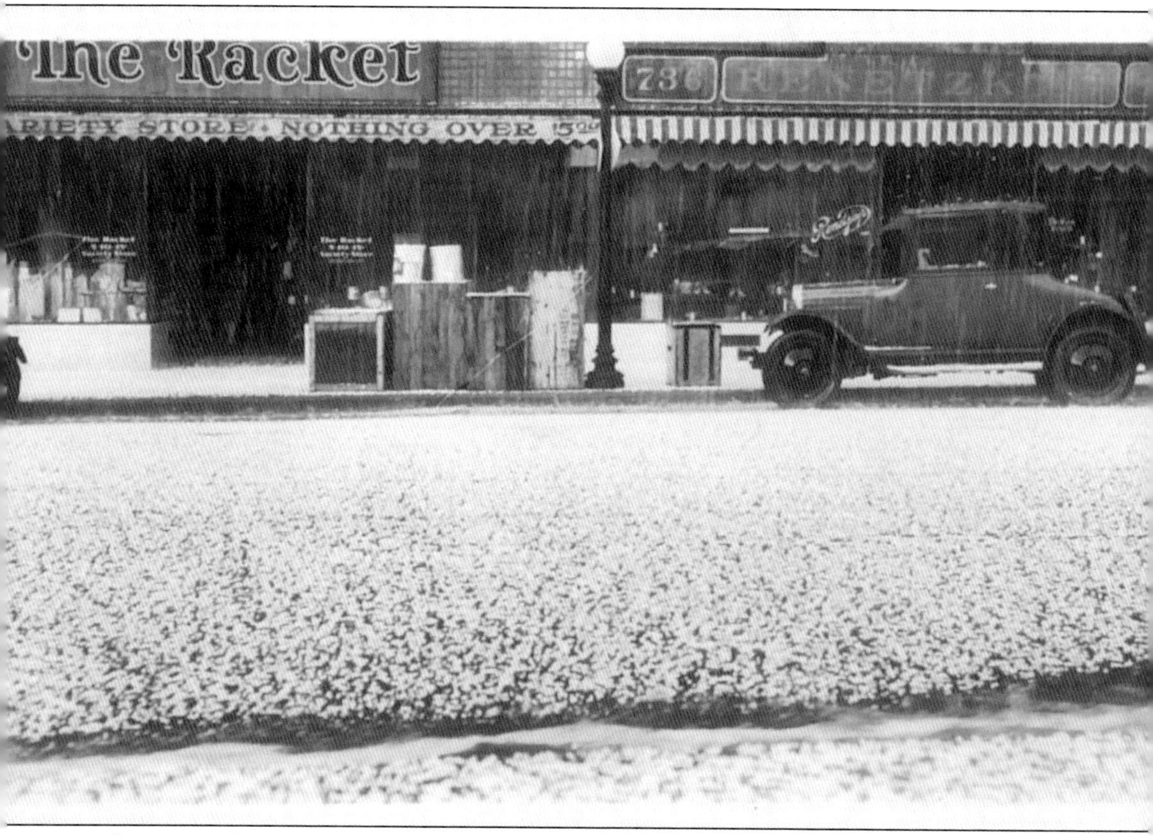

This postcard captures the great hailstorm of San Luis Obispo on June 6, 1922. Insurance photographer Frank Aston captured this moment in history, believing that "many people would be filing claims for broken windows, damaged automobiles or who knows what." His instincts were proven correct: he had over 20 requests to photograph damaged property from this storm.

Part I

San Luis Obispo

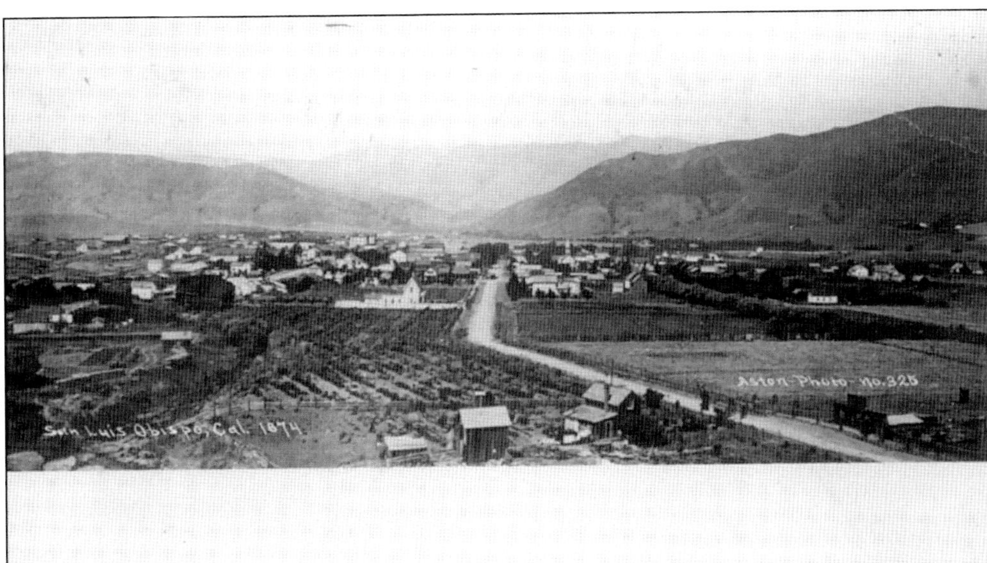

Not far from being a "one-road" town in 1874, the agricultural heritage of San Luis Obispo is apparent in this postcard as the majority of the land in the central basin is dedicated to farming. The Spanish Mission settlement has not grown much since its founding one hundred years prior.

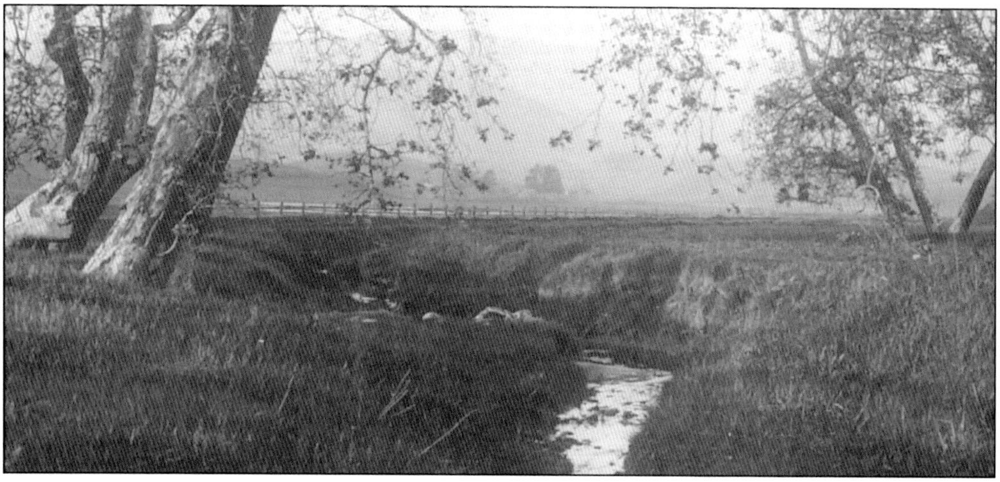

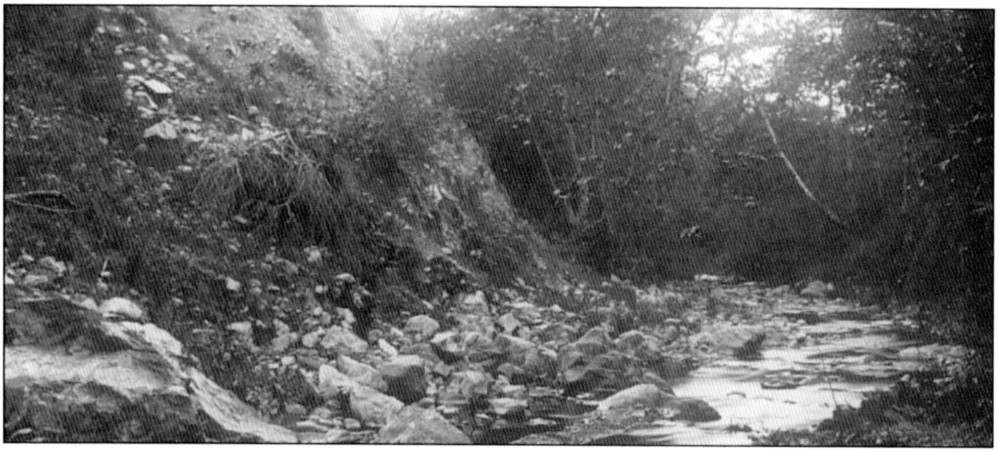

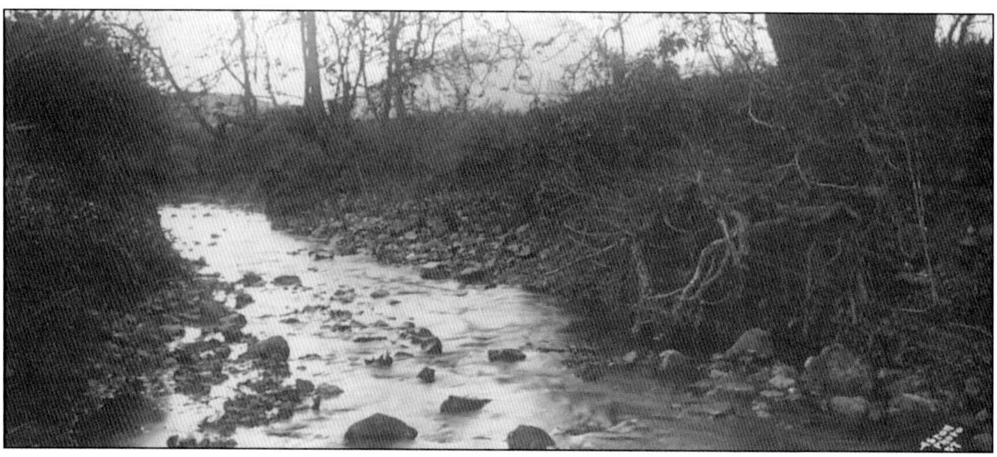

The San Luis Creek not only brought the necessary fresh water that the Father Junipero Serra needed for farming, but also provided access to meats. The first inhabitants of the Mission were able to fish year round and hunt for a variety of game. The creek was essential in the formation of the community at the early stages of development.

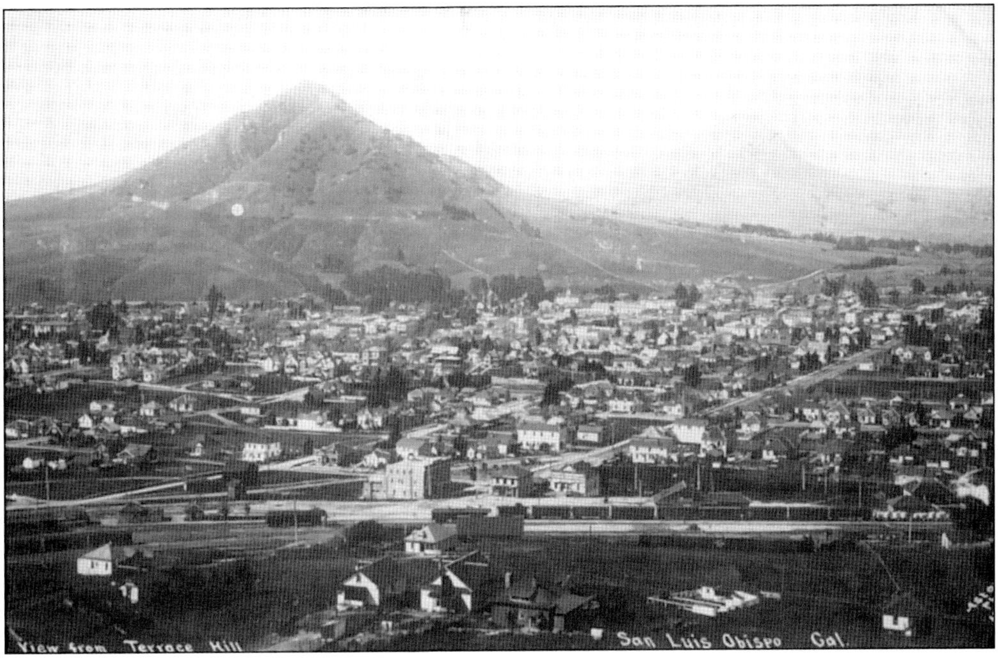

These images, taken in 1902 from atop Terrace Hill, are a testament to the fantastic growth of San Luis Obispo. This booming period began with the arrival of the stagecoach in the 1860s and skyrocketed as the first of the Southern Pacific Rail Roads or "Iron Horses" in the late 1880s replaced the beast-driven mode of transportation.

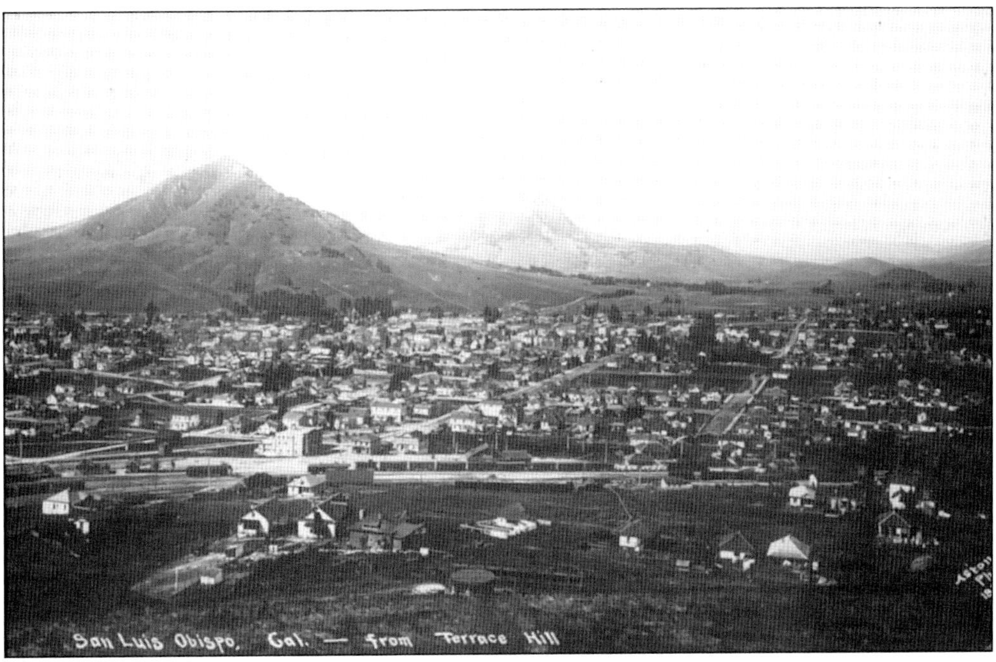

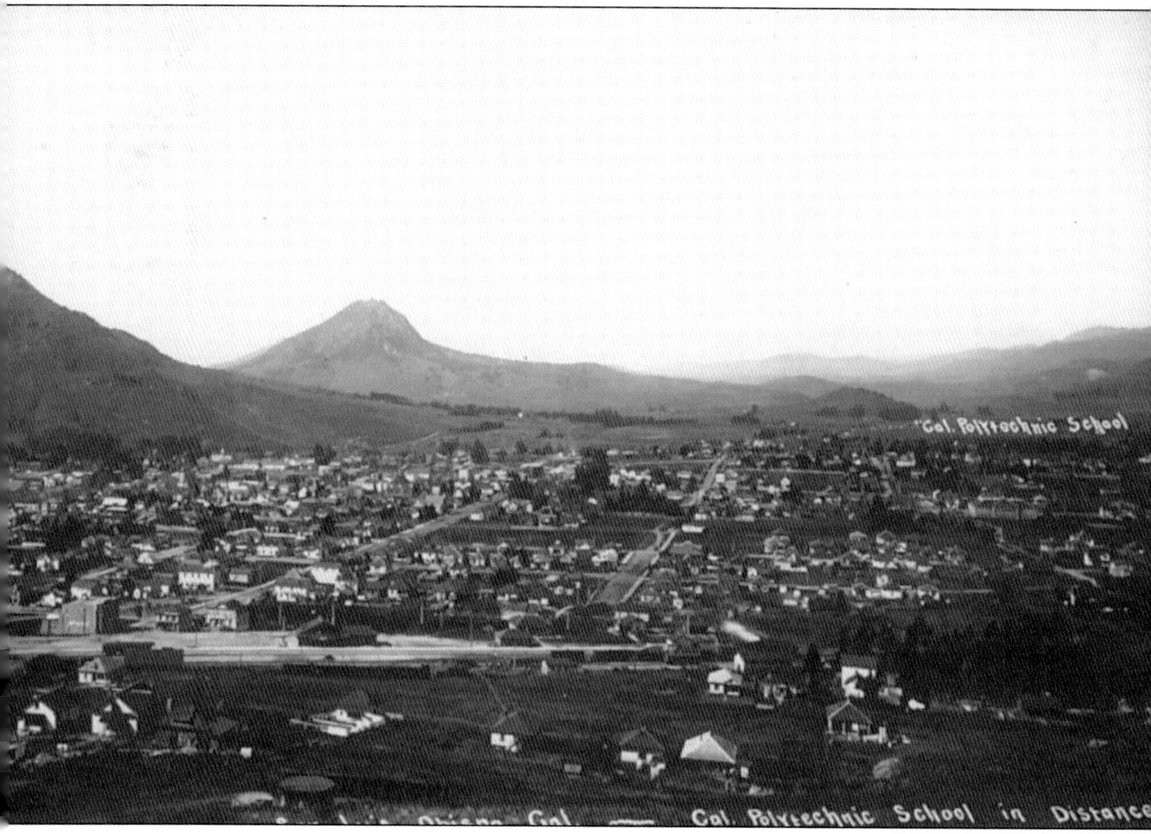

The significance of Cal Poly was anticipated even before the first classes began. This picture was taken in 1902, one year prior to the first day of class in October 1903. Note the location of the school in the distance. It appears isolated on its original 220-acre agricultural campus, which today is nearly 10-times in size.

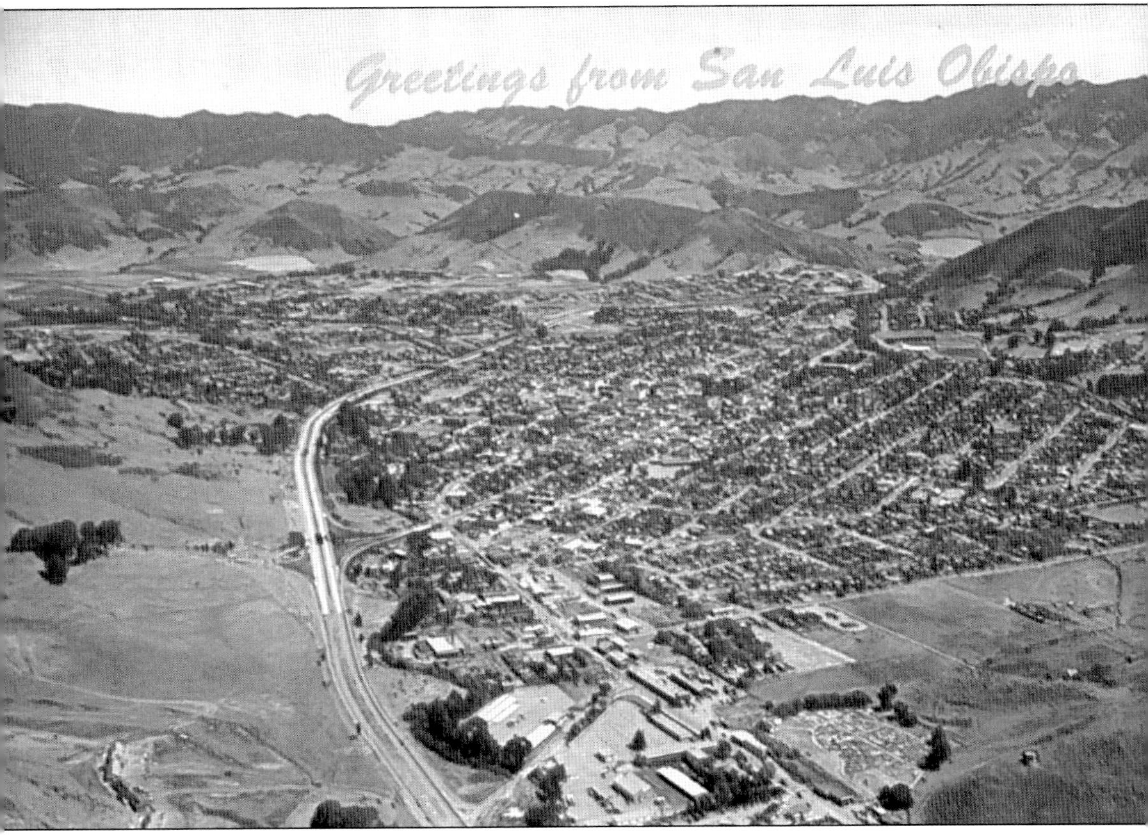

This postcard from the early 1960s is of a San Luis Obispo with a population of nearly 30,000 inhabitants. Cal Poly is hardly distinguishable in this postcard, located at the upper left-hand side of the city itself. U.S. Highway 101 and California State Highway 1 connect on the south part of town; the two highways' routes directly through the city played a vital role in its development.

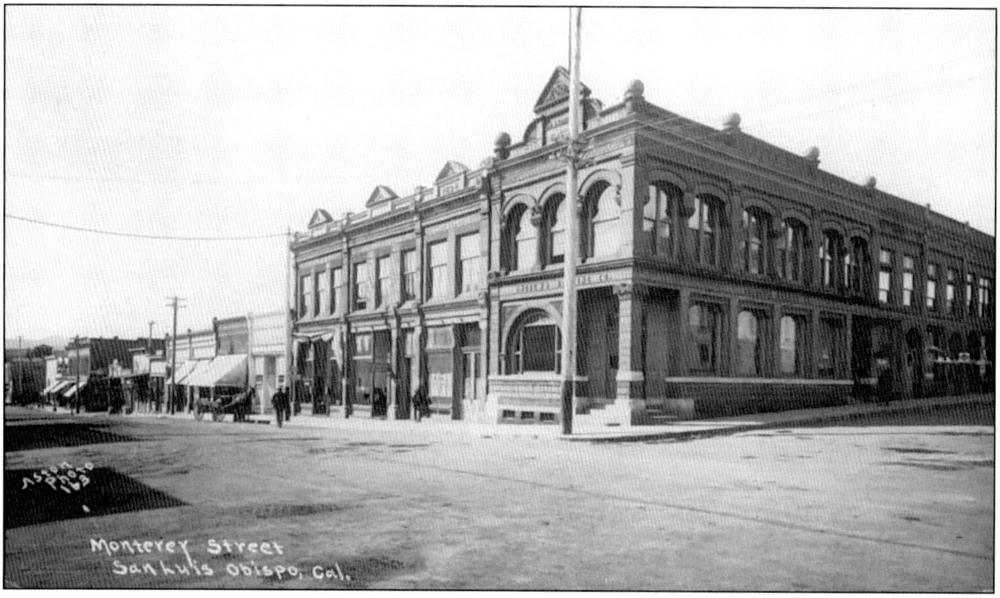

Monterey Street was the center of commerce and trade in 1899 as the J.P. Andrews building's architectural prowess suggests. On the left-hand side is the former centerpiece of San Luis Obispo's 19th-century downtown; the Central Hotel is dwarfed in comparison. Within the Andrews Building is the Luis Steen Electric Light Fixtures Company, and its lone electric wire crossing Monterey Street.

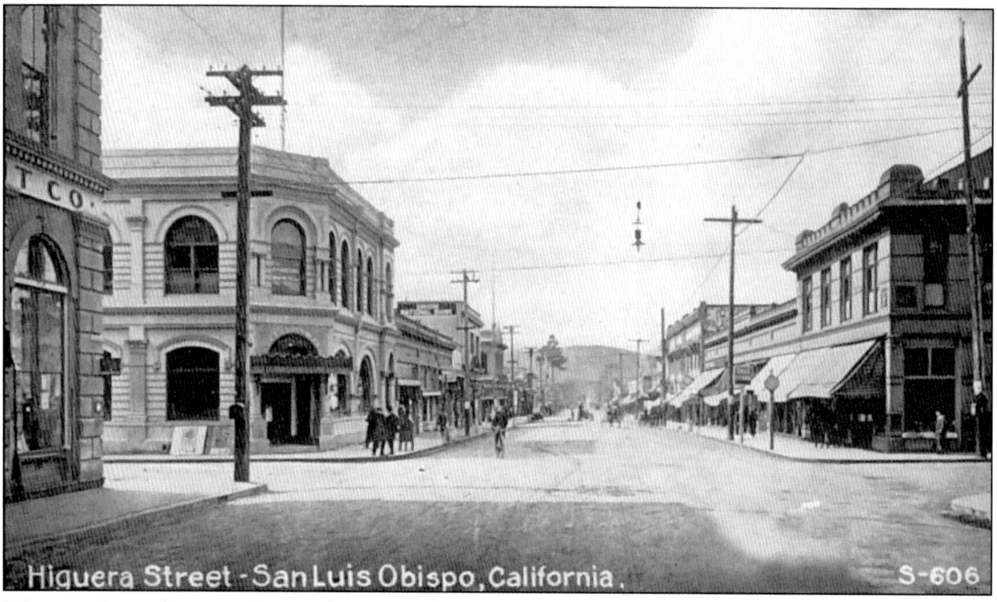

Higuera Street became the city's "second" street by 1910. At the time of this postcard, 1911, over 40 businesses occupied this wide road, which was designed to provide an eight-horse team ample space to make a U-turn at any point in the business district. Note the electric light over the intersection, which appears to be suspended in mid-air. This safety feature added in 1909 was illuminated during the first four hours of darkness each night, and the first two hours before dawn the next morning.

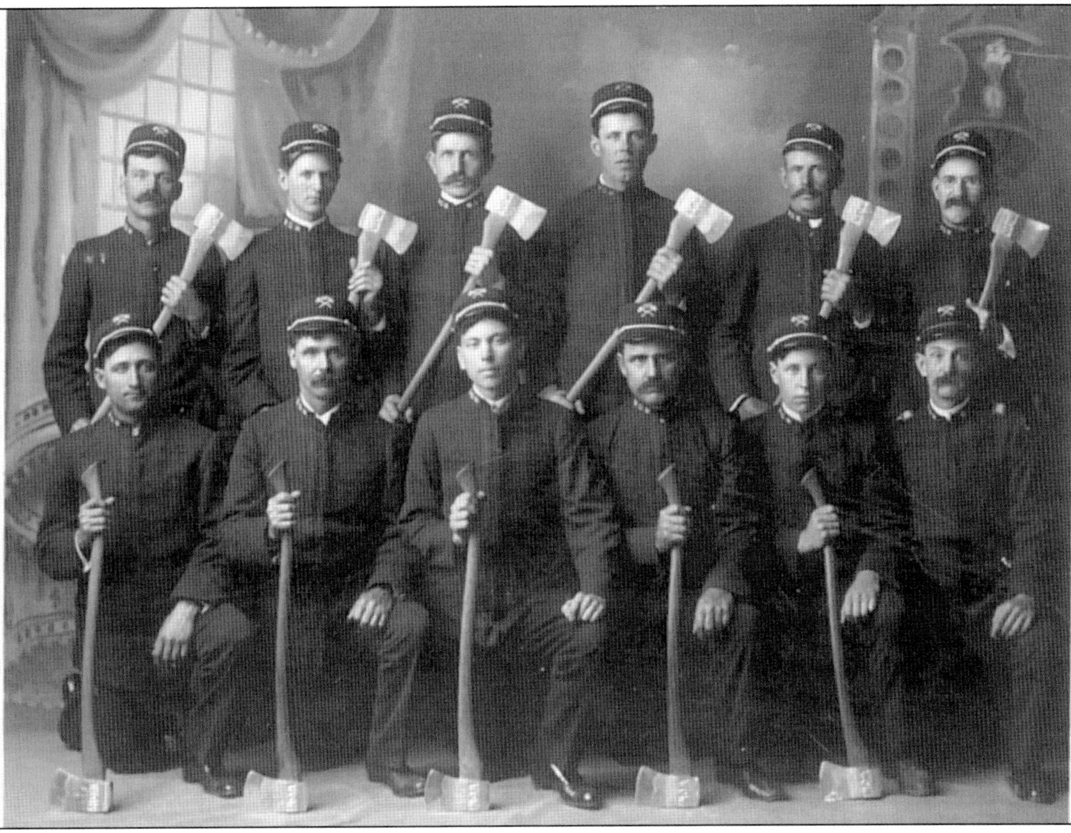

Pictured above are San Luis Obispo's first "professional volunteer fire fighters." The California National Guard had trained these brave men, and this photo commemorates their successful completion of training and subsequent initiation in 1900. By 1917 their numbers increased to 25, as being a member of the team was a well-respected pursuit.

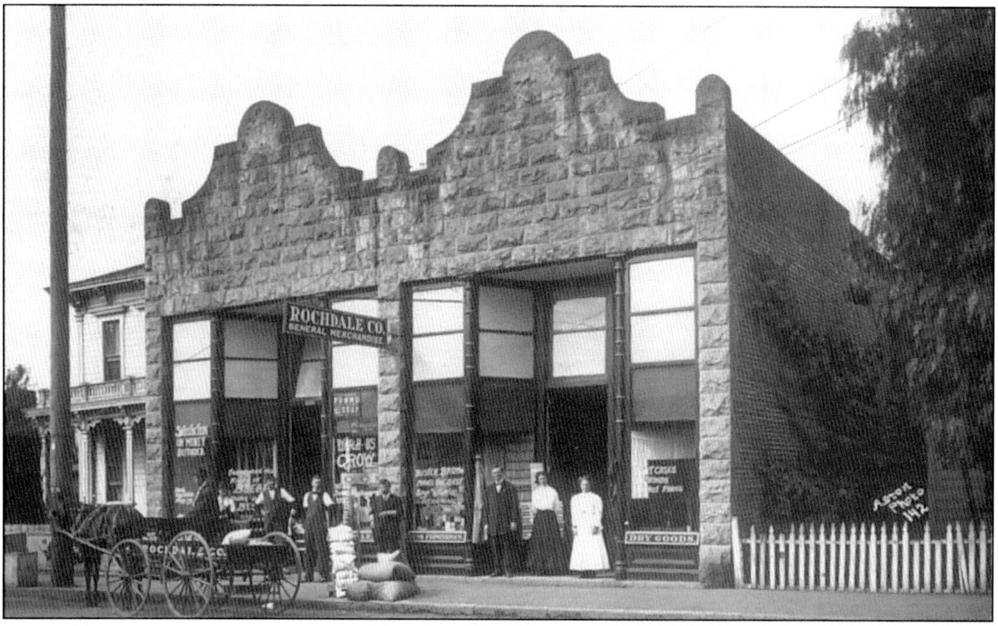

Rochdale Company, General Merchandise was San Luis Obispo's first authentic all-goods store. With the sale of food products, home furnishings, dry goods, clothing, and nearly anything else that Mr. Rochdale (pictured in the center wearing gloves) could sell to the public. This full service merchant even delivered his goods via horse and buggy. Postcard image taken in 1902.

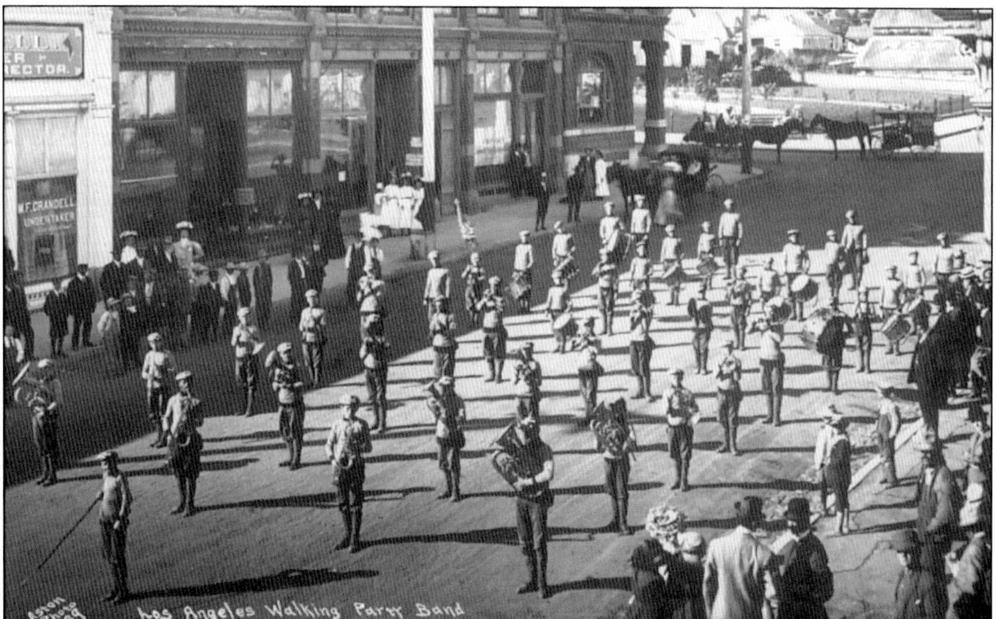

The Los Angeles Walking Party Band parades through the downtown in 1901. Interesting to take notice of are the members of the band, which included in their ranks African Americans.

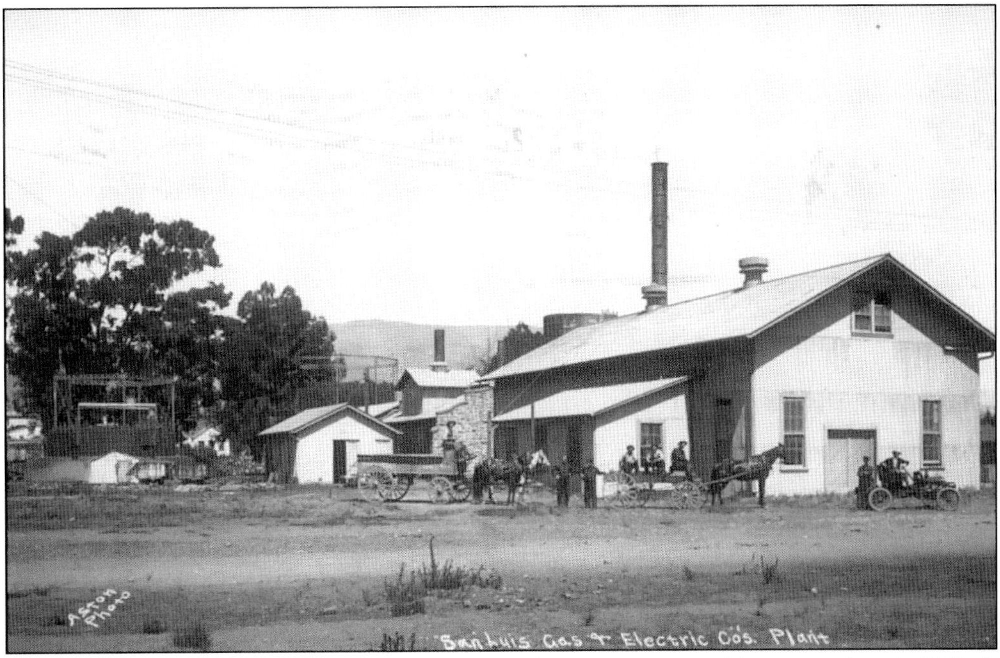

The San Luis Gas and Electric Company completed construction on this power plant in 1903. It was the sole generator of power for San Luis Obispo until 1905, at which time Cal Poly built its own power plant.

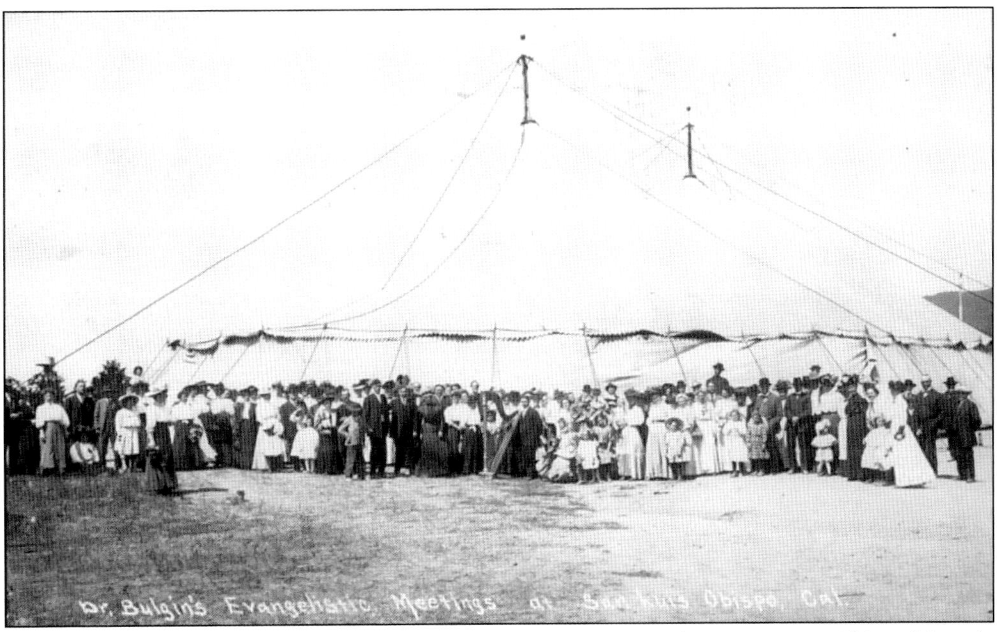

In 1905 the "Spiritual and Evangelical Leader" Dr. Bulgin brought to San Luis Obispo his style of "Christian re-Birth." These retreats were typically four-day events, which focused on the Christian's duty of hard-work, bible reading, and brotherly love. The Dr. Bulgin pulpit preached "only the most true to Christ's teachings would find success in this life, and reward in the next." The minister is standing to the immediate right of the harp.

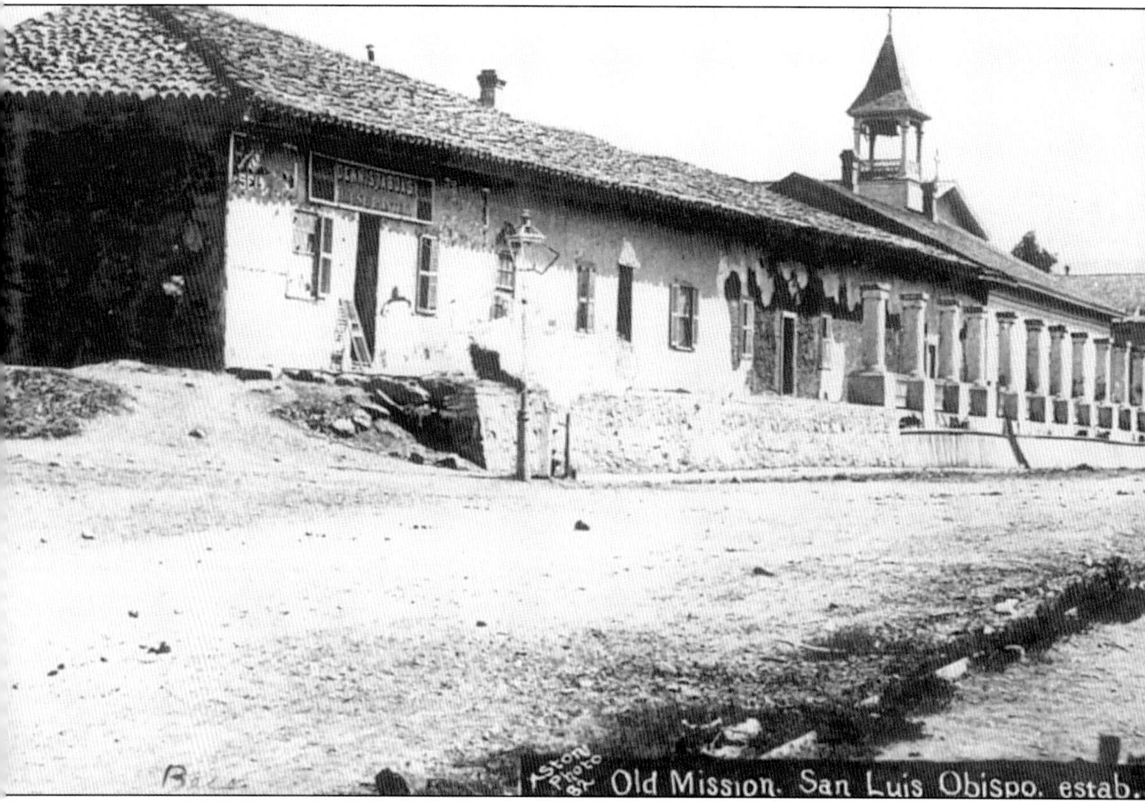

This 1903 photo of the "Old Mission of San Luis Obispo" records the first efforts in the 20th century at restoring the building. Even though the Mission had become somewhat dilapidated over the course of 125 years, Roman Catholic Mass was held there, without interruption. The painter in charge of this early restoration, Dennis Taboas, has his company sign hanging over the rear entry.

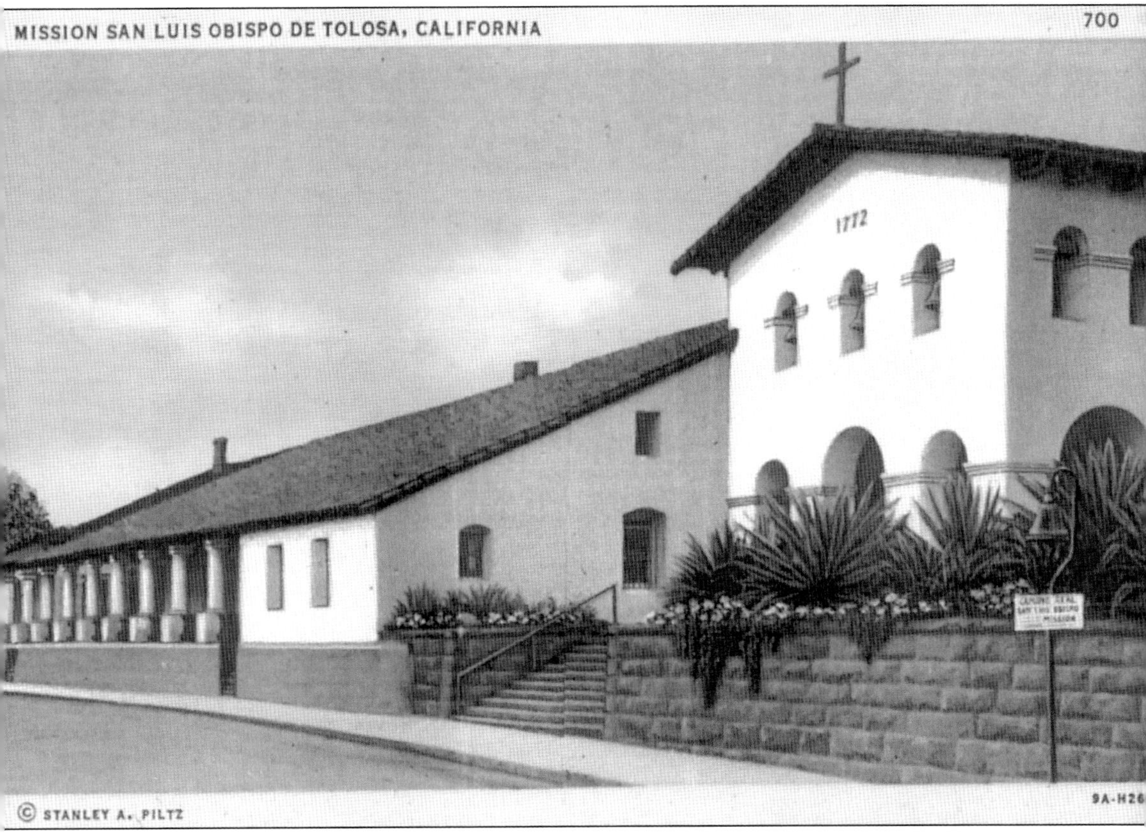

This artist rendition of the Mission in 1950 shows the completely restored building, which after World War II became the central tourist attraction of the city. Nearly 100,000 visitors were drawn to this spot in 1951, with each successive year witnessing more and more tourists.

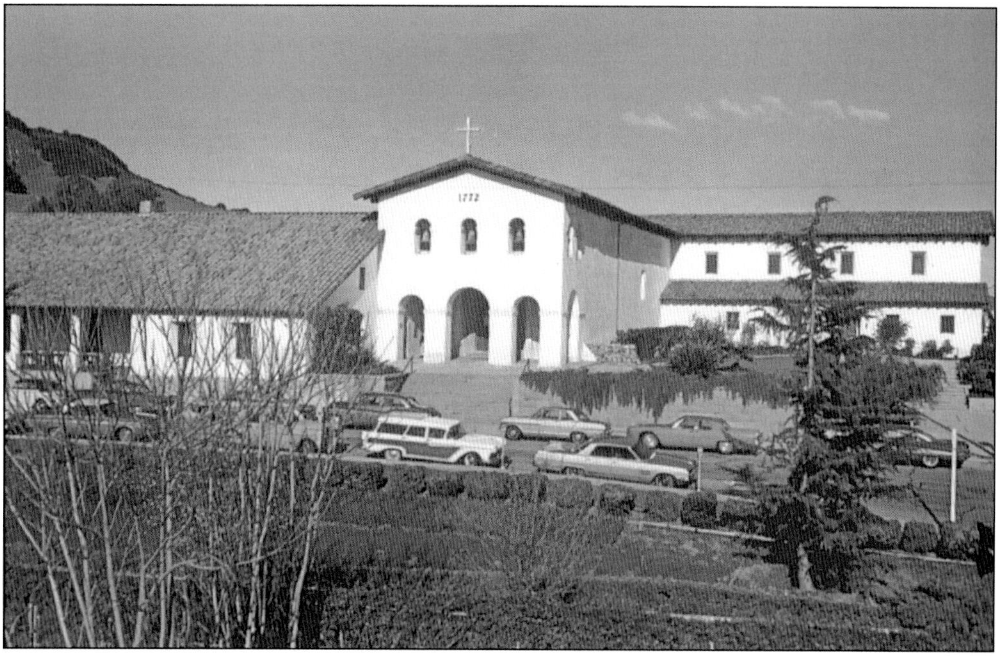

The utilization of the Mission as a Catholic church continues today. This is a 1960s postcard of a Sunday Mass in progress at the Mission.

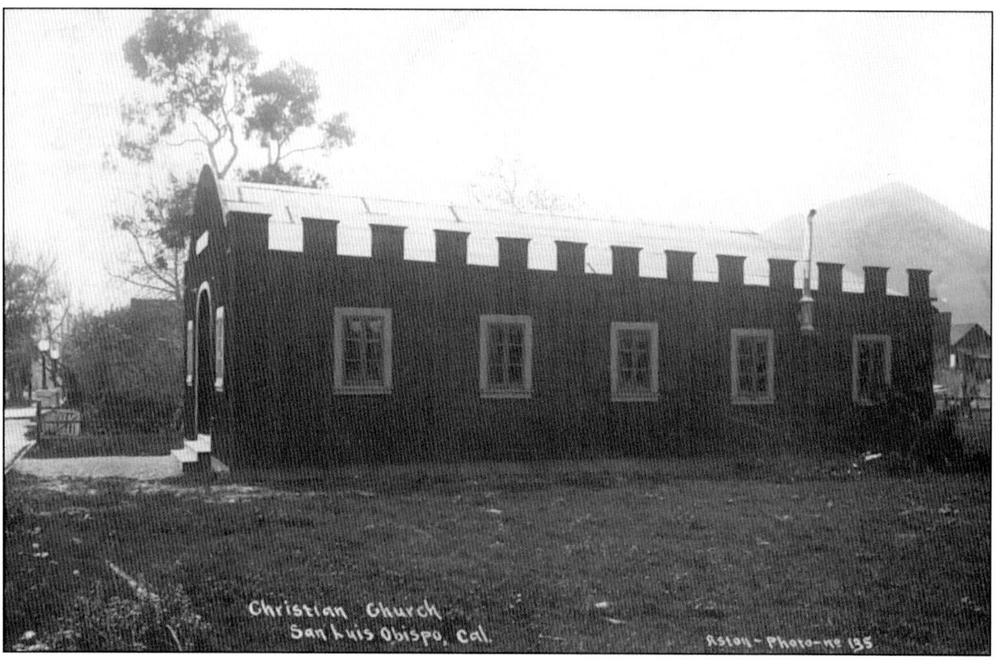

The Christian "non-denominational" church of San Luis Obispo had just recently completed the addition of their heater and boiler when this photograph was taken, *c.* 1905.

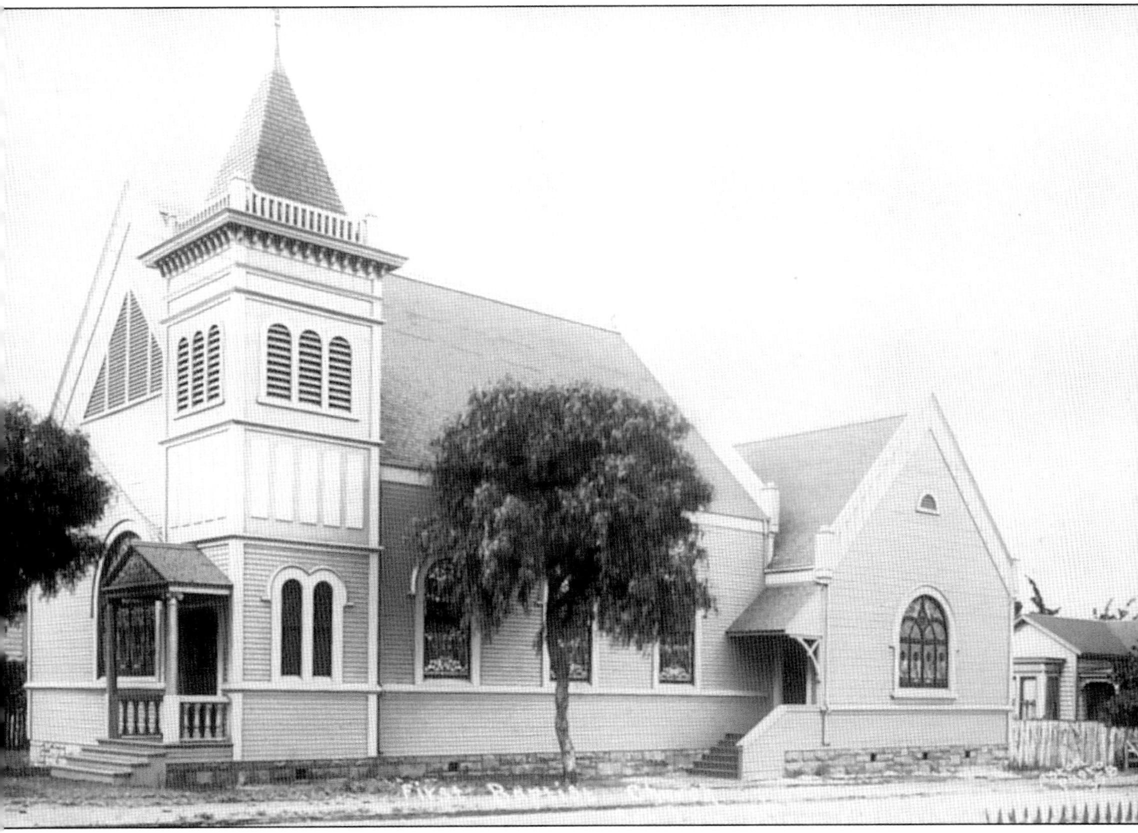

For many years the "pride" of San Luis Obispo's dedication to religion was reflected in the fine and well-kept First Baptist Church. This photo was taken in 1908.

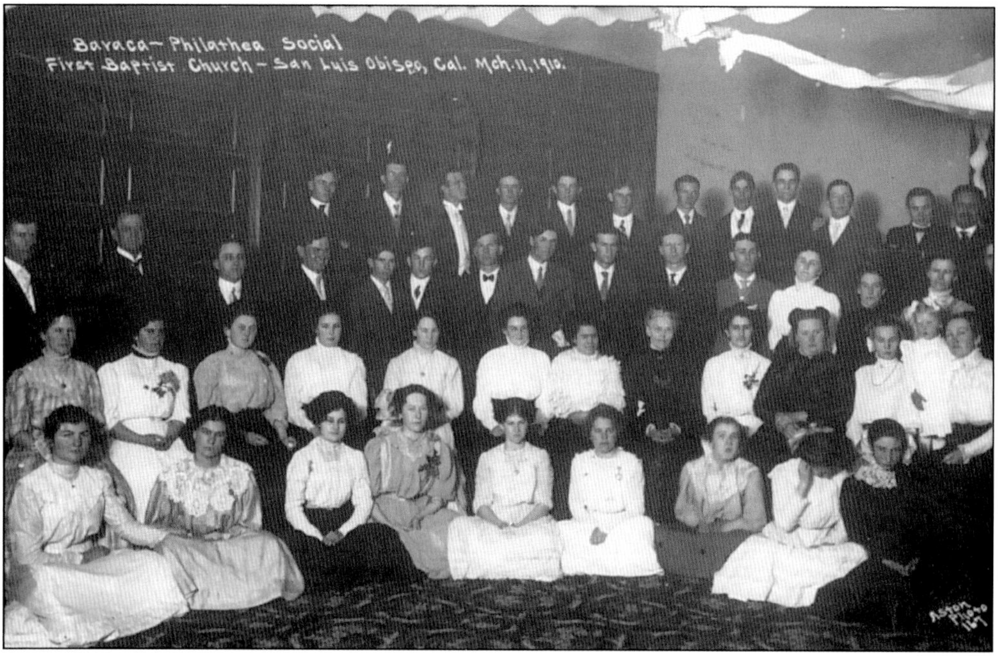

The extremely active congregation of the First Baptist Church holding one of its Baraca-Philathea Socials, on March 11, 1910. The First Baptist Church boasted a congregation of over 1,000 souls by the year 1912, making it the second largest fold in San Luis Obispo at that time.

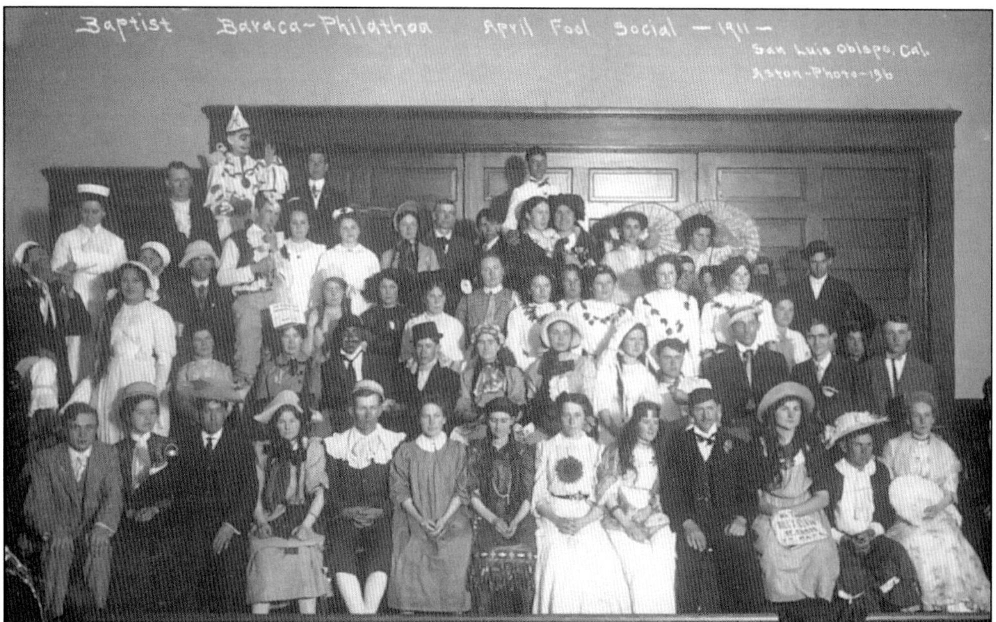

The First Baptist Church's Baraca-Philathea "Special April Fool's Social" on April 1, 1911, attracted such a large number of participants that the event spilled outside of the hall and onto the grounds of the church.

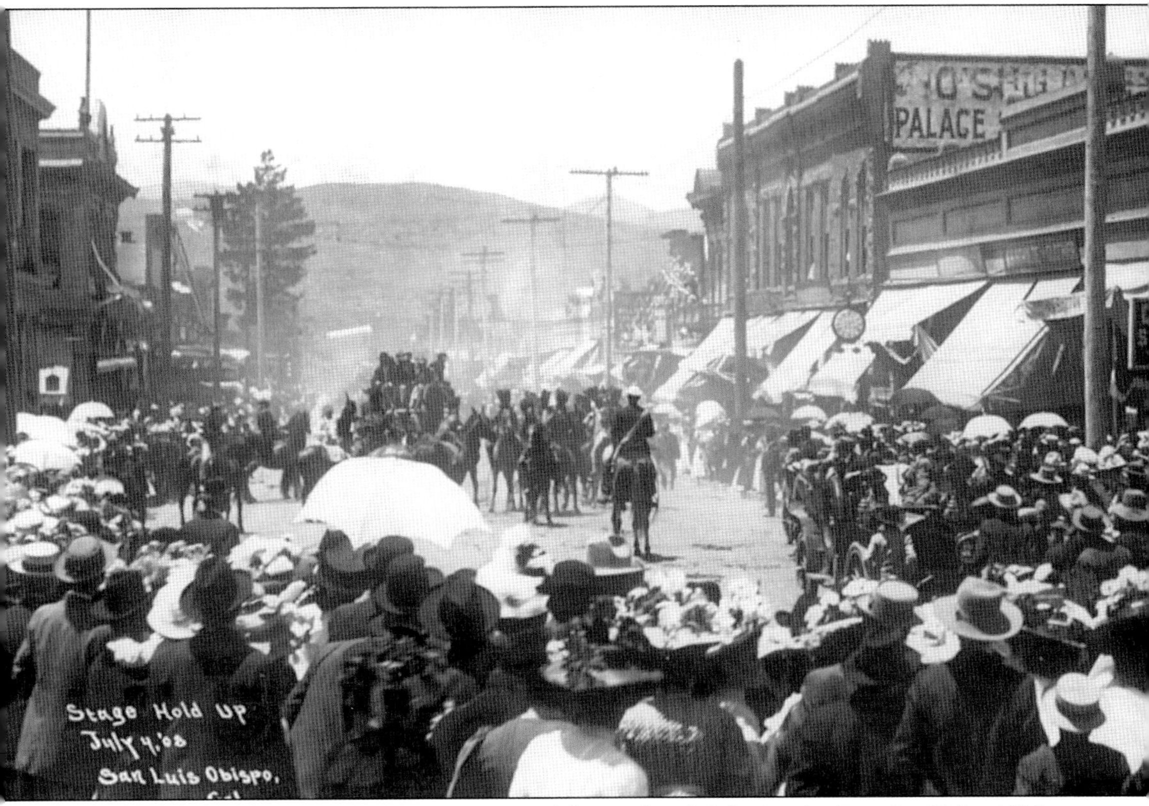

San Luis Obispo was not a town that focused solely on church life. On the Fourth of July, 1908, the city put on quite a show in the downtown. Beyond the typical parades and band music, a stagecoach hold-up was reenacted. However, things went amiss when the actors depicting Indians were intoxicated beyond their ability to control themselves. When one of these "Indians" accidentally injured another, a fight broke out. The downtown crowd, unaware that the entire event was staged, contributed to the action by attacking two of the "Indians." One man was accidentally shot, another fell off his horse; neither man suffered any severe injuries and therefore no legal charges were brought up.

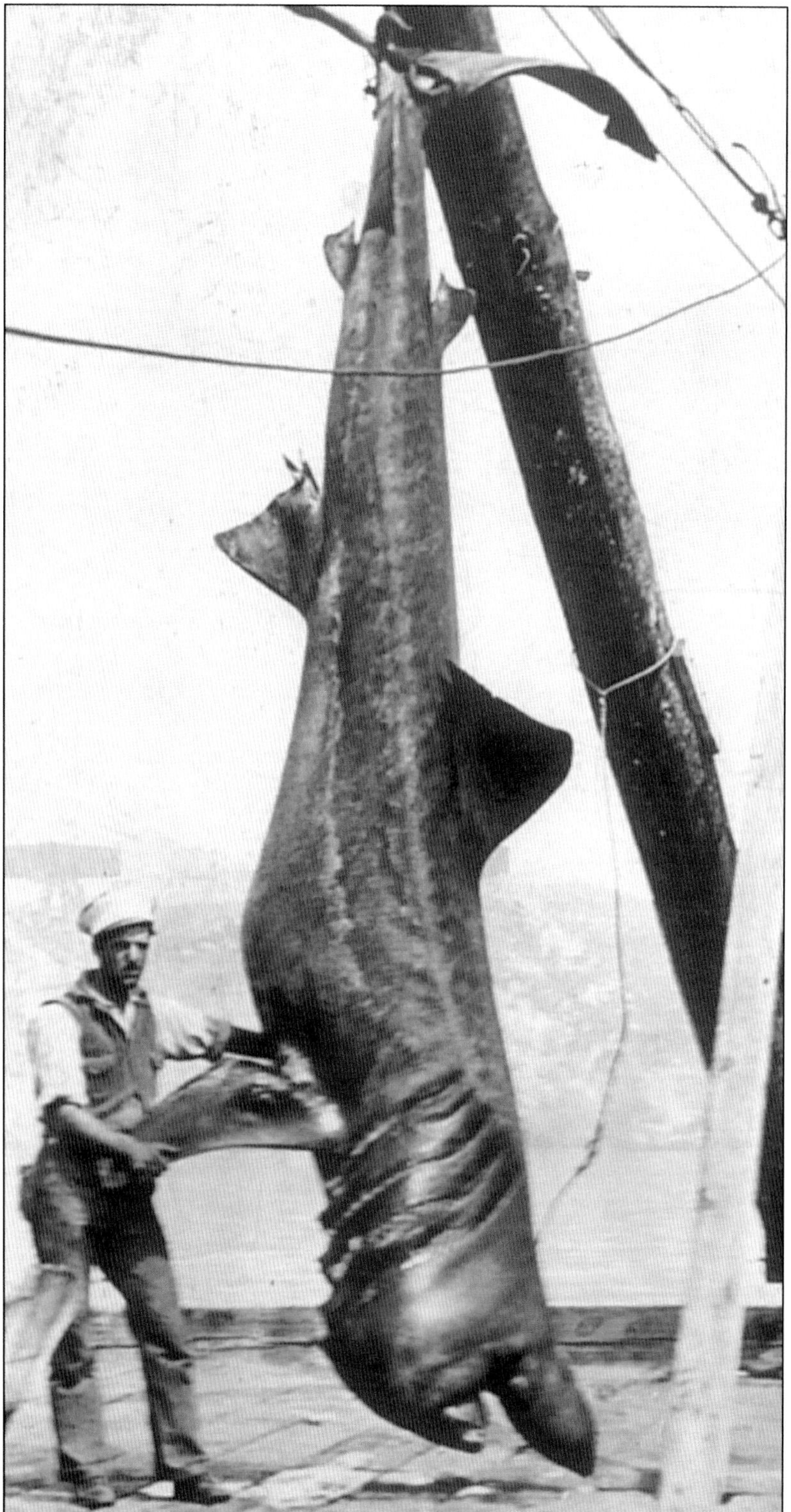

This 20-foot basking shark was caught off the Pismo Beach coast in 1906, and led to many shore-fishermen pouring onto charter boats attempting to catch another one of the Pacific Oceans great fish.

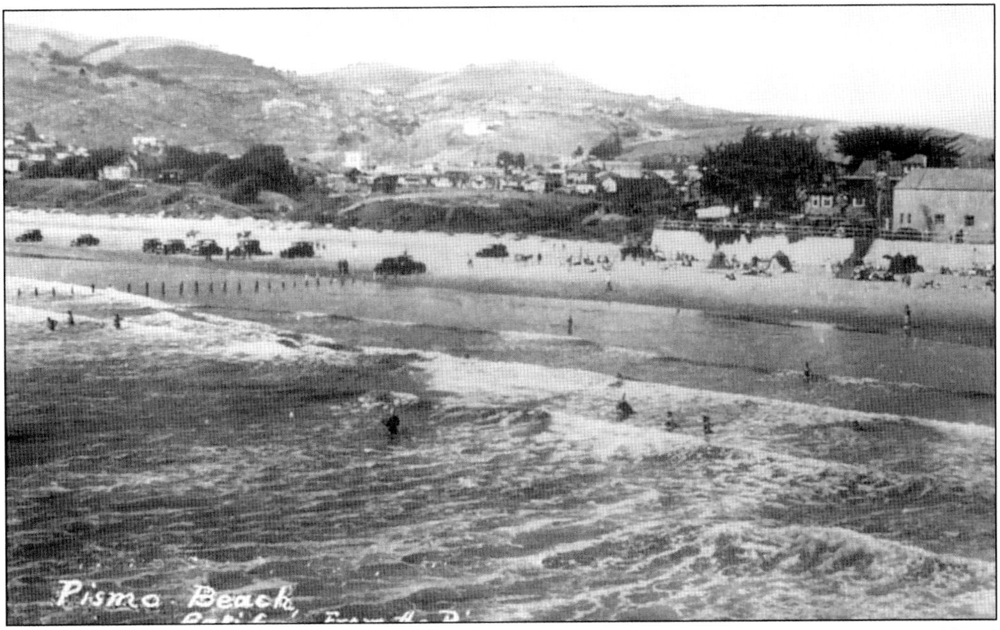

Pismo Beach grew tremendously during the first 50 years of the 20th century. This wide and long sandy beach brought in vacationers from all over the United States and other nations as well. The beach town was easily accessible from the main roads, and its close proximity to San Luis Obispo made it a popular beach retreat for the locals. This postcard is from the early 1930s.

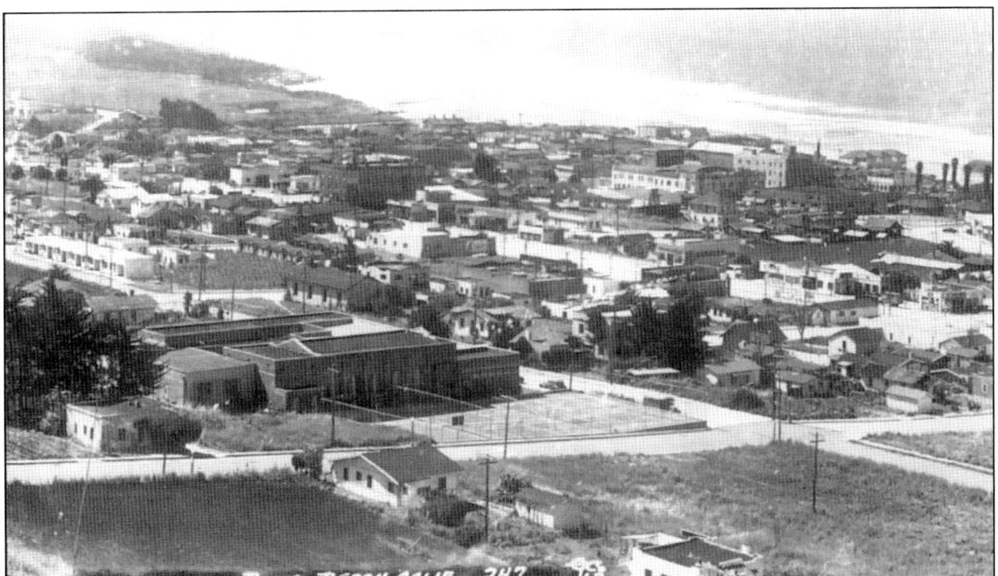

By the 1950s Pismo Beach had not only blossomed into a city in its own right, but also as a center for the bohemian movement which was sweeping the country at that time. The temperate climate and relatively low cost of living ($500 would buy an acre just outside of town in 1952) made it a popular home for the emerging Beat Generation. It remains today as a popular counterculture beach community.

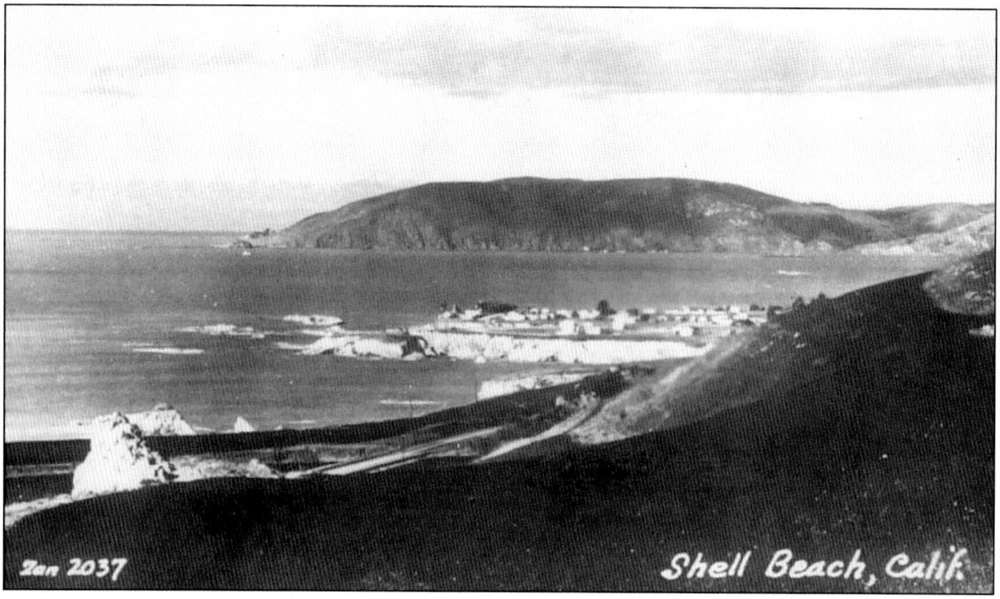

Shell Beach has continuously been a popular retreat for locals. With much less notoriety than Pismo Beach, this tranquil ocean community remains one of the more naturally intact points along the San Luis Obispo County coastline.

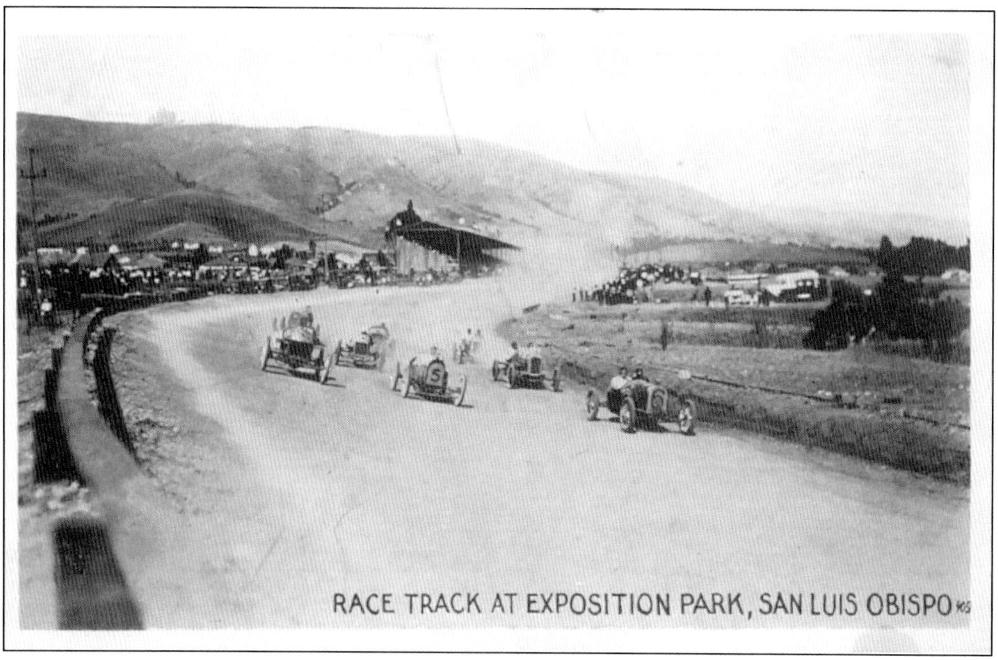

The race track at Exposition Park in San Luis Obispo was host to many spectacular car races in its day. This Saturday race in 1922 had 18 entrants, with only 6 participants actually crossing the finish line. Multiple wrecks were very common during the races, which attracted over 1,500 spectators to these spring and summer events. At one race in 1923, 12 of the 14 entrants either crashed or the cars simply came apart as they competed for the first place finish.

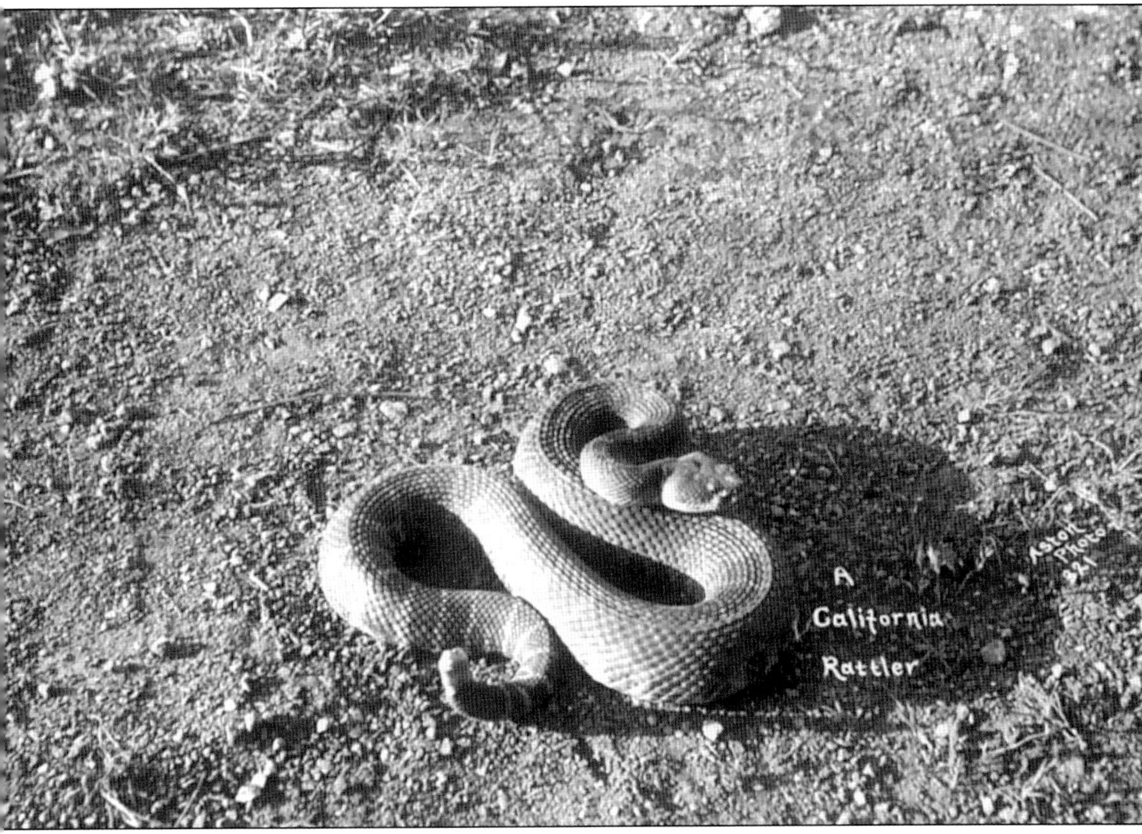

Photographer Howard Aston snapped this picture of a rattlesnake on his property in August 1907, and sent this postcard to his mother, Elizabeth Aston, in Ohio.

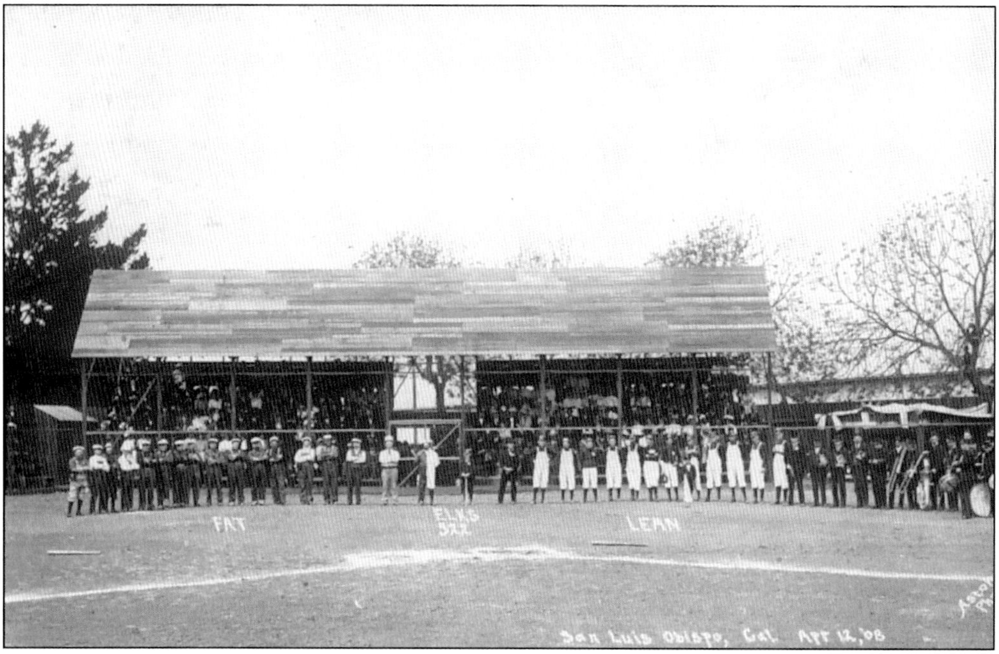

Opening day at the Elks Lodge 322 as the Fat and Lean teams took the field on April 12, 1908. The final score that day: Lean—3, Fat—0.

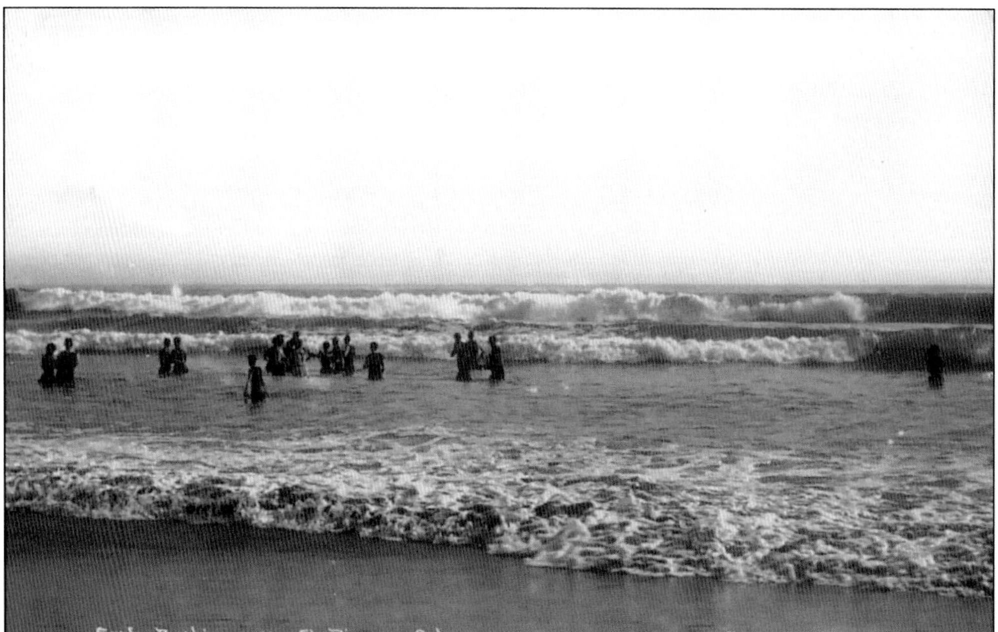

Citizens of San Luis Obispo seek relief from the hot August summer sun at the beach in 1908. Many of the churches organized beach outings during the summer months, which commonly saw temperatures in the mid-80s and above for weeks at a time.

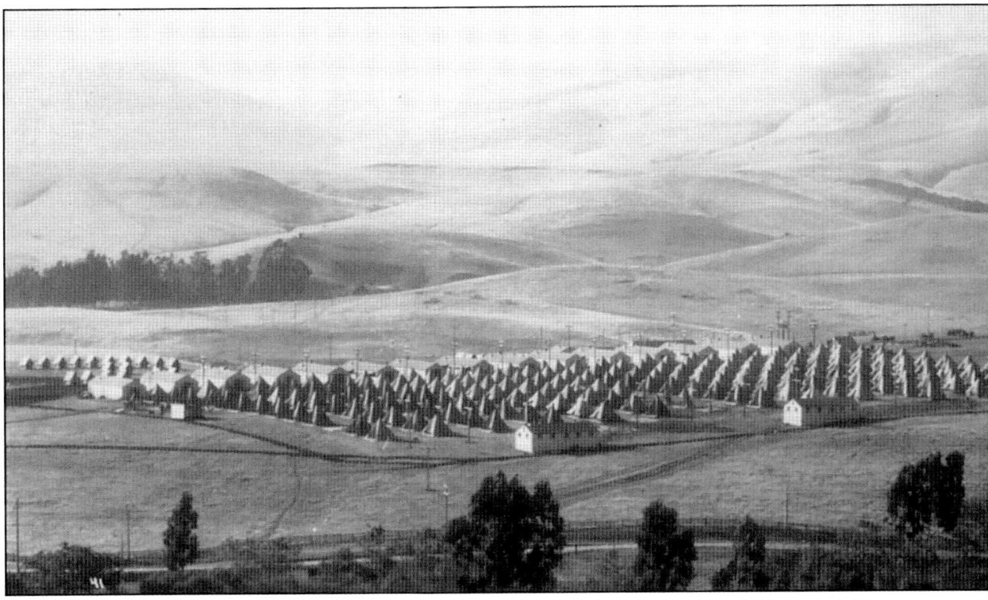

Camp San Luis Obispo is the original home of the California National Guard. This postcard is of the tents reserved for the freshly minted privates, *c.* 1910. At the time that this picture was taken nearly 2,000 men trained at Camp San Luis Obispo each year. The nearby cities of San Luis Obispo and Morro Bay filled with Guardsmen on their weekend leaves. During the World War I training years, the businesses, predominantly the saloons, would be drained of their inventory by the close of Saturday night. The churches would also note "full houses" every Sunday, as all men were permitted the right of practicing their respective faiths. At times the religious trainees practiced "all the faiths that the towns could offer."

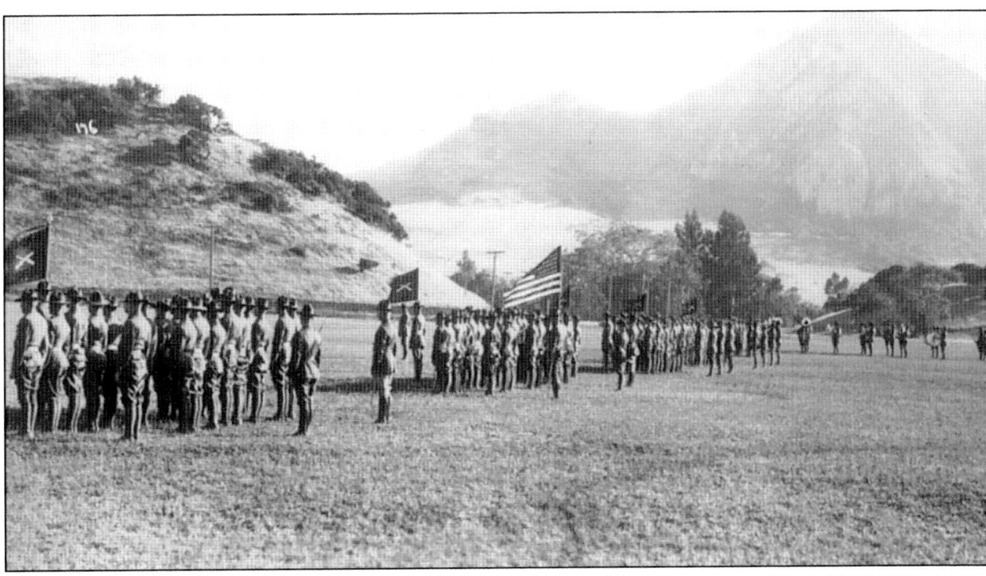

The infantry practicing on the California National Guard parade grounds, *c.* 1910. The camp would grow tremendously during World War I, as it became one of the major training grounds on the West Coast for America's entrance into that fight.

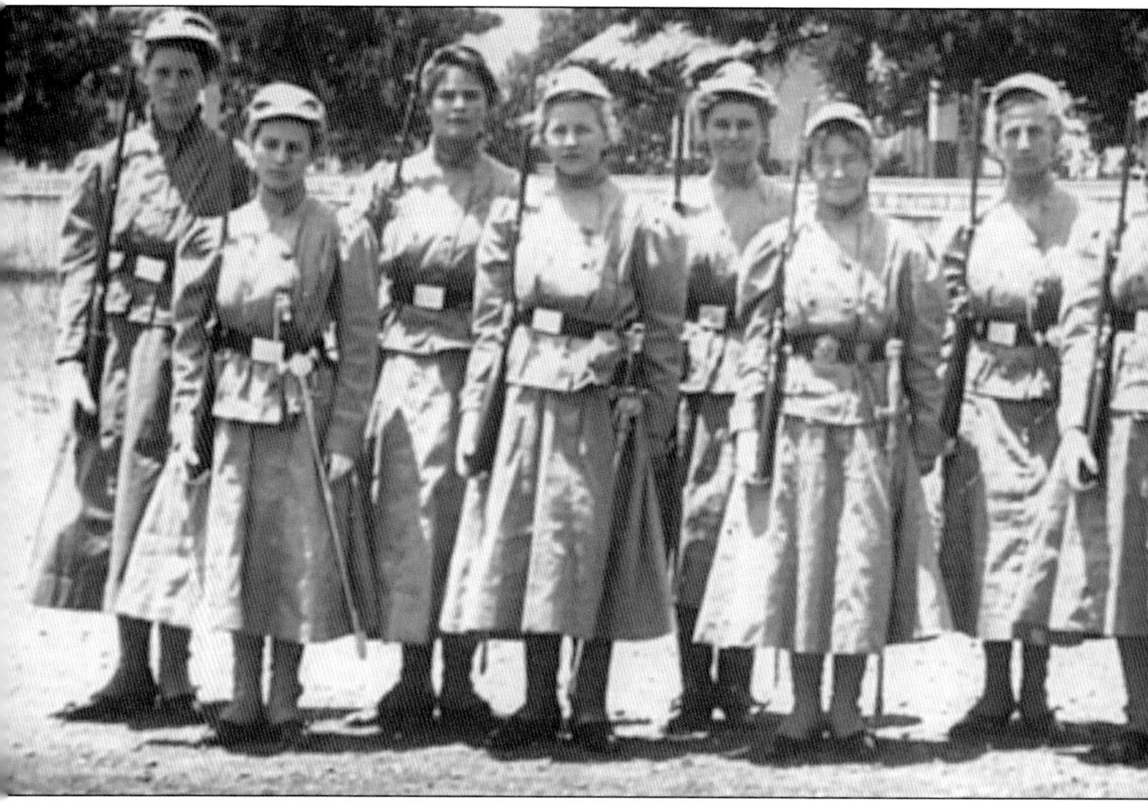

Even the girls were able to show their metal. This squad of eighth graders practices its military maneuvers, just in case the men need help. The motions are Advance, Draw, and Thrust. "Look

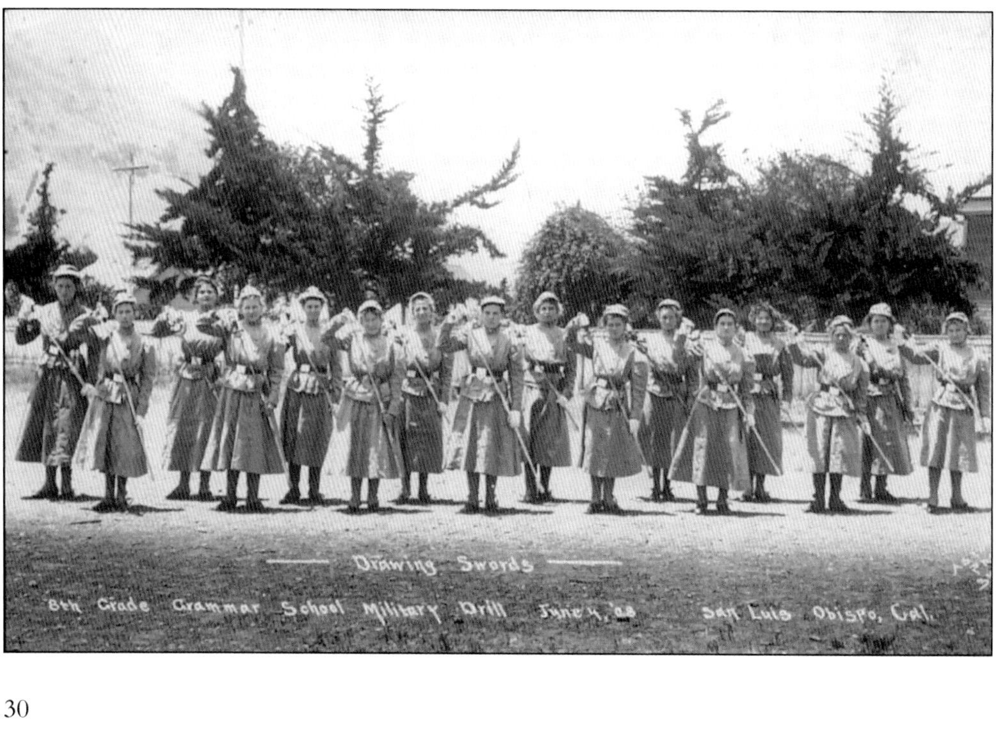

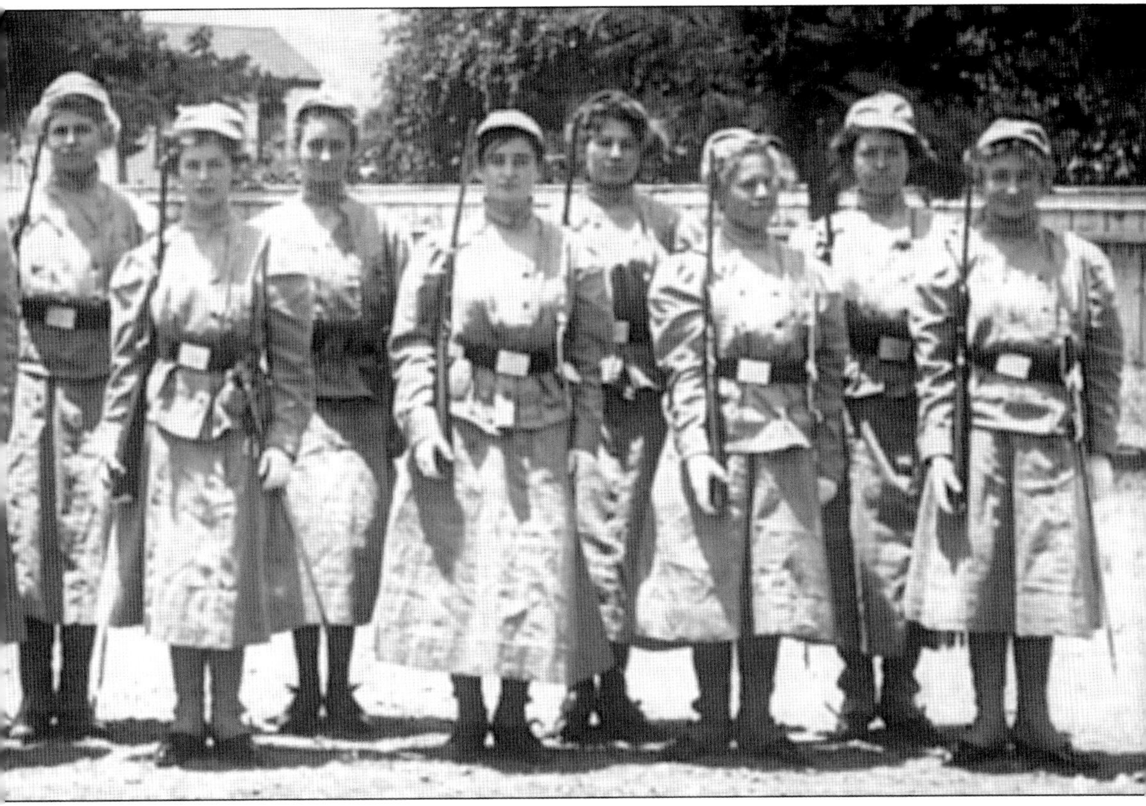

out!" came directly after Thrust! June 4, 1908.

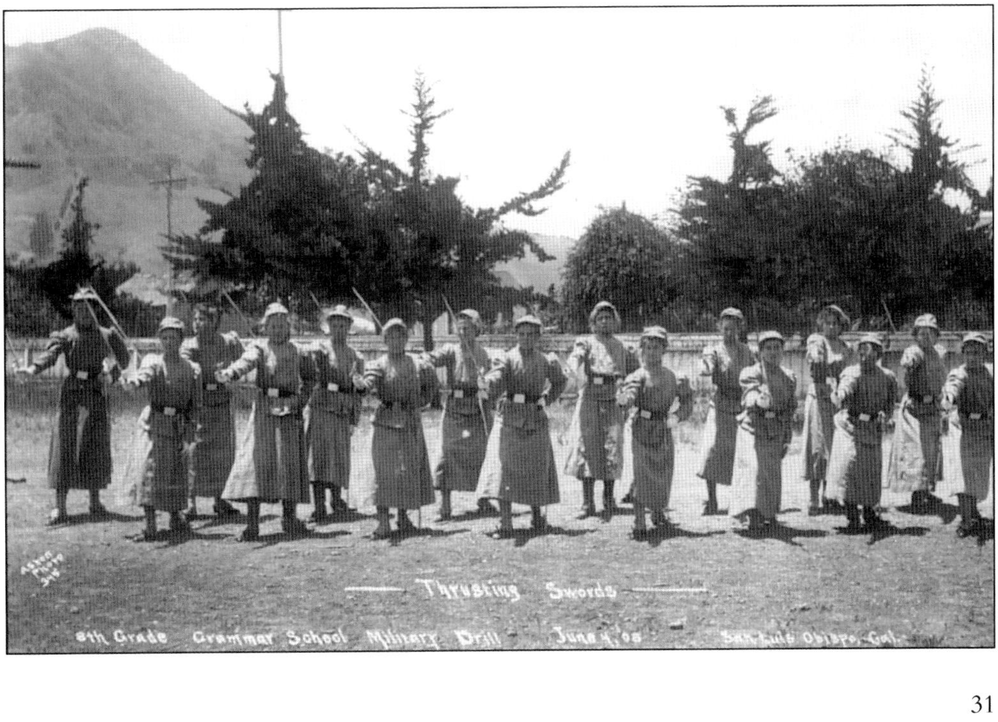

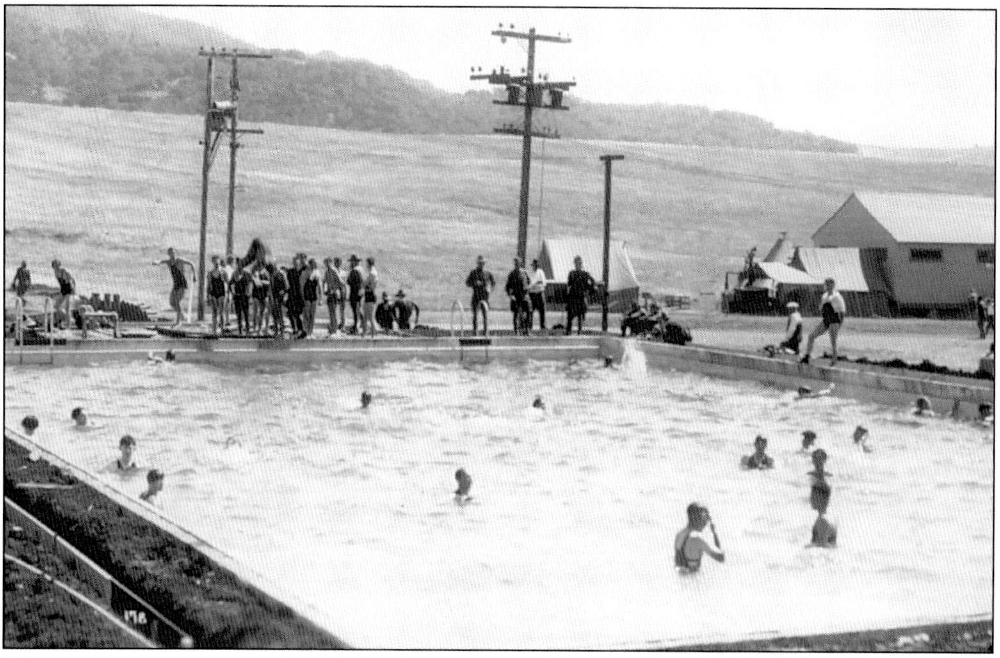

After a long day of marching, the infantry gets a chance to cool off in "The Plunge" at the National Guard Camp, *c.* 1910.

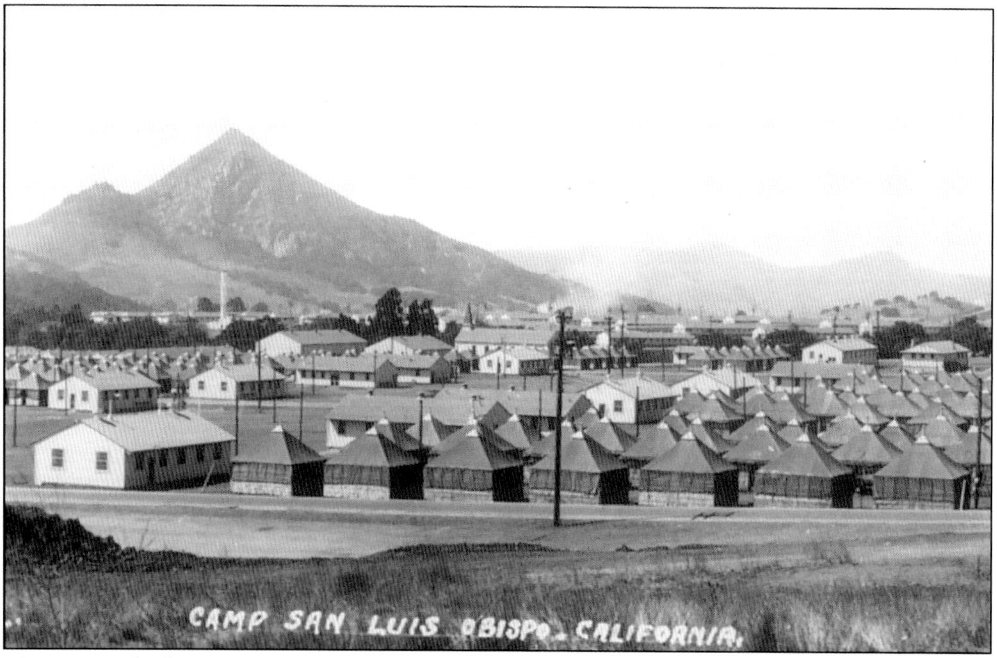

This postcard of Camp San Luis Obispo captures the unplanned growth of the military facility with the number of temporary buildings surpassing the number of permanent buildings, *c.* 1919.

Private Joe Burns had this photo-postcard taken mid-way through his training for the Great War at Camp San Luis Obispo. He was 19 years old in this image, and only four weeks away from crossing the Atlantic. Burns was one of the lucky ones who returned home from the war.

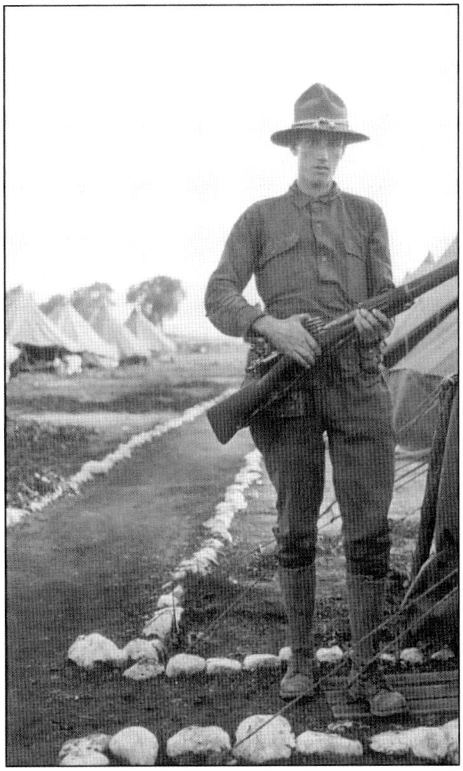

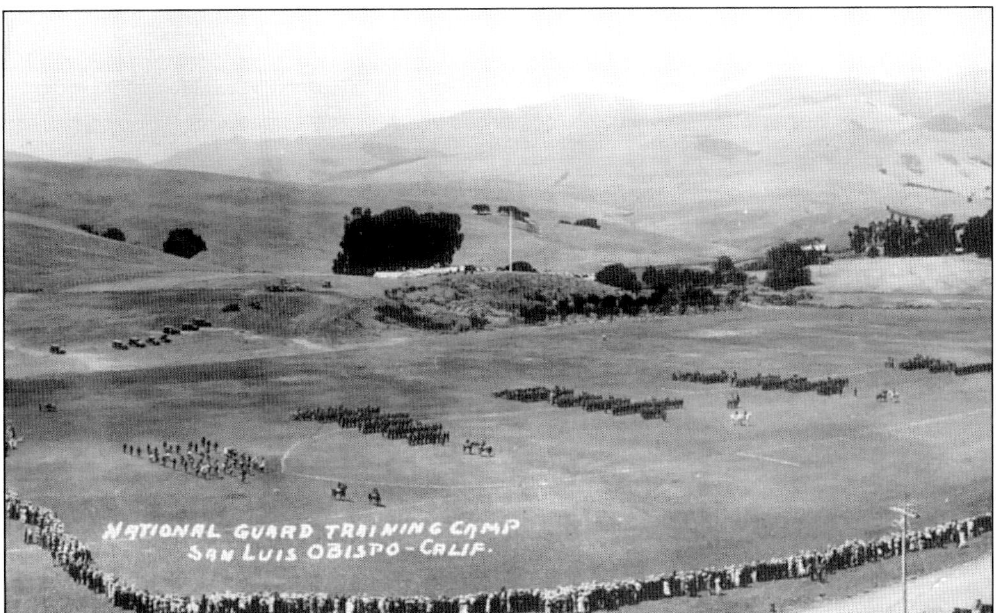

At the close of World War I, the training facility was returned to the state of California from the federal government, and training for the California National Guard resumed. This 1923 postcard is of the final parade of that summer's 255-member graduating class of National Guardsmen. Nearly 2,000 spectators and family members turned out for the event.

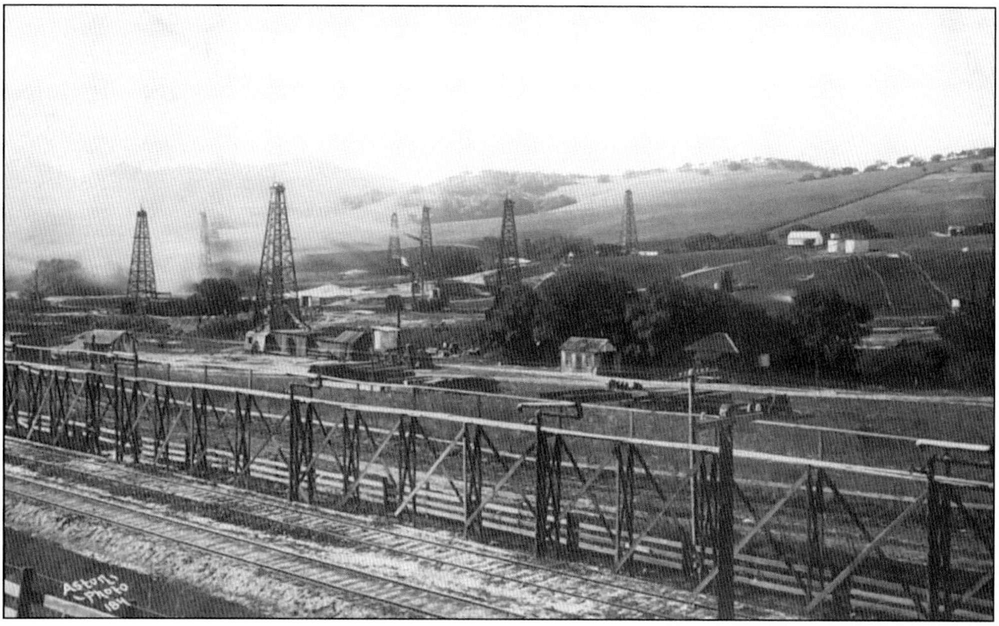

In 1903 Union Oil Company of California opened their operations in San Luis Obispo. The addition of this company into the economy was a huge boost. Nearly 500 new jobs were created within the first two years. Union Oil took advantage of the central location of San Luis Obispo, and lobbied with great intensity for the U.S. Navy's refueling rights.

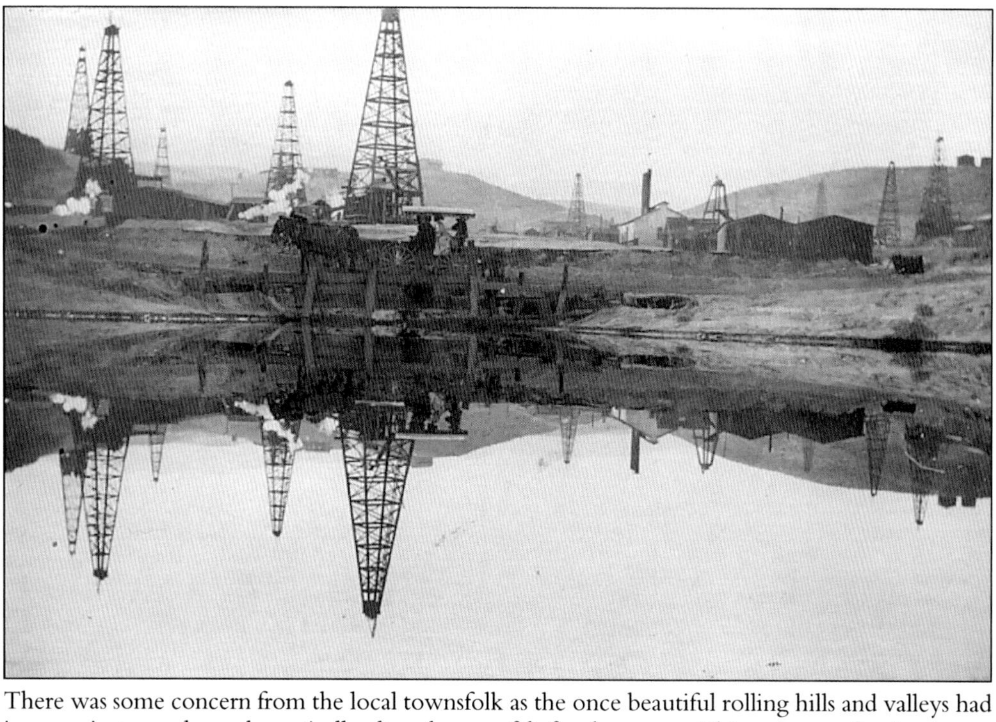

There was some concern from the local townsfolk as the once beautiful rolling hills and valleys had in some instances been dramatically altered, some felt for the worse. This unique reflecting image of the oil fields, taken in 1906, bears testament to their concern.

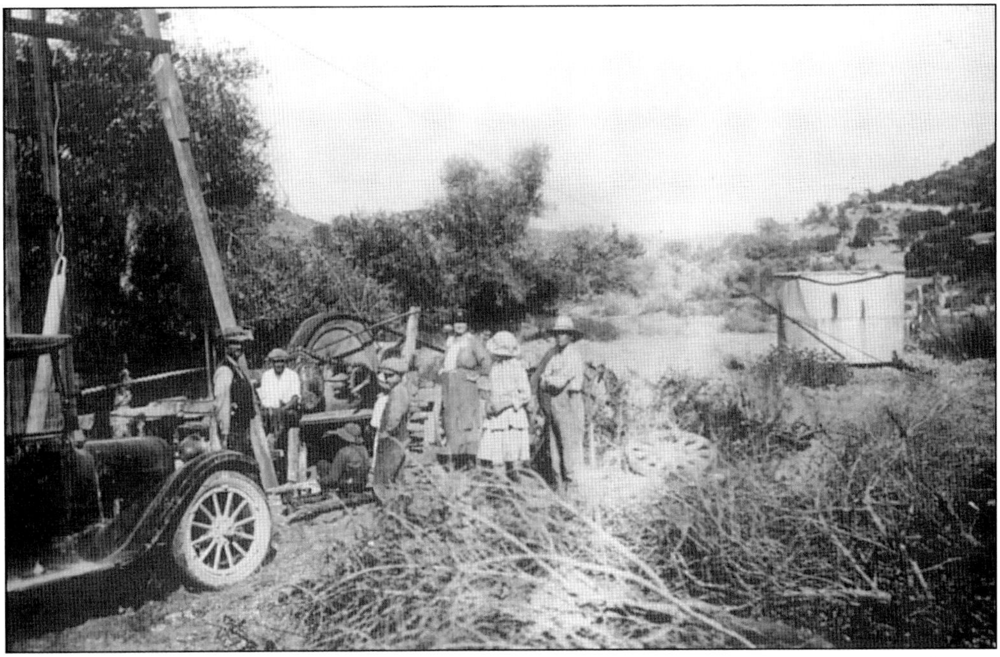

This postcard commemorates the completion of an oil-drilling rig. The gentleman standing in front of the automobile and the one seated facing the camera and wearing a white shirt, are representatives from Union Oil. The family, to the right of these men, were the proprietors of the land who were leasing this section of their property to Union Oil, *c.* 1912.

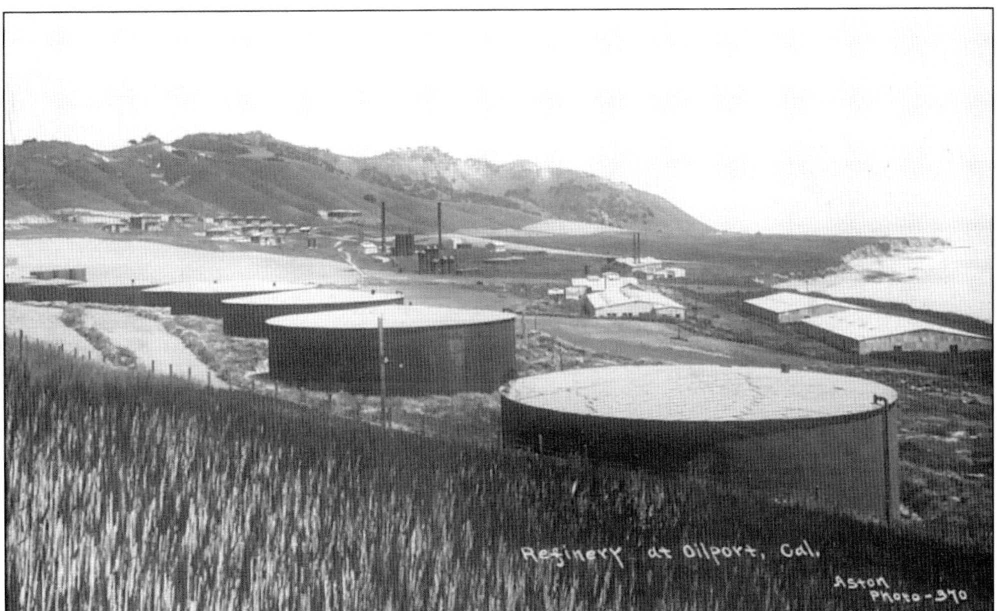

Union Oil drilled, refined, and stored at San Luis Obispo and its community of oil tanks, drills, and refineries came to be known as Oilport. The refinery and storage facility of Oilport was billed as the largest in the world at the time of these postcards, *c.* 1907.

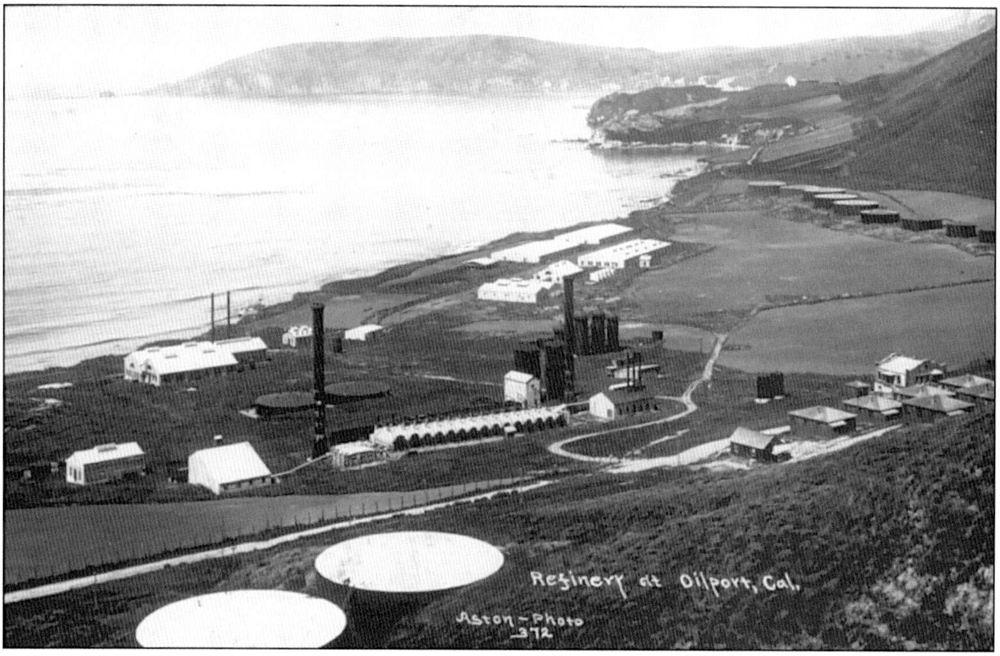

Above and below are oilport images taken *c.* 1907.

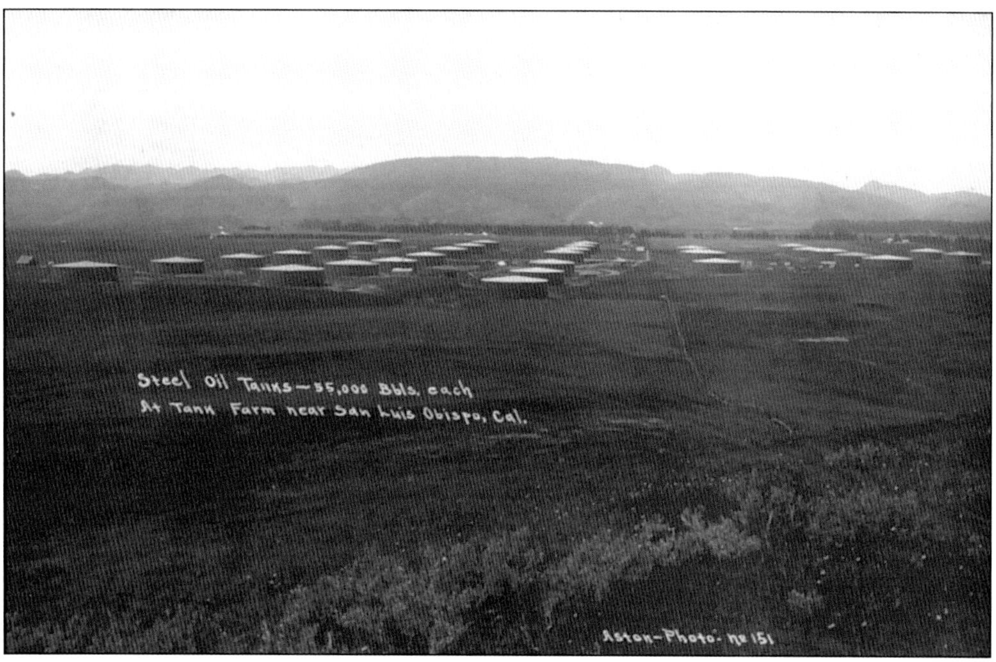

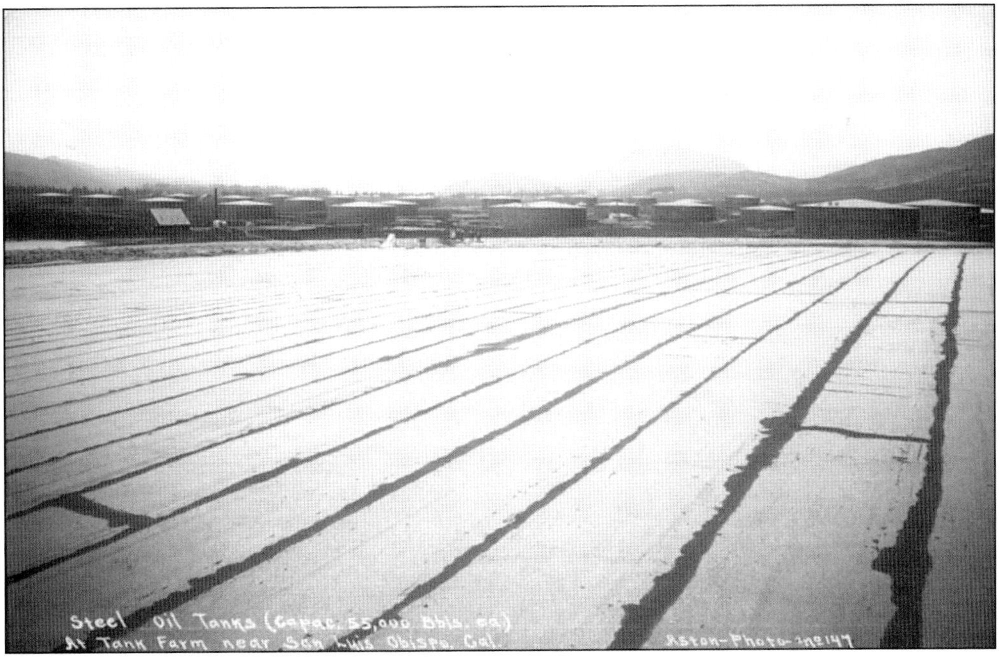

Above and below are more oilport images taken *c.* 1907

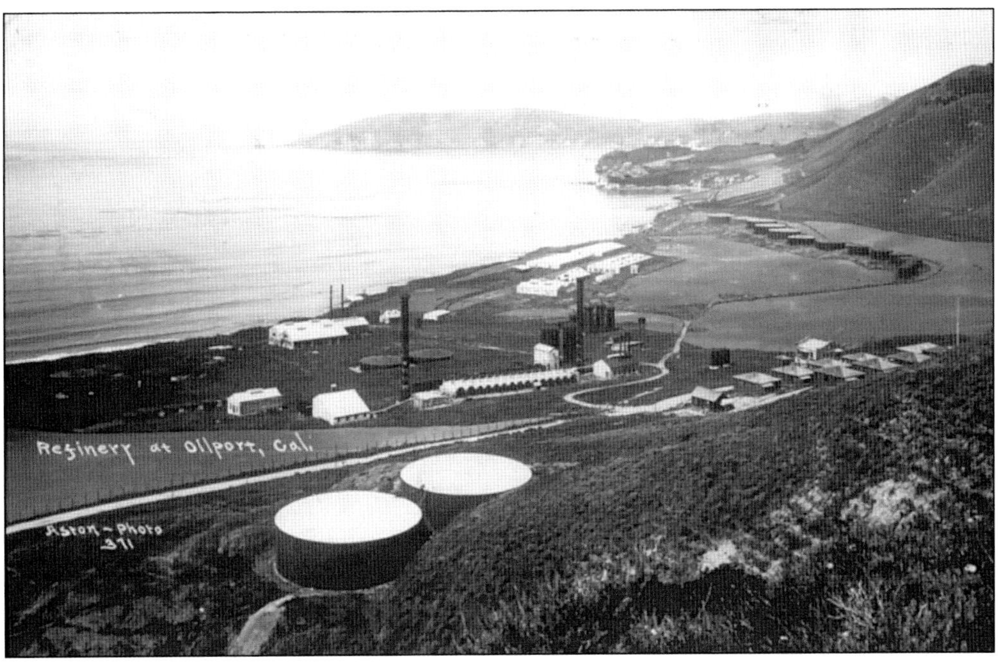

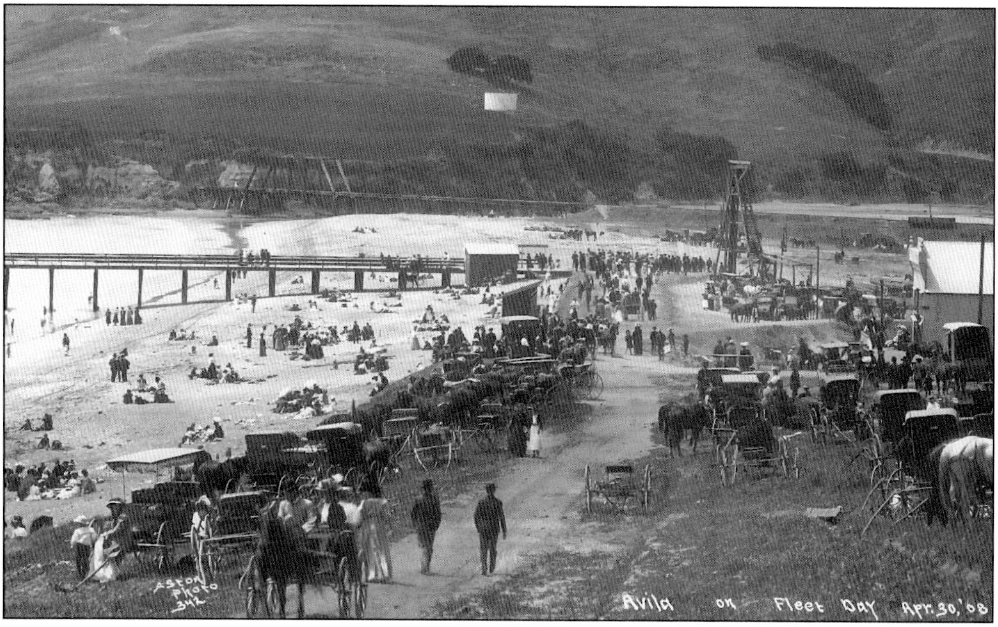

On April 30, 1908, President Teddy Roosevelt rewarded Union Oil and sent the "Great White Fleet" through San Luis Obispo. There was great anticipation of the arrival of the fleet, which had just returned from its tour around the world. Nearly all the businesses closed for the event and

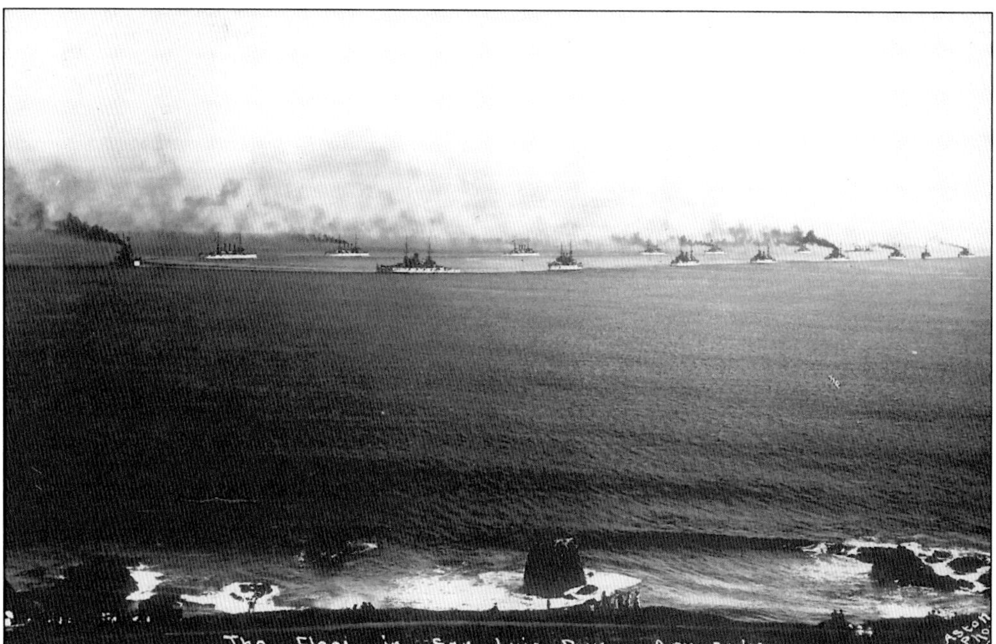

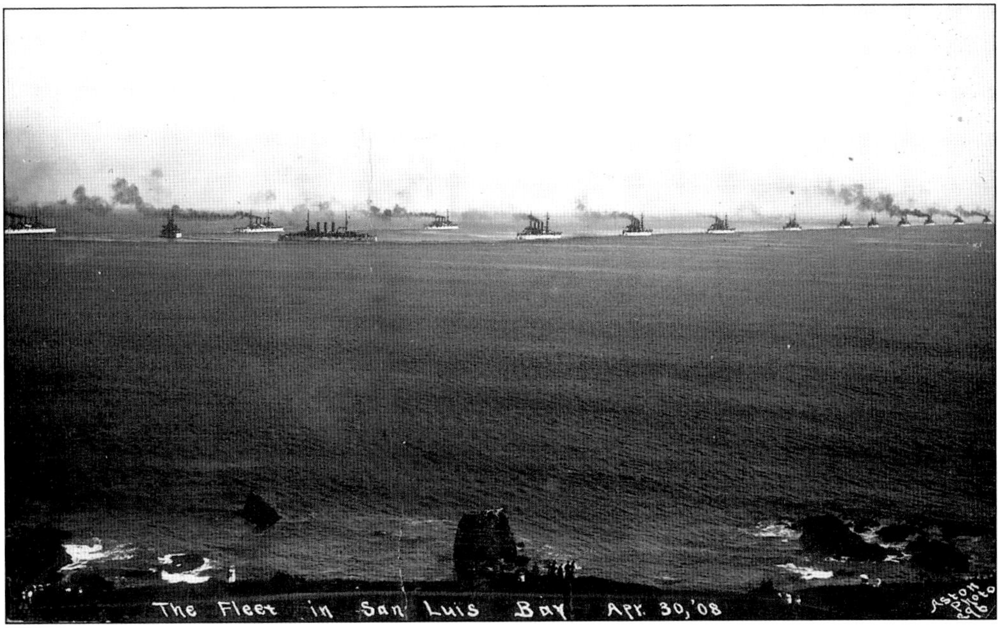

all the schools dismissed class, as one educator noted that "the students probably would not have gone to class anyway, and perhaps a few of the teachers as well."

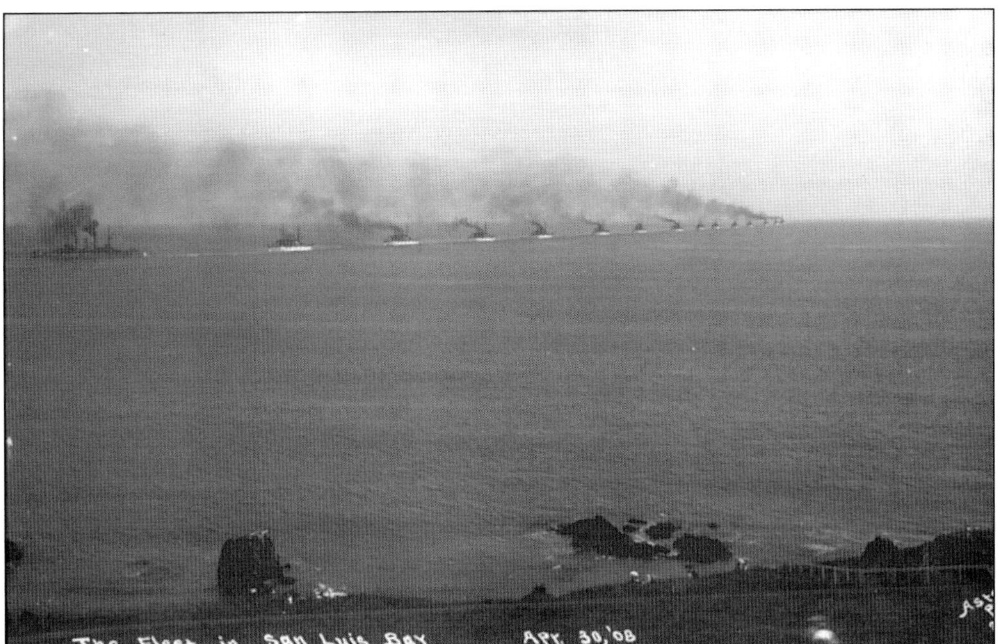

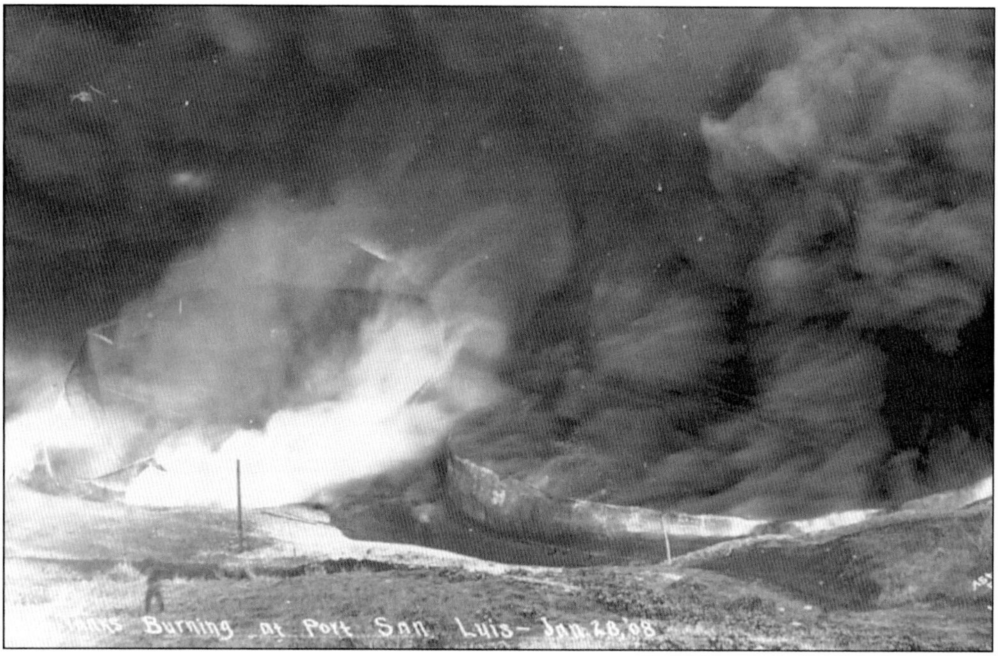

The year 1908 was a traumatic year for the Union Oil Company, in spite of the arrival of the "Great White Fleet." On two occasions there were massive fires at the oil tanks. The first occurred on January 28, 1908, and lasted for three days. The smoke covered the sky, and as photographer Frank Aston noted, "the black smoke raced to cover the sky, and its foul stench took away my appetite long into that day." #36.

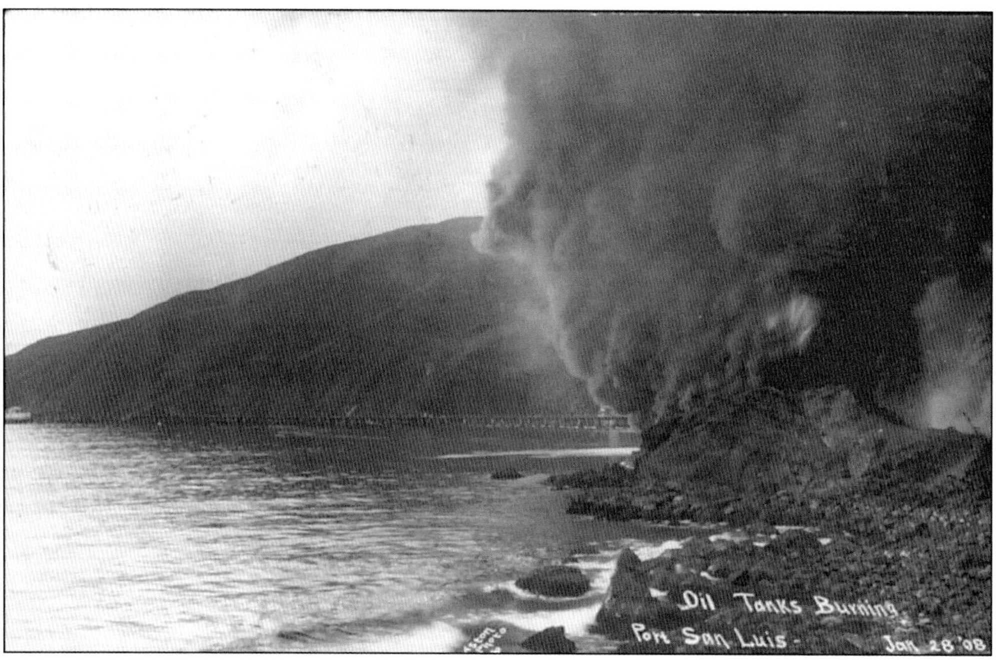

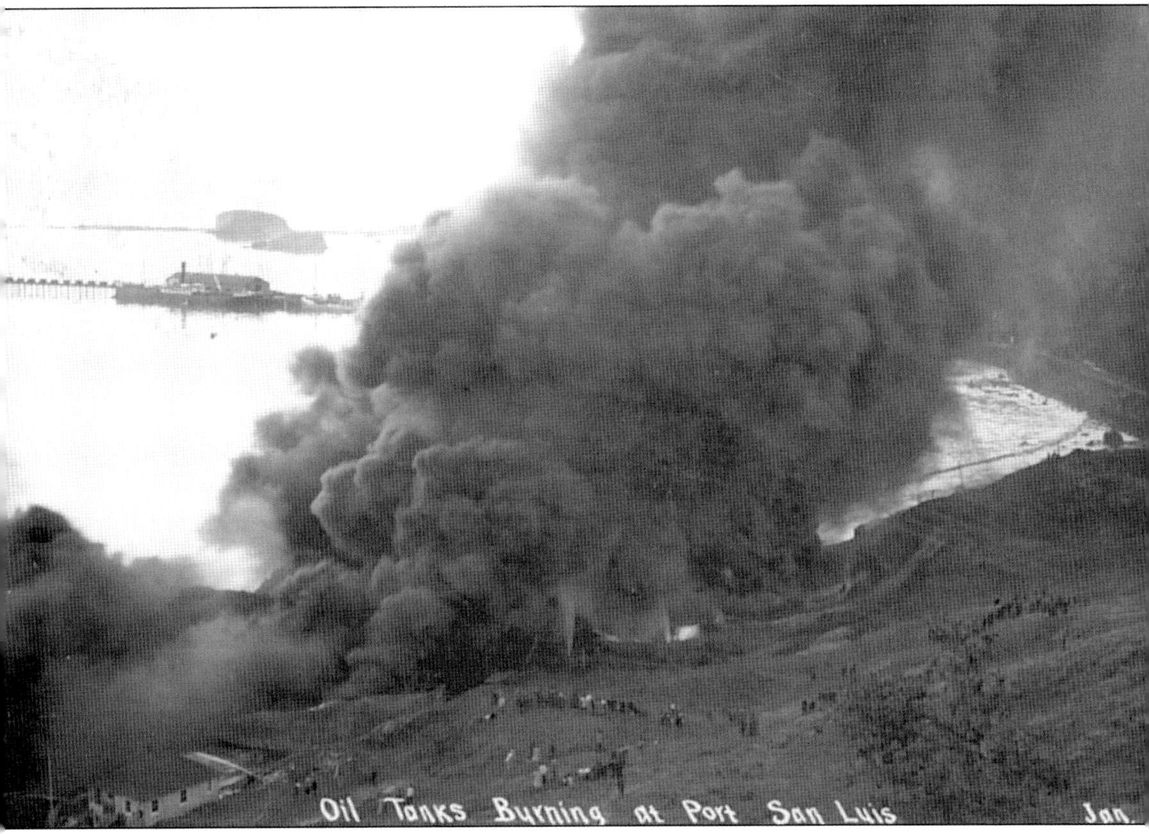

The towering black smoke attracted quite a mass of on-lookers from town. At one point the photographers, Frank and Howard Aston, estimated that "nearly 500 people, in addition to those who were fighting the fire, stood precariously close to the flames, smoke and fumes, as though they were under a trance." The crowd is somewhat visible in the foreground of these postcard images.

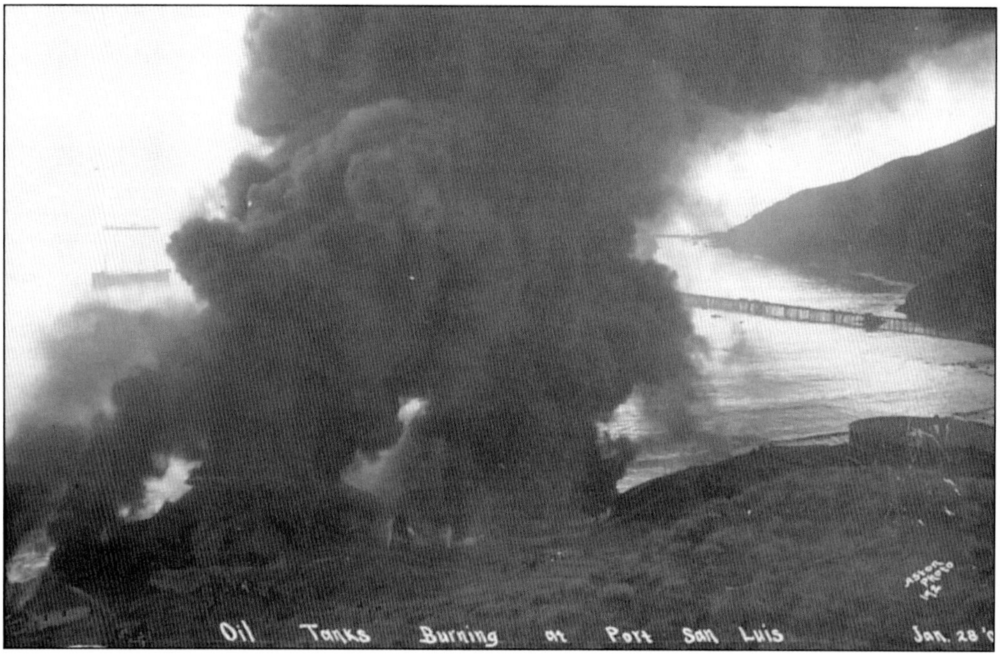

Many of the workers' families poured out to the location, looking for their loved ones, while many others simply came out to see the spectacle unfold. Photographer Frank Aston noted that by the time he had left the scene of the fire his clothes not only smelled of the putrid stench that

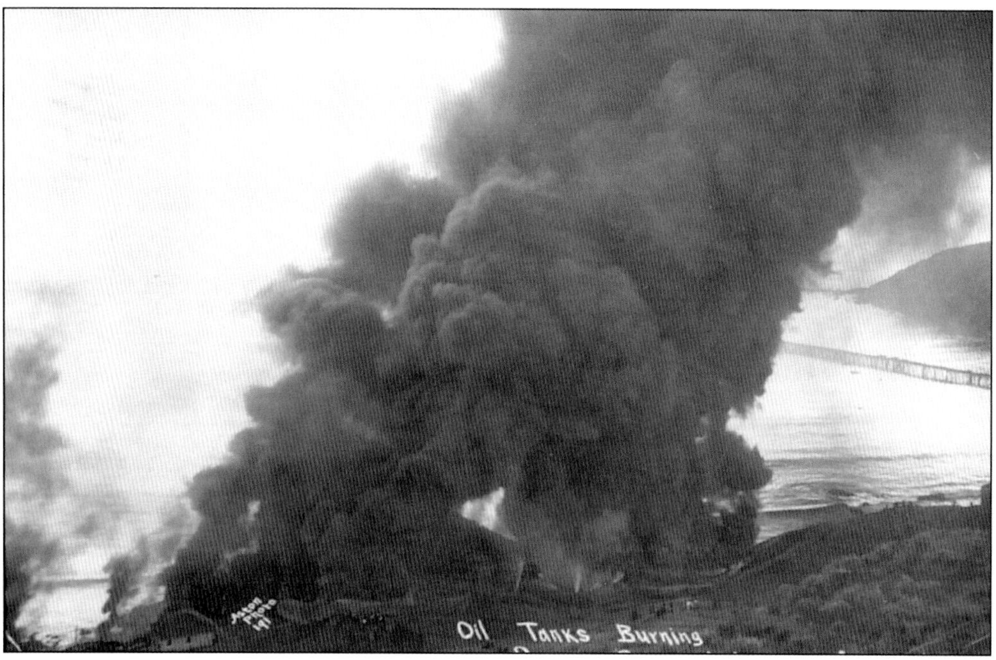

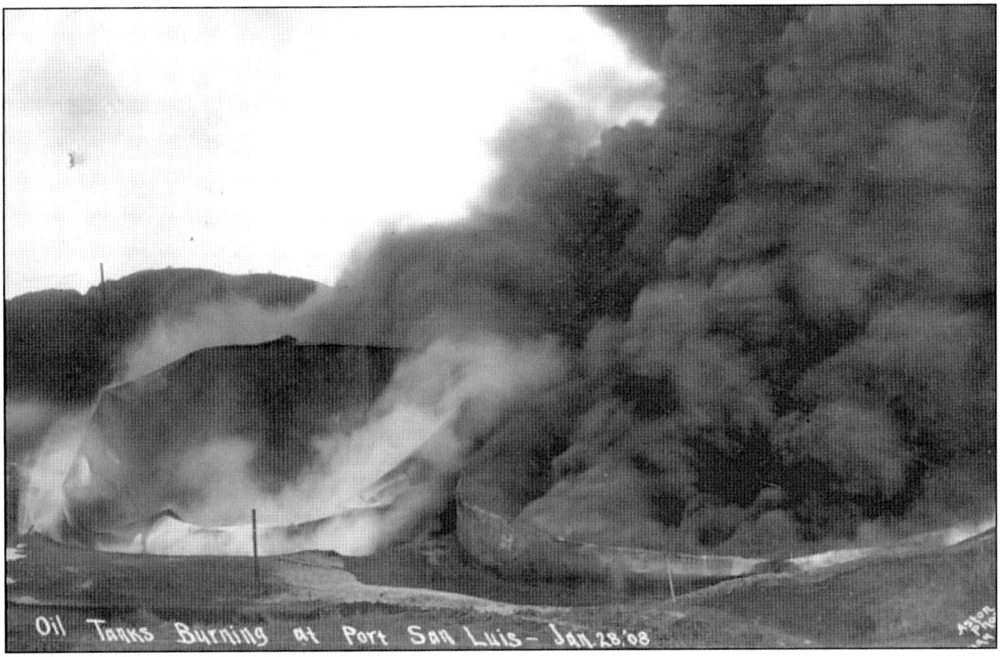

filled the air, but that he and his camera lenses had been covered with the effects of the smoke due to the swirling winds. It was the greatest disaster the community had faced up to that time, and it was one event that would repeat itself in less than six months.

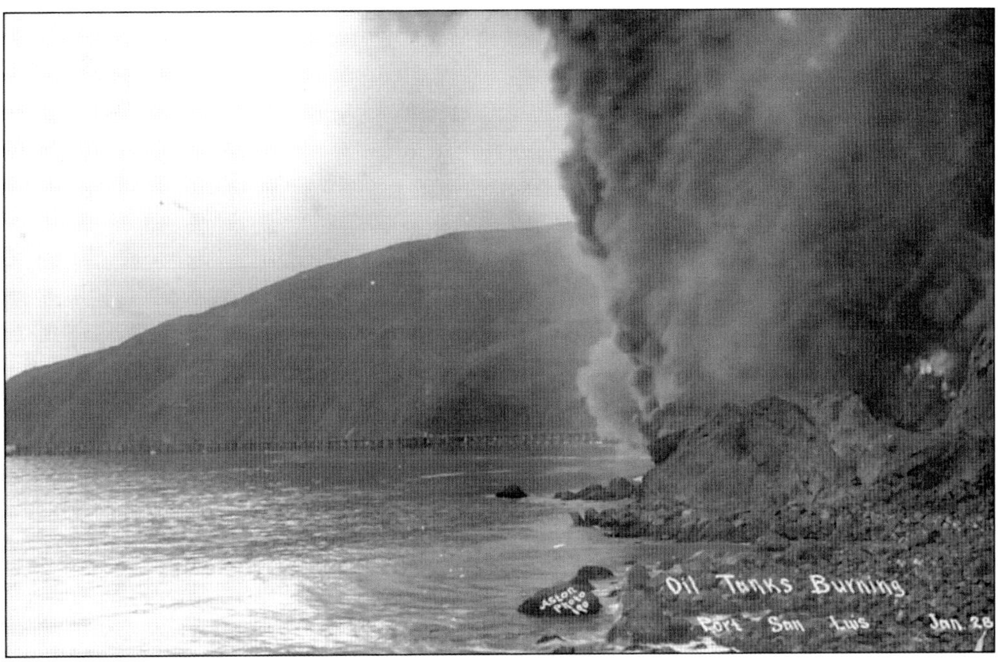

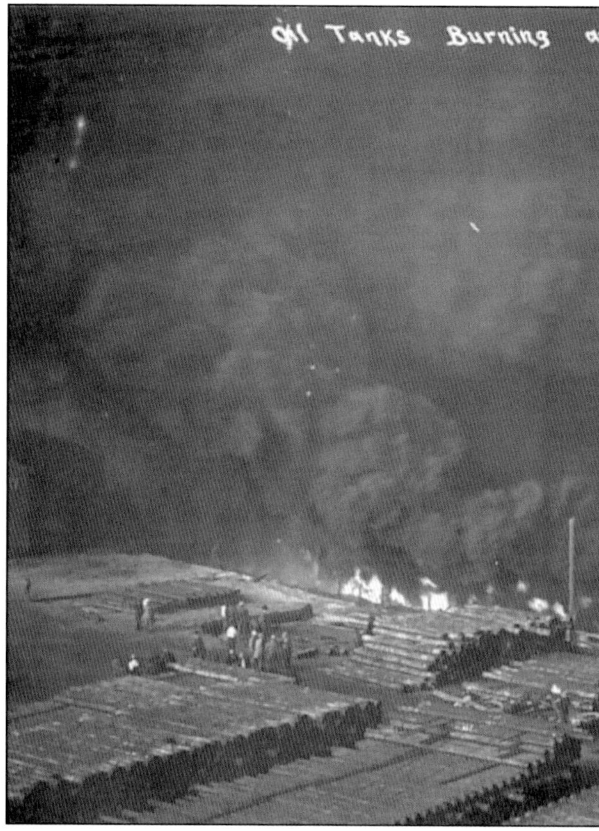

Tragedy struck again at the oil fields on July 15, 1908. Just two-and-a-half months after the arrival of the "Great White Fleet," the second fire for Union Oil broke out. This time the fires raged for nearly one week.

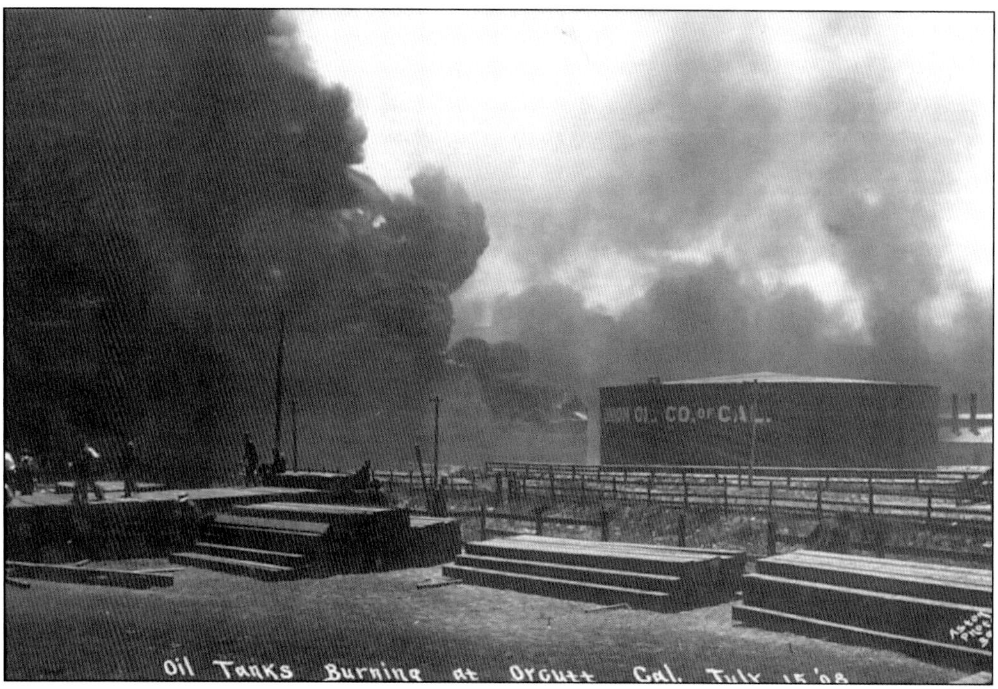

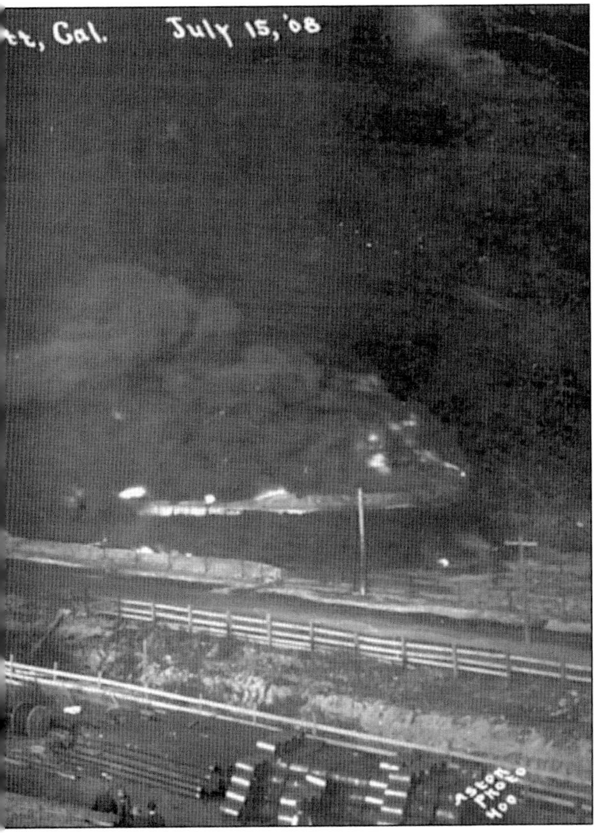

Also, this time it happened during the middle of the summer. As photographer Frank Aston pointed out "the intensity of the heat, even at a distance of fifty yards or so, made my clothes so hot that I thought I might catch on fire too!"

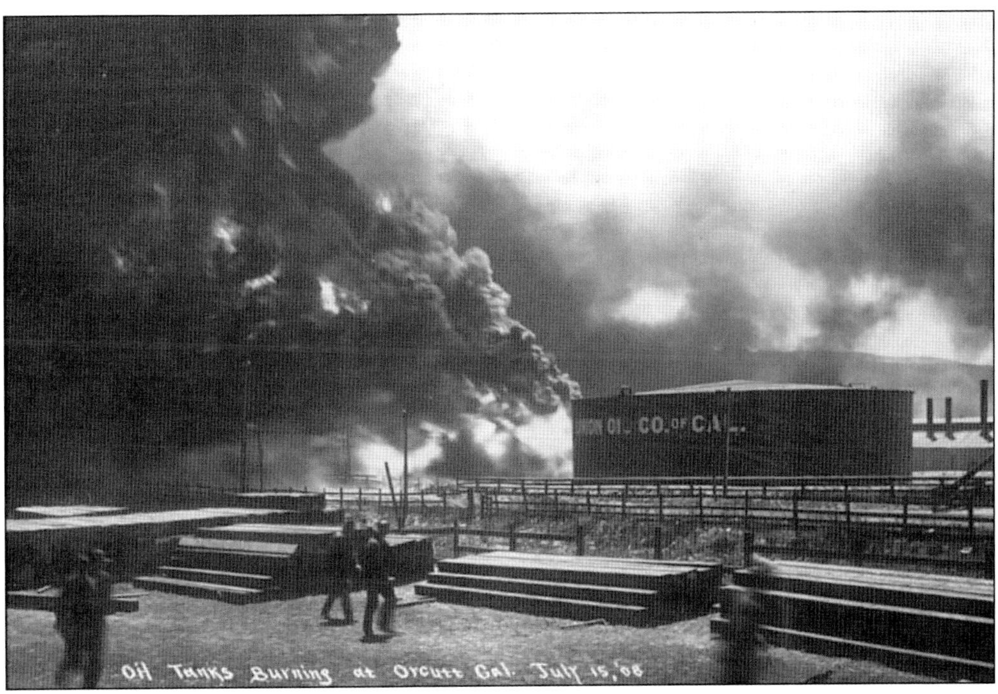

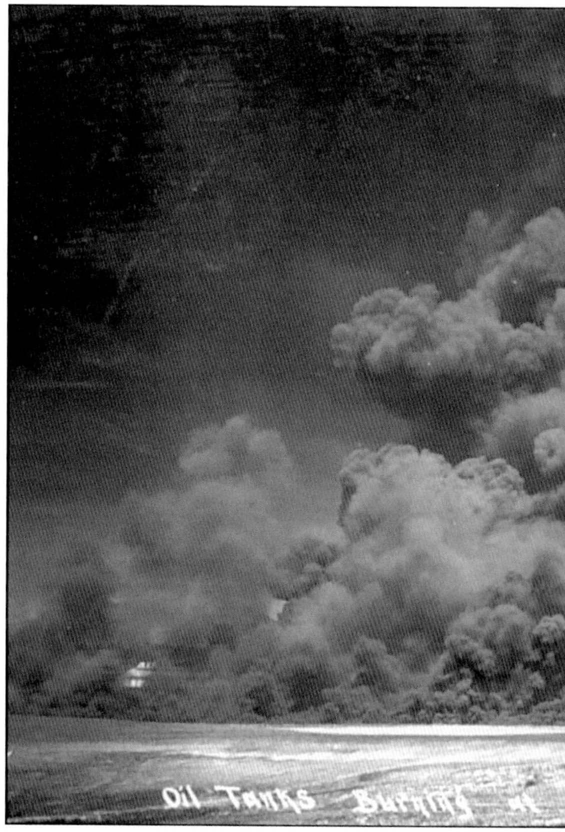

This fire covered the sky with smoke, turning San Luis Obispo's days into a prolonged state of darkness. After the third day, the situation gradually came under the control of the fire fighters and oil workers at this facility, which was billed as the world's largest oil storage facility.

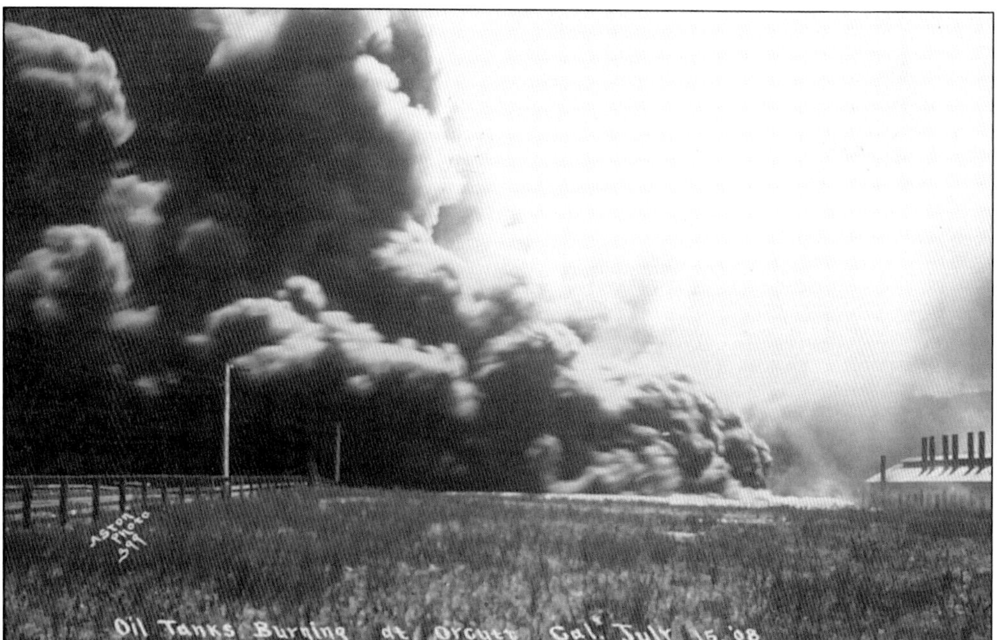

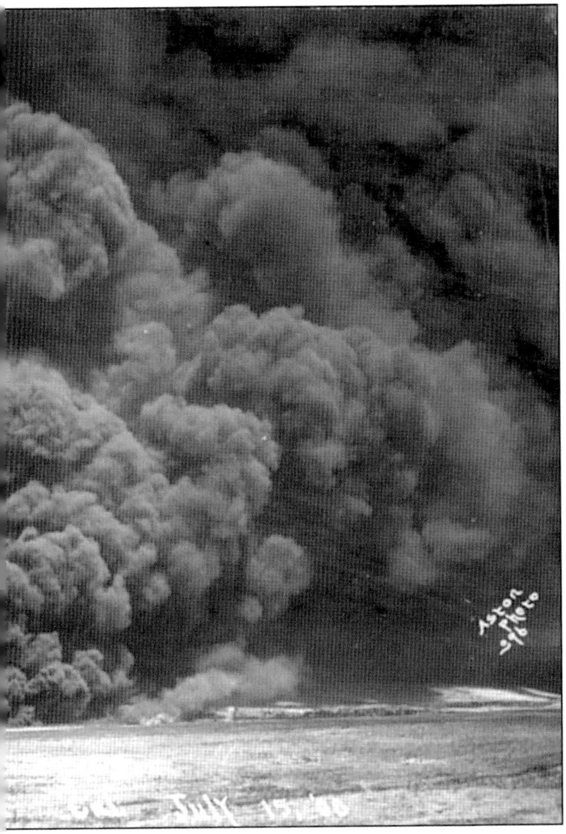

It took nearly six months to tabulate the bill for the fire, with insurance estimates ranging from $250,000 to over $1 million.

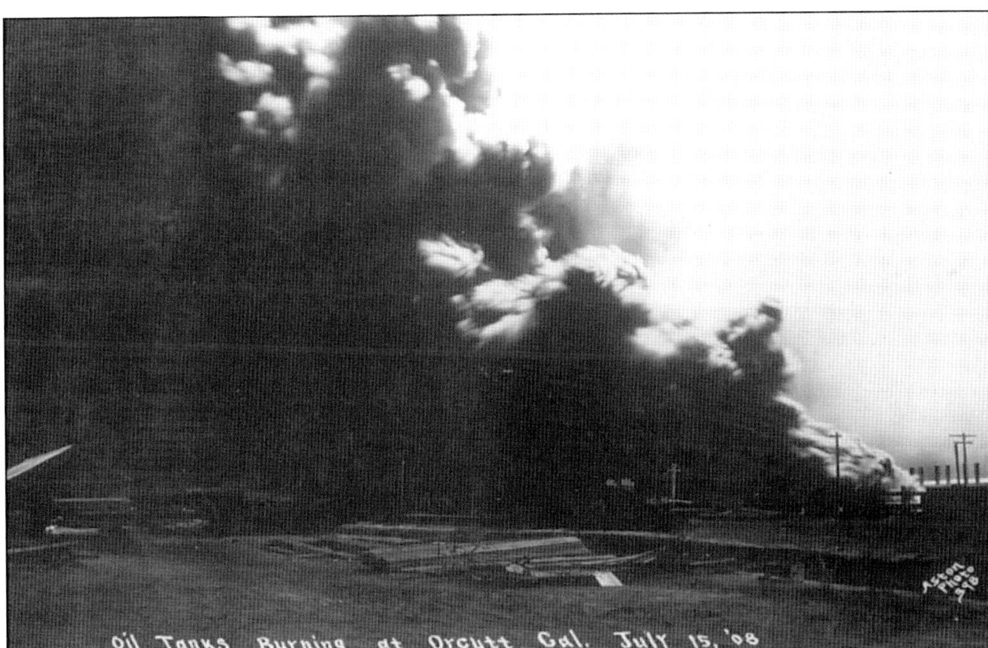

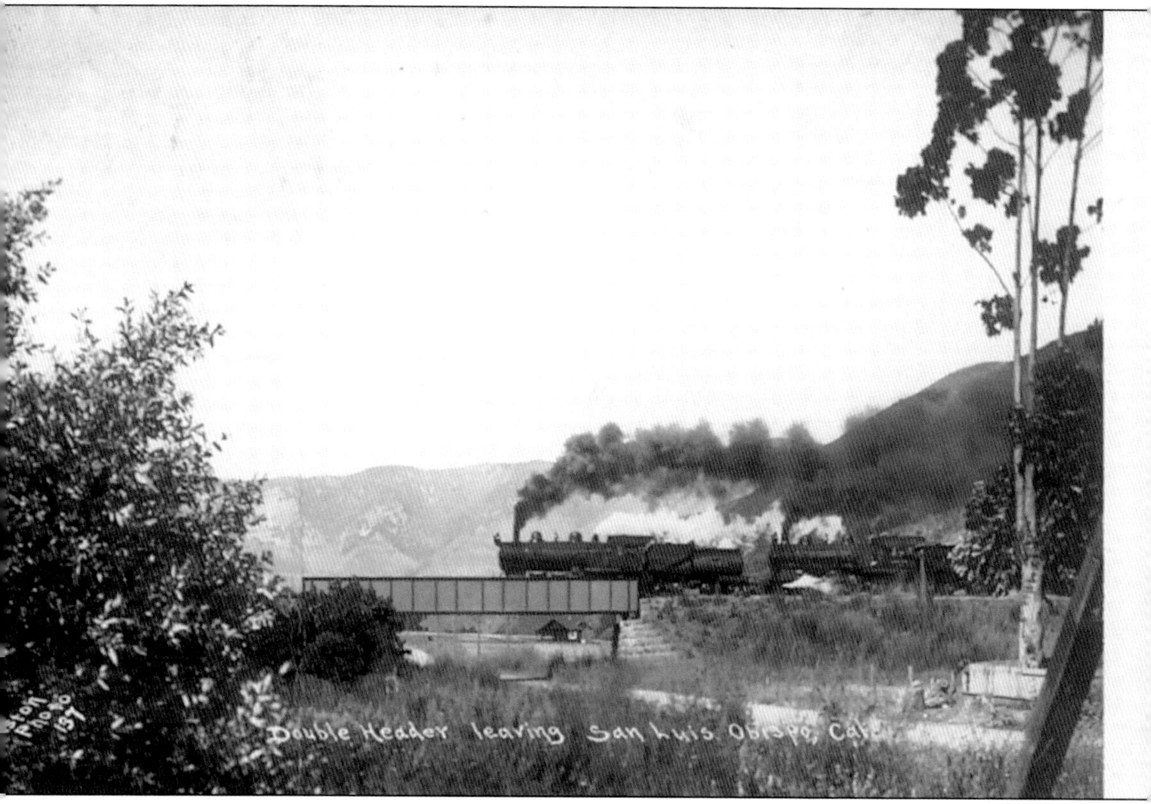

The schedule of trains through San Luis Obispo at the beginning of the 20th century increased considerably. The greater demand for the Southern Pacific to carry goods and passengers led to the common use of the "Double Header" that employed two engines instead of simply one, *c.* 1902.

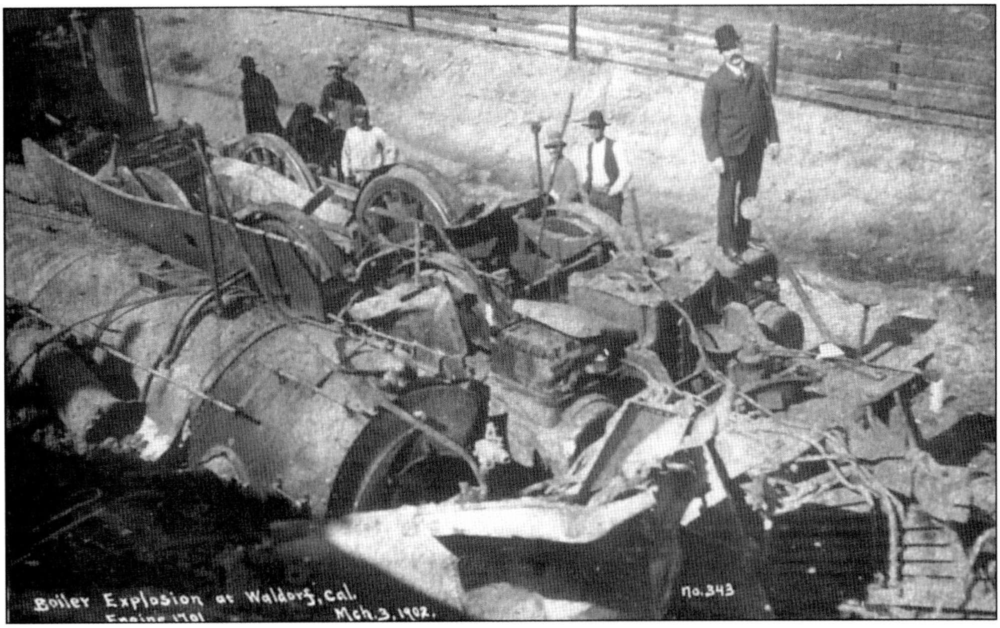

In the first decade of the new century, San Luis Obispo bore witness to two train wrecks. The first occurred on March 2, 1902, due to an "extremely overworked boiler that exploded, taking two souls with it." The explosion of Engine 1701 was great enough that fragments were found over 100 yards away.

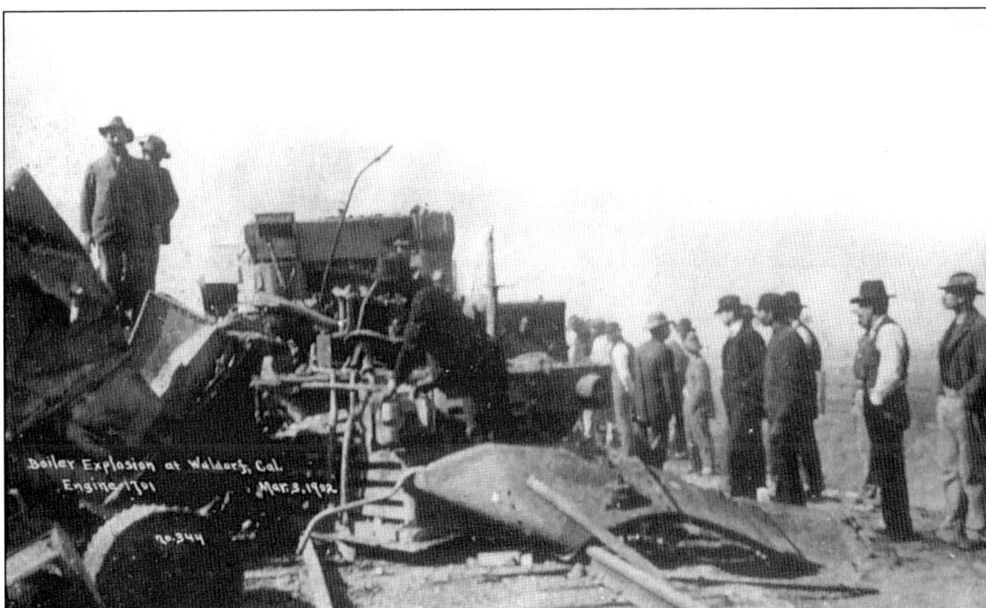

Insurance agents, investigators, and onlookers survey the damage. There had been speculation that sabotage had been the culprit for this particular accident. With accusations ranging from "children tinkering around with the train when it was at the station" to "former stagecoach owners, out of business and plenty angry with the trains that took their place." No person was ever officially charged with any crime in relation to this accident.

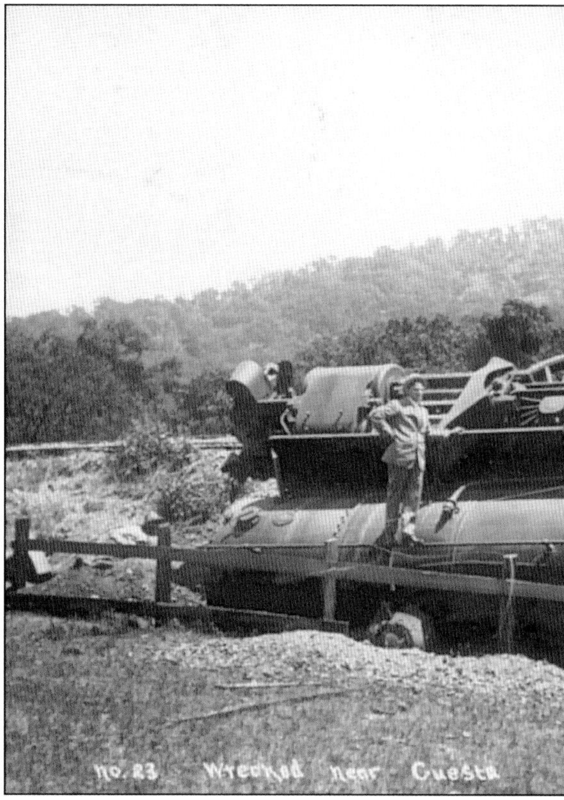

On May 22, 1908, a single engine en route to link up with a particularly heavy load in need of a second engine derailed due to irregularities in the tracks. It was later speculated that people had been taking out the spikes as souvenirs at the location of Engine 23's wreck.

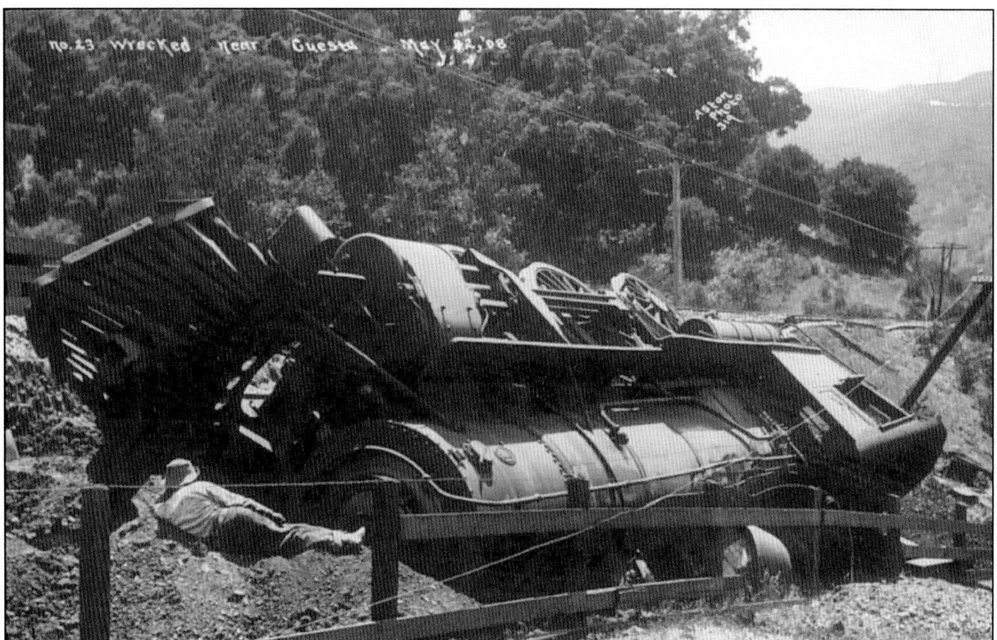

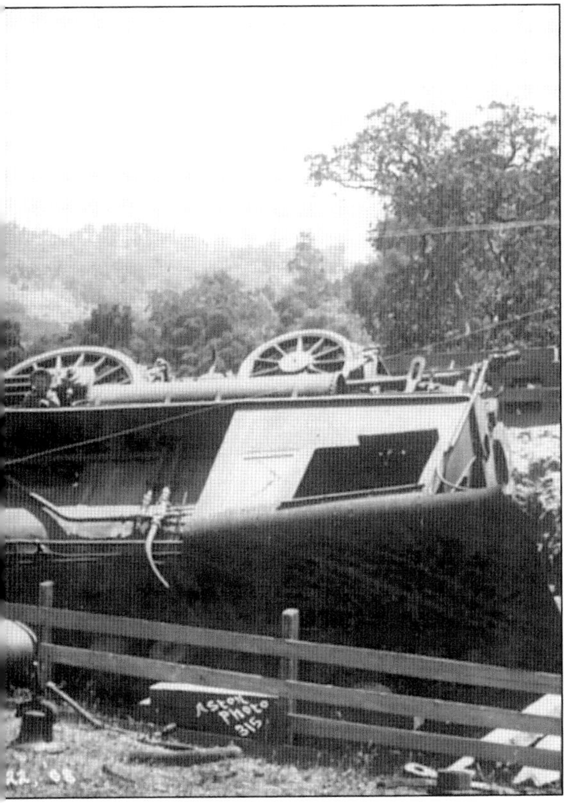

Ten signs were posted along the tracks that ran through San Luis Obispo County, reminding people that any interference with the trains or their tracks was formerly a capital offense in California and remained a felony that the State would prosecute to the fullest extent of the law.

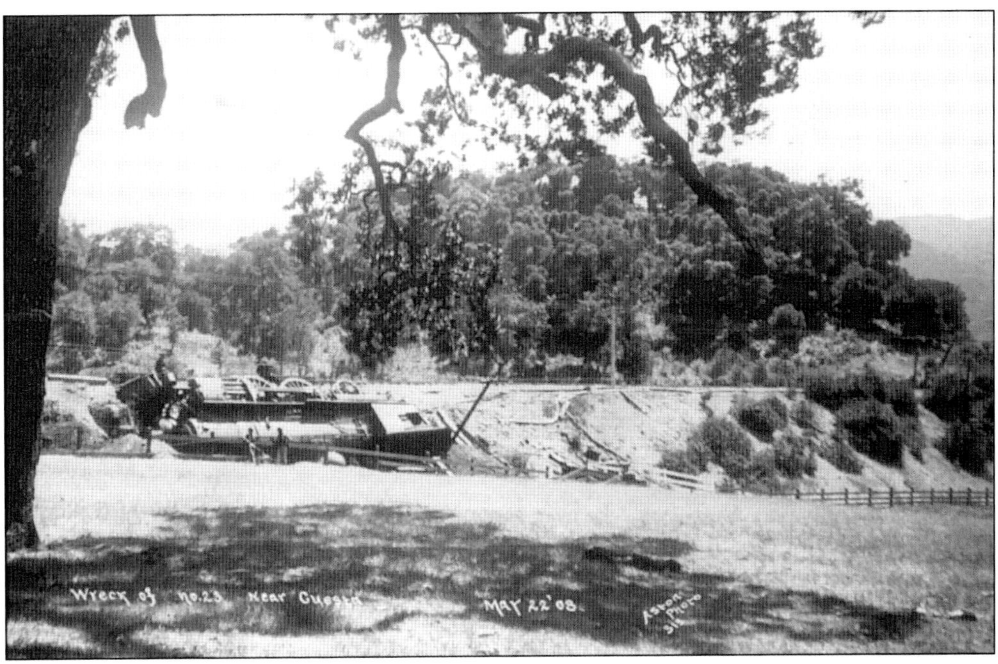

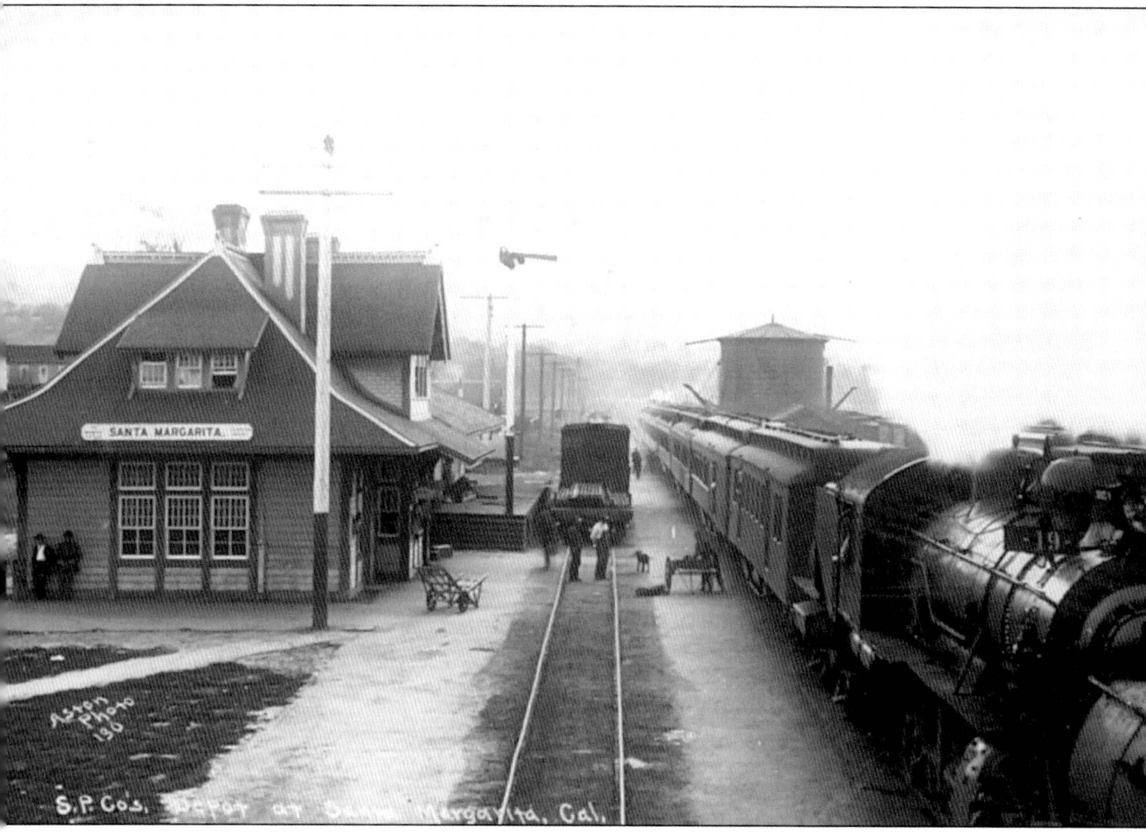

The town of Santa Margarita, just a few miles north of San Luis Obispo, began to add considerably to its population after the arrival of the Southern Pacific's rail station in 1900. The city became situated on the former Rancho location, in the central part of the valley.

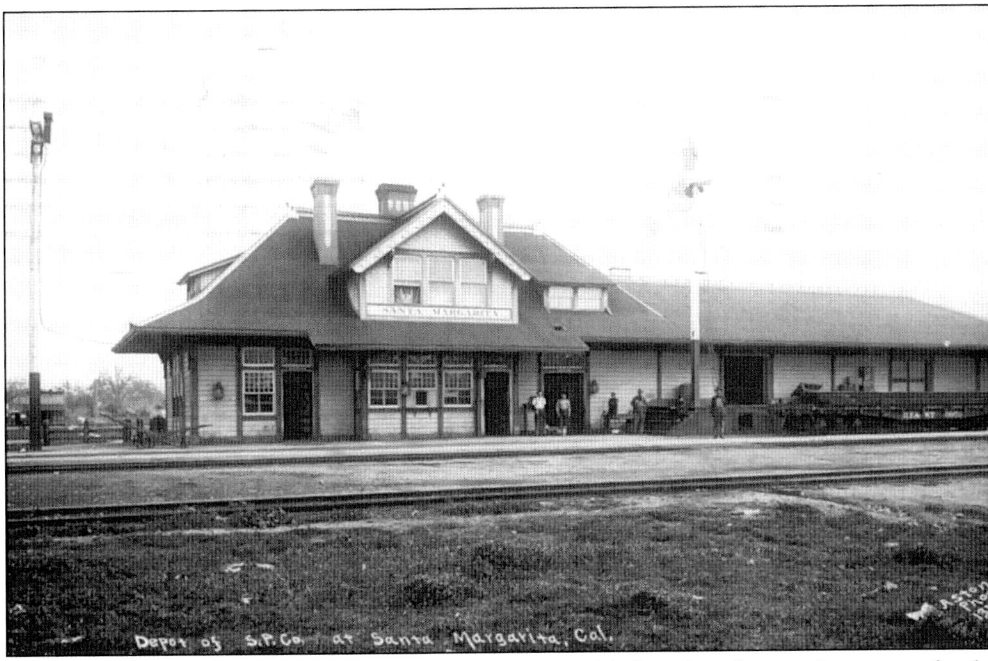

The Depot of the Southern Pacific at Santa Margarita, 1901, functioned not only as a stop for the railroad, but also as the telegraph center and post office.

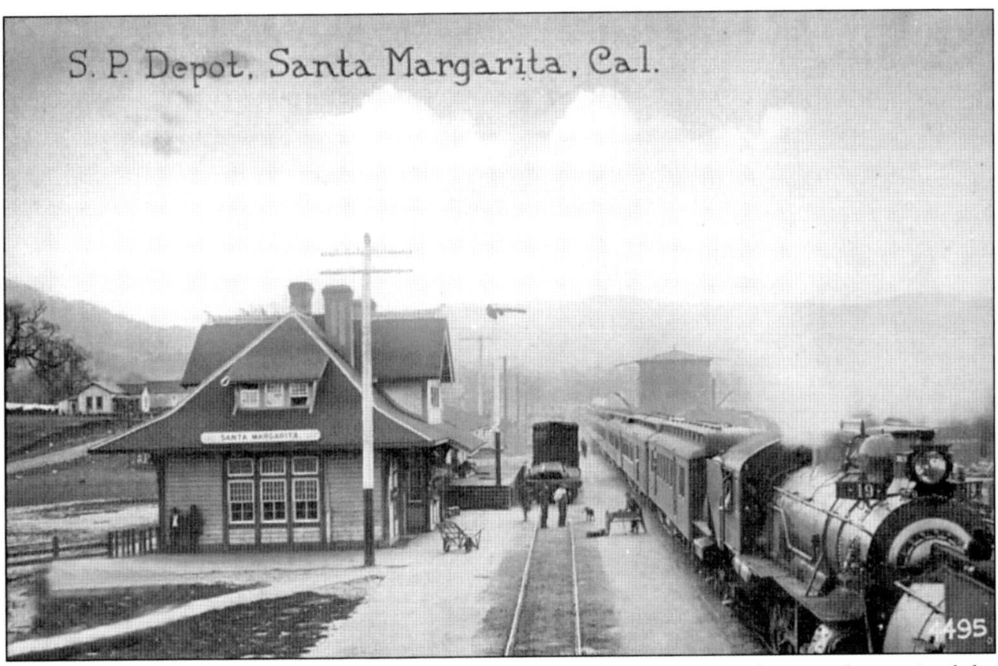

At the time of the postcard, 1905, the Southern Pacific Depot had 10 employees who serviced the 40 stops that the railroad made each week.

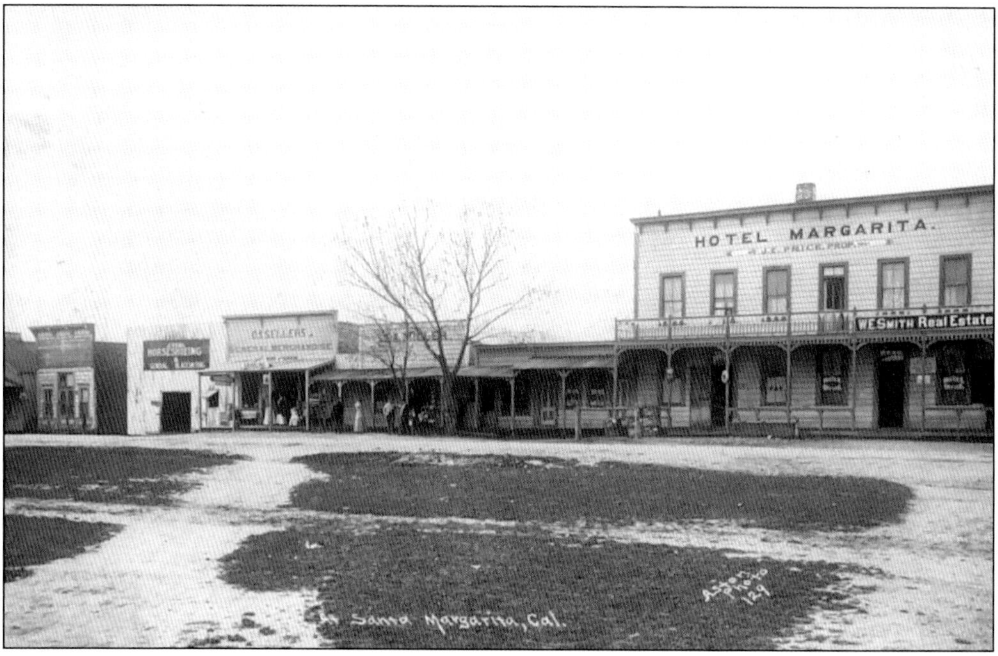

The downtown of Santa Margarita in 1907 boosted of having a "hotel, a few saloons, a handful of stores, and more than enough restaurants."

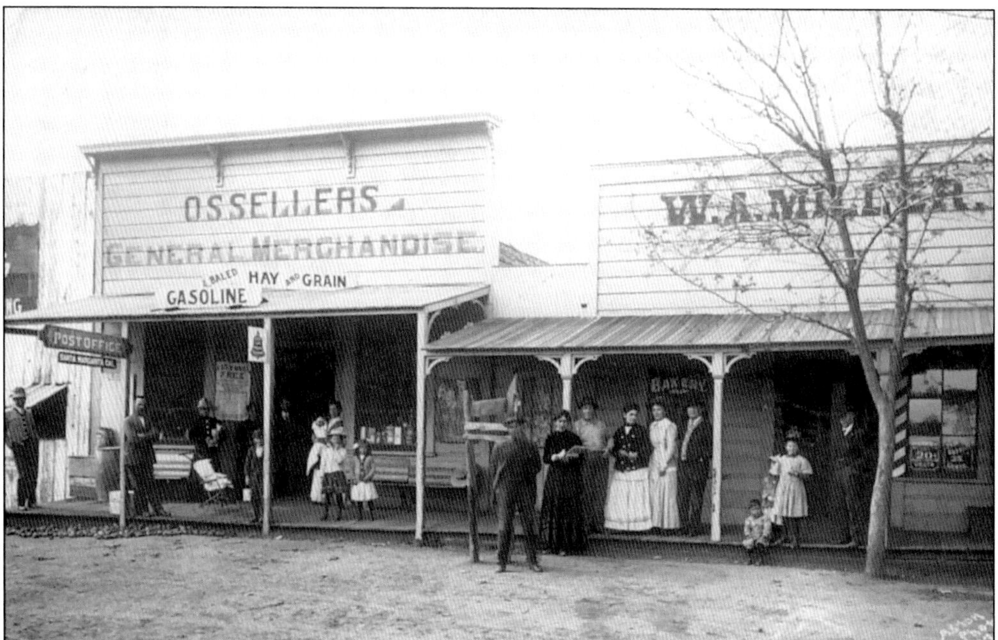

O.S. Sellers General Merchandise began carrying two new commodities for San Margaritans in 1907: gasoline and a long distance pay phone. The advertisement in the barber's window carries the price of a shave for 20¢ and a hair cut for one quarter.

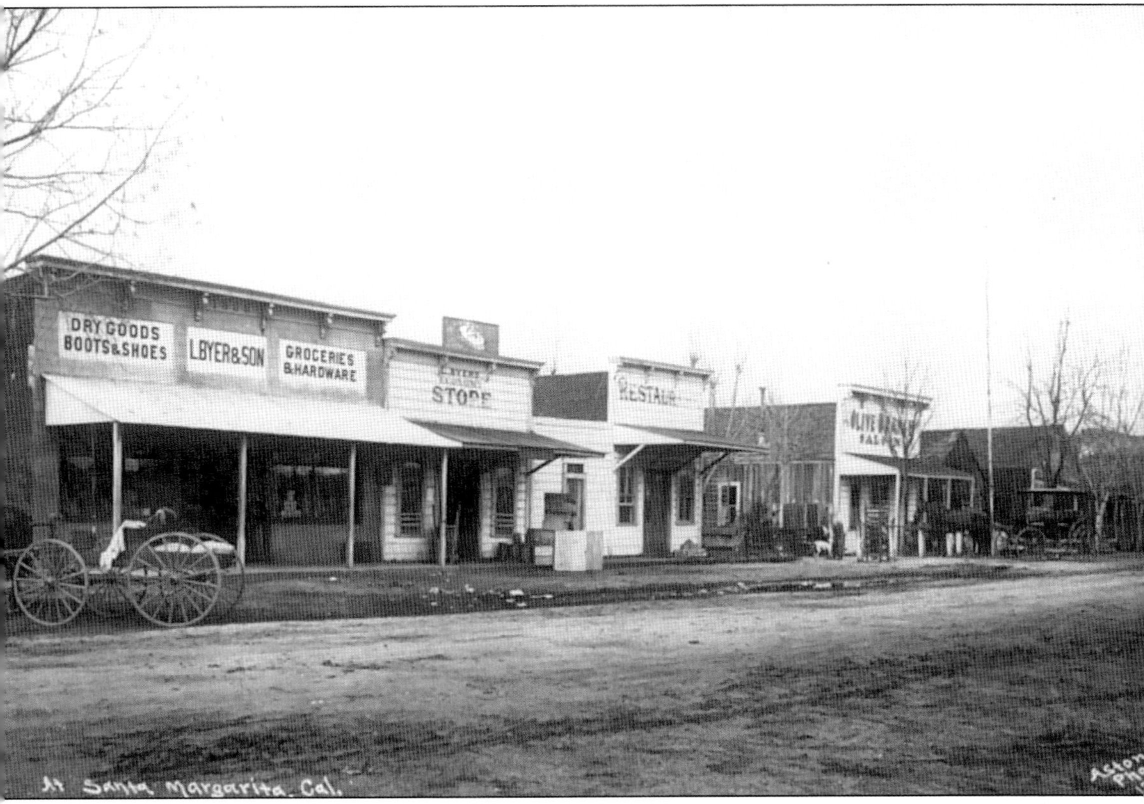

L. Beyer and Son General Store recognized the need for a discount outlet in Santa Margarita, and opened such a business directly next door to their regularly priced items. Also interesting to note was the name of the saloon—"Olive Branch." Perhaps this bar was one of the instruments aimed at keeping the peace at the turn of the century in this California whistle-stop town.

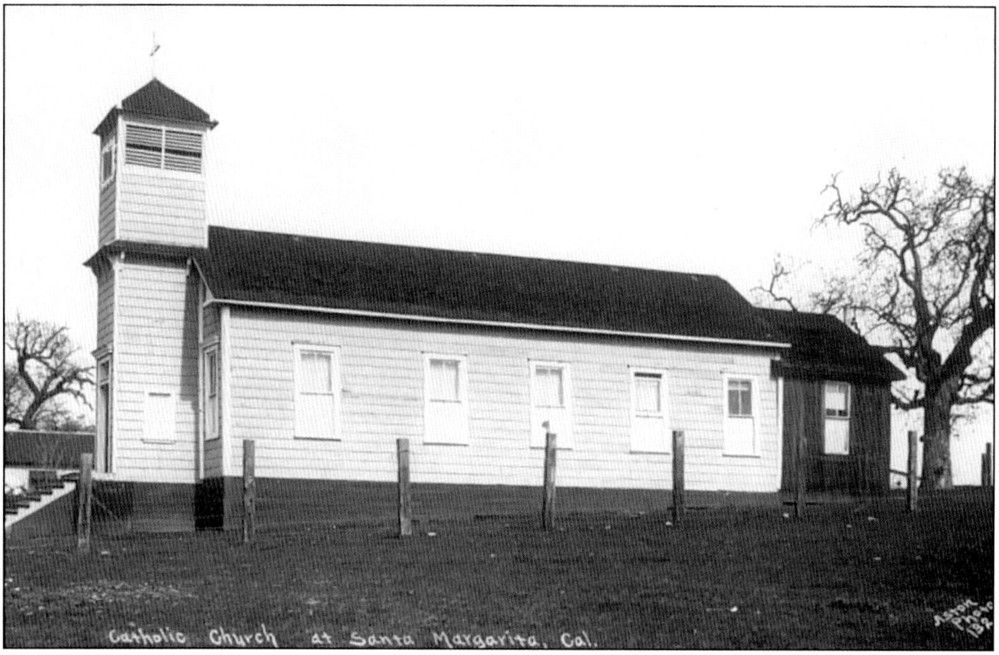

The Catholic Church in Santa Margarita had a strong following in 1904. In that year the congregation was able to pool their resources for the addition of a Sunday school classroom in the rear of the church.

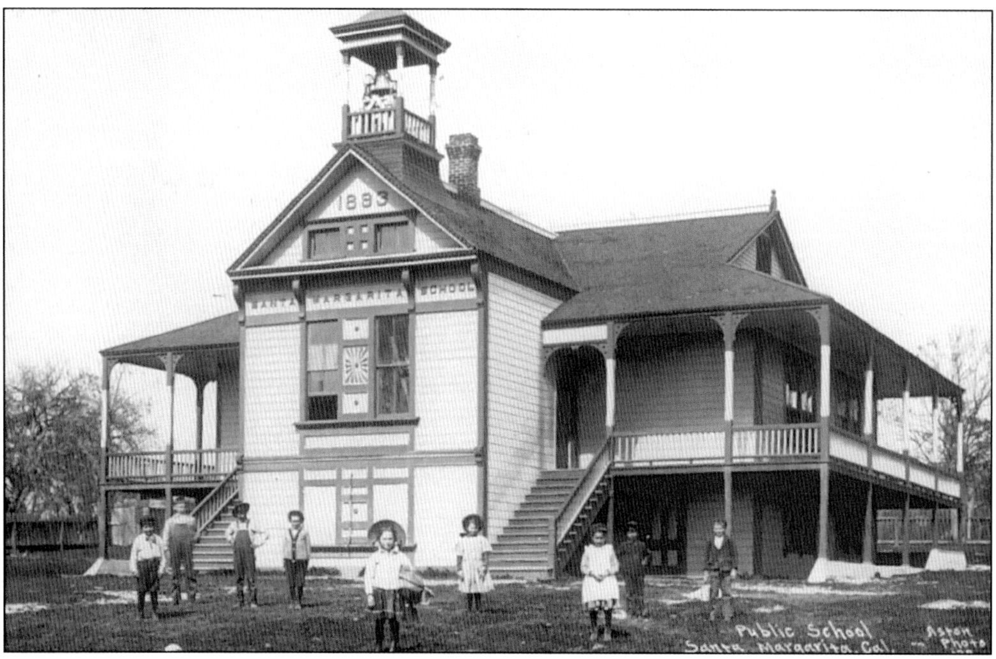

Santa Margarita began erecting their six-room schoolhouse in 1893; it was completed that following year. The enrollment at the time this picture was taken in 1903 tallied 46 students.

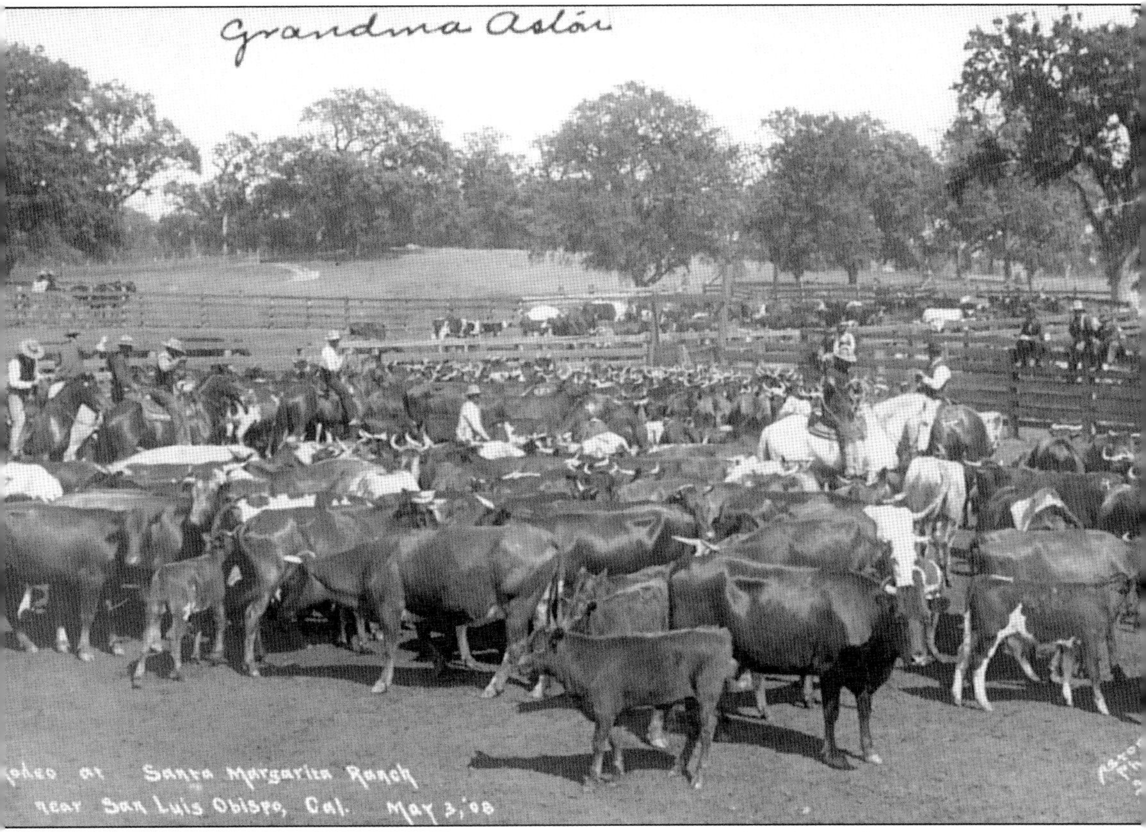

The biggest event each year in Santa Margarita was the Barbecue and Rodeo at the Santa Margarita Ranch, which was held the first weekend of May 1908.

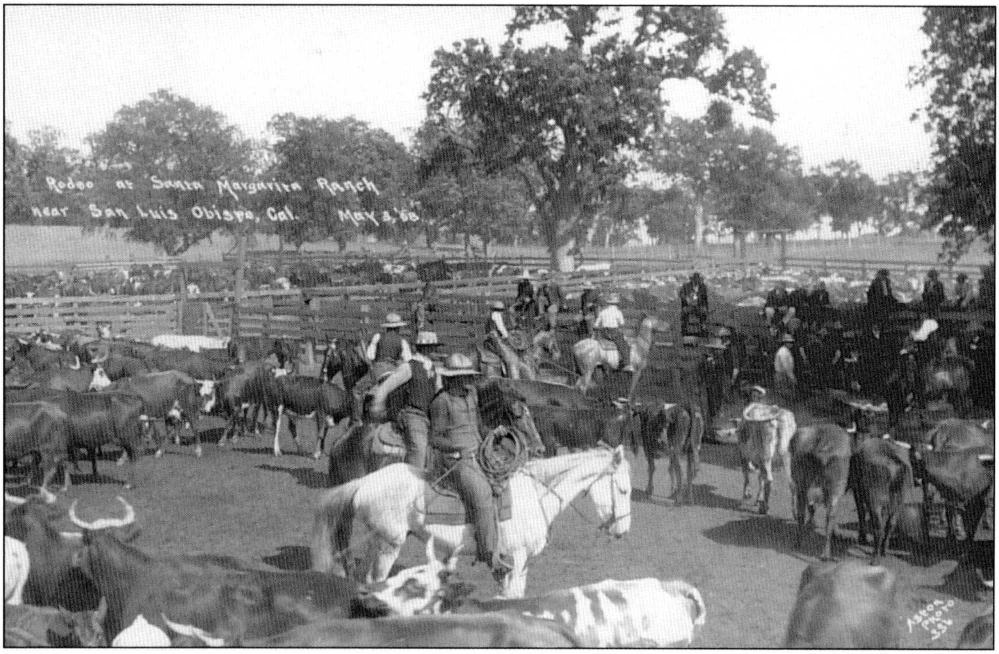

The rodeo at Santa Margarita Ranch brought in contestants from all over central California, and in the event recorded by this postcard, May 3, 1908, two cowboys had traveled all the way from Wyoming, and two other "former ranch hands turned financiers" from San Francisco.

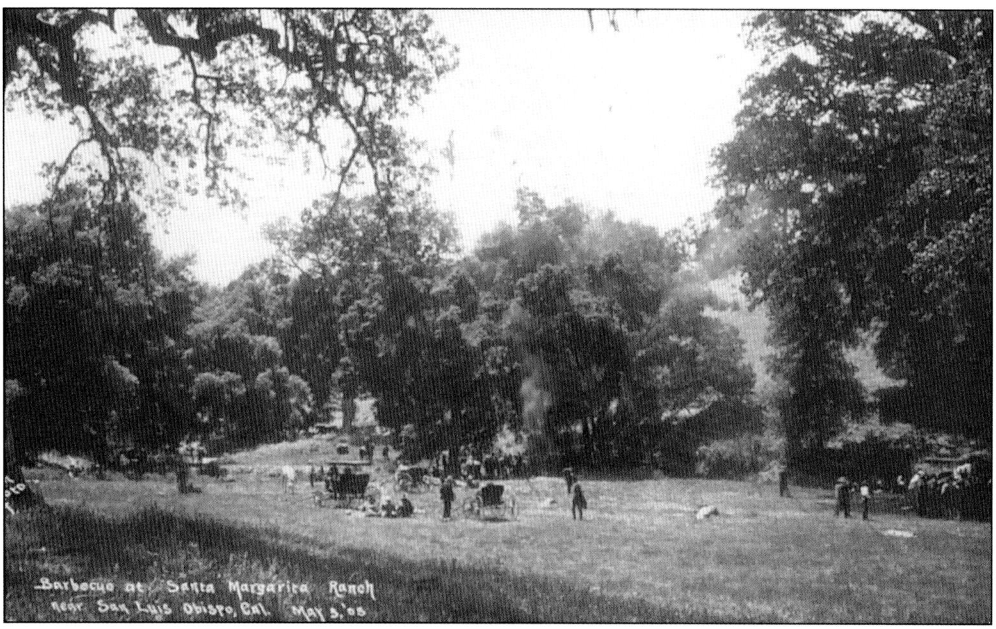

The barbecue was the capstone on the day's events, with more than a few of the calves filling the stomachs of the tired rodeo participants and their families, May 3, 1908.

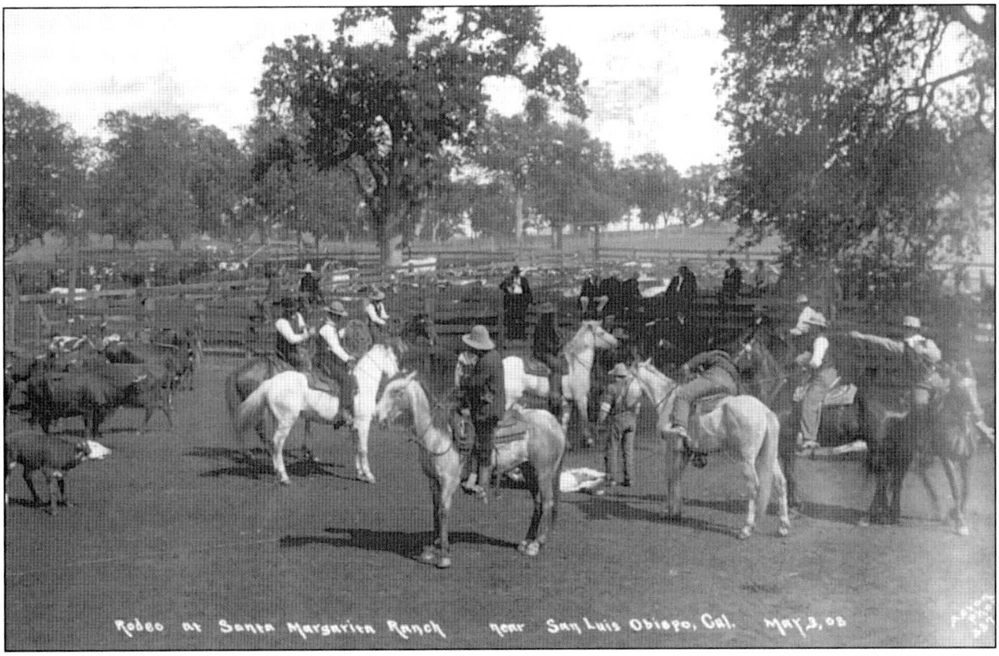

Pictured above is the catching one of the calves for the barbecue pit.

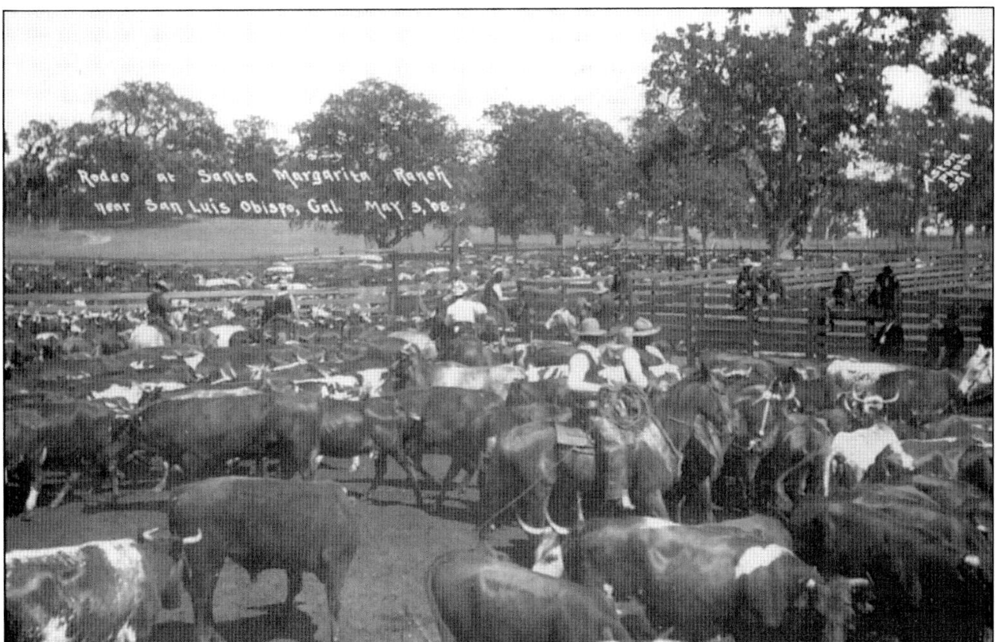

Here are more heads of cattle than these cowboys can handle.

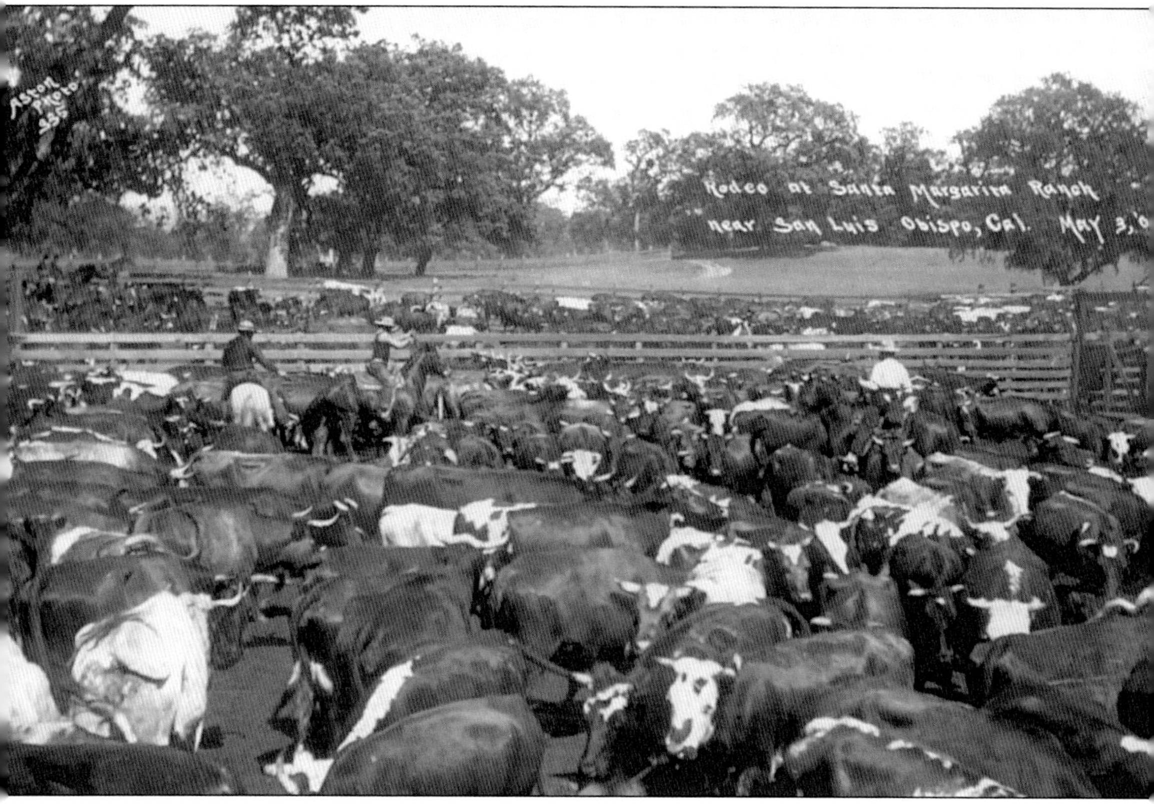

Three cowboys set their lassos on a calf in quite a crowd of beef.

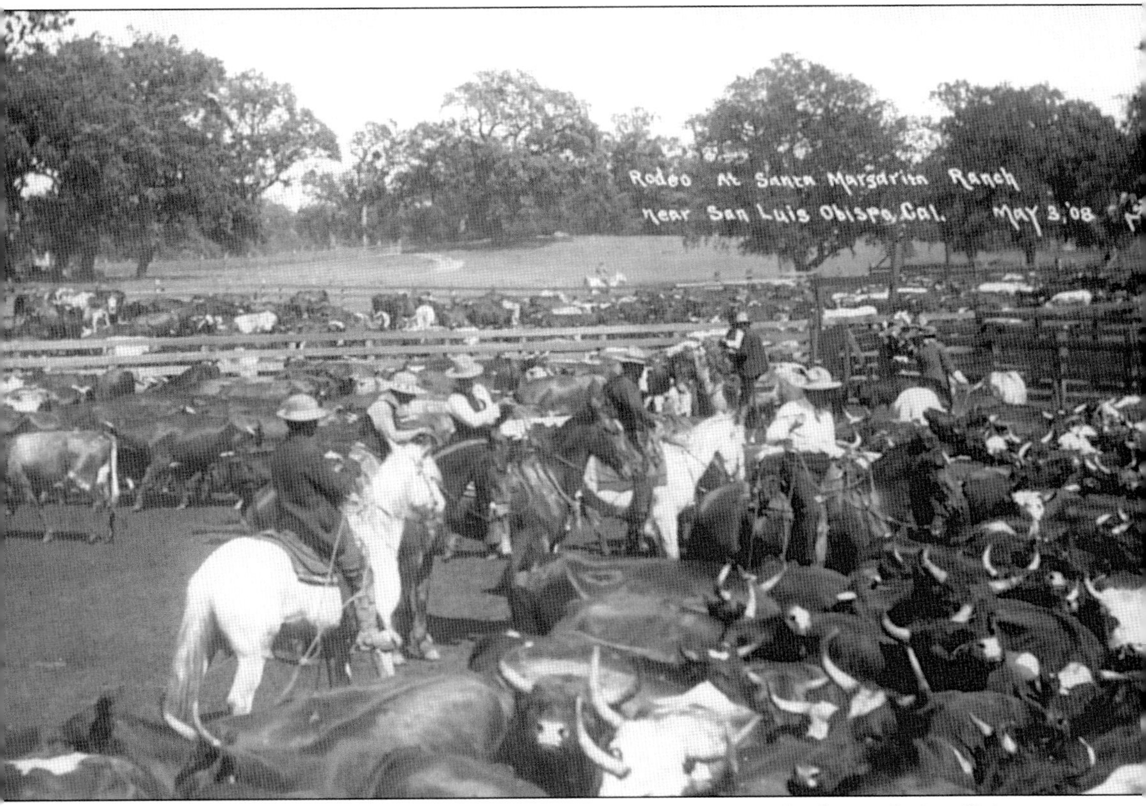

Corralling the herd was an event where the cowboys were judged on their efficiency and flamboyance.

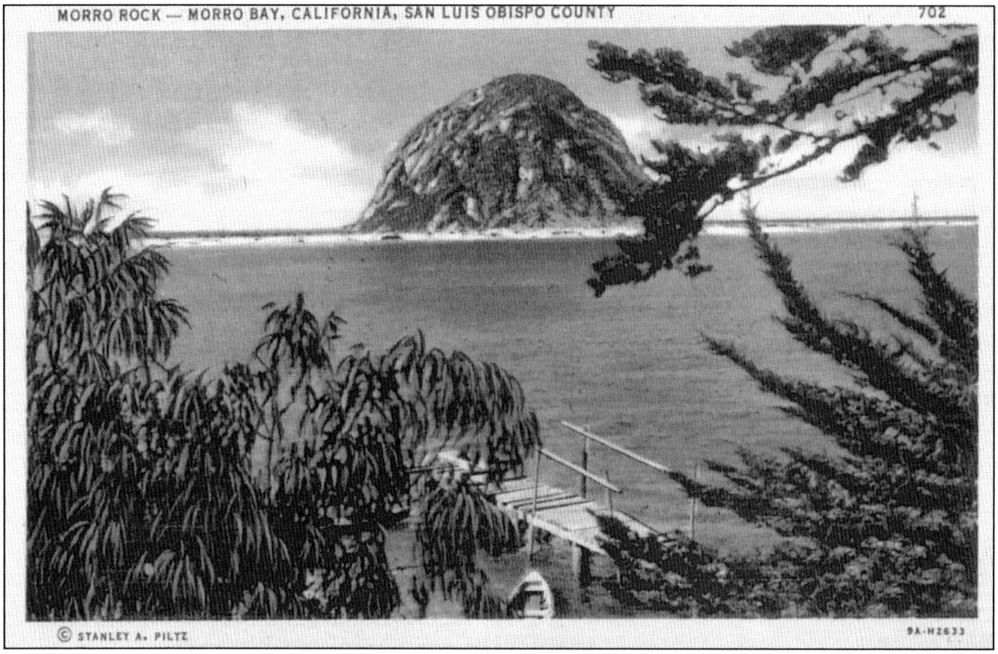

Morro Bay is centrally located on the Pacific between Santa Margarita and San Luis Obispo. These postcards are artists' renditions of the great Morro Rock and the Morro Bay, *c.* 1900. Morro Rock, the "Gibraltar" of the California Coastline, was still an island at this time. Now, a man-made causeway connects the 576-foot high mighty rock and California State Historical Landmark, Number 821, with the mainland. Morro Bay is no longer the tranquil "two-vessel" harbor that this postcard commemorates. On any give day hundreds of ships, from the commercial and tourist fishing industries to ocean yachts, now fill the small harbor.

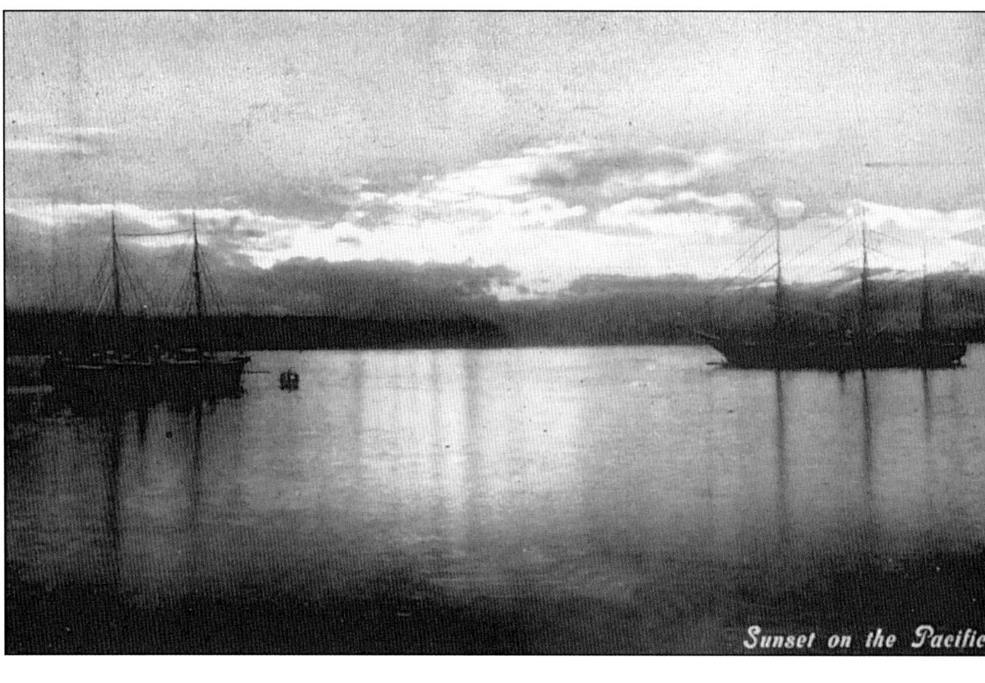

Part II

The California Polytechnic School

In San Luis Obispo from 1895 to 1900 a new "professional" school to educate and train young men and women in the specific fields of agriculture and homemaking was planned, employing an innovative and progressive curriculum entitled Agricultural Engineering and Home Economics. These academic courses would focus not only on teaching the rudimentary skills needed in these fields, but also encourage innovation and the entrepreneurial spirit.

Myron Angel, a local newspaperman, is credited with the initial concept of developing the polytechnic, and forming the local board of trustees to govern its development. A consensus on the coursework amongst the planning commission of town leaders during this initial stage was never reached. This gridlock was finally overcome in 1900 when the agricultural education expert Dr. Leroy Anderson, Ph.D. from Cornell University, was contracted to "fully develop a modern and professional academic curriculum and environment, conducive to the further advancement of engineering needed for all areas in agriculture, to include a modern household."

The first year of instruction at Cal Poly, as it came to be called quite early on, was conducted by a faculty of three, including the director, Dr. Anderson, who taught agriculture and animal and dairy industries. The first matron of Cal Poly, Gwendolyn Stewart, was educated at Stanford University, where she earned a B.S. in domestic science. Oscar Heald, project supervisor of the construction of the buildings at the school and graduate of the Throop Polytechnic Institute, was retained by Anderson to give instruction in the areas of carpentry and iron works.

Cal Poly eventually evolved from its status as a high school, and into a junior college, and then finally into the California Polytechnic State University.

Pictured on the following two pages are images of the California Polytechnic School.

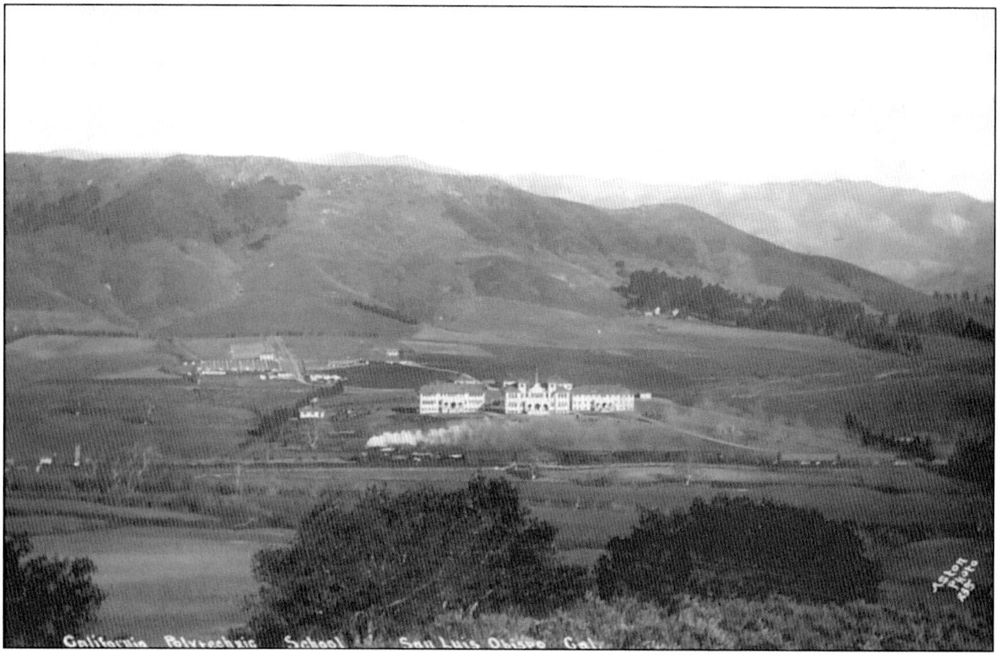

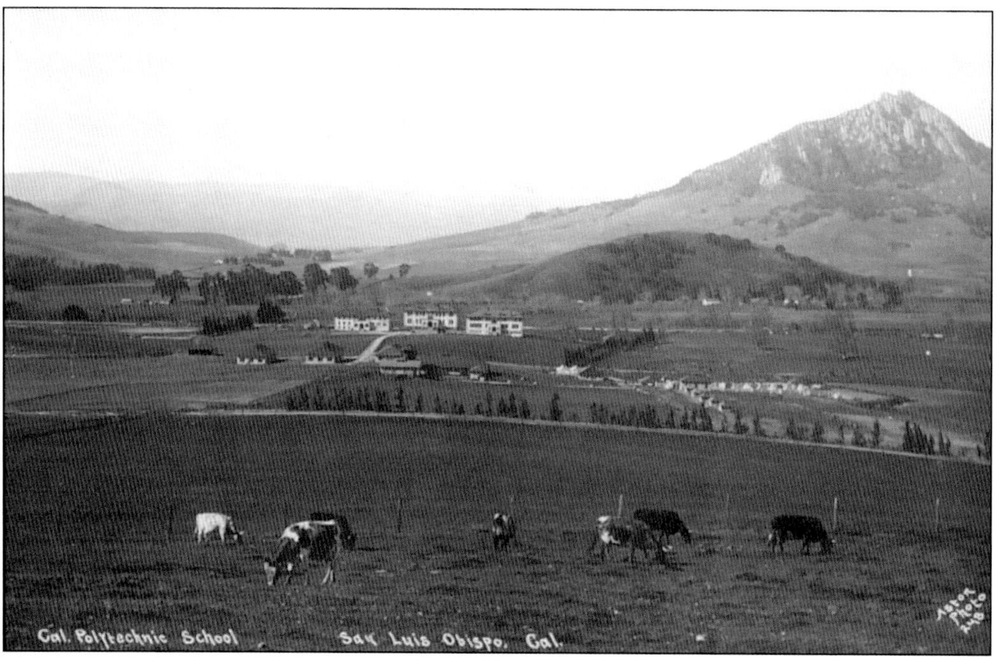

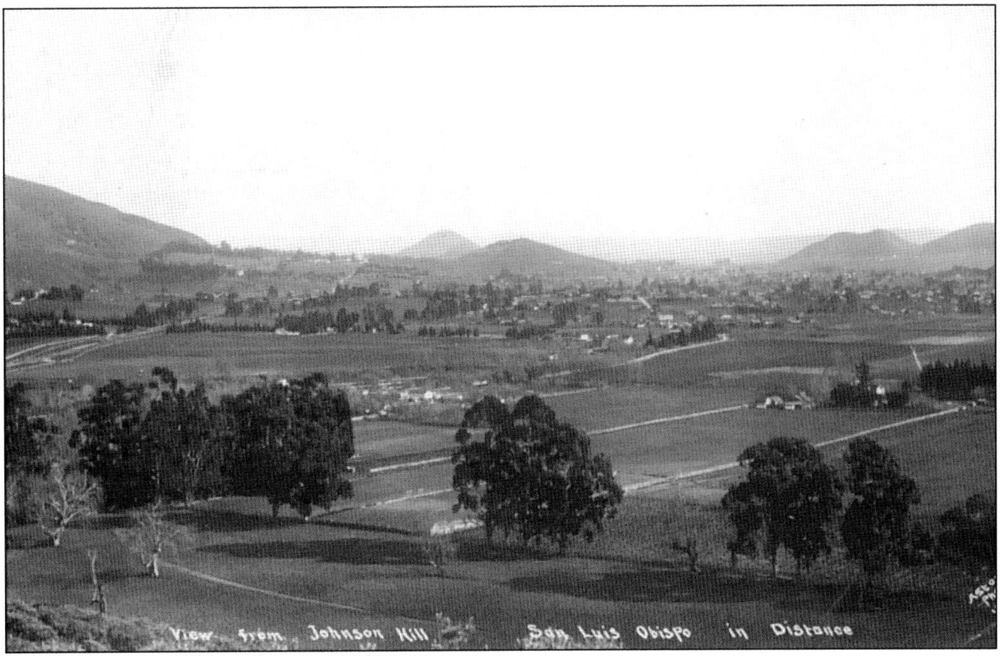
View from Johnson Hill San Luis Obispo in Distance

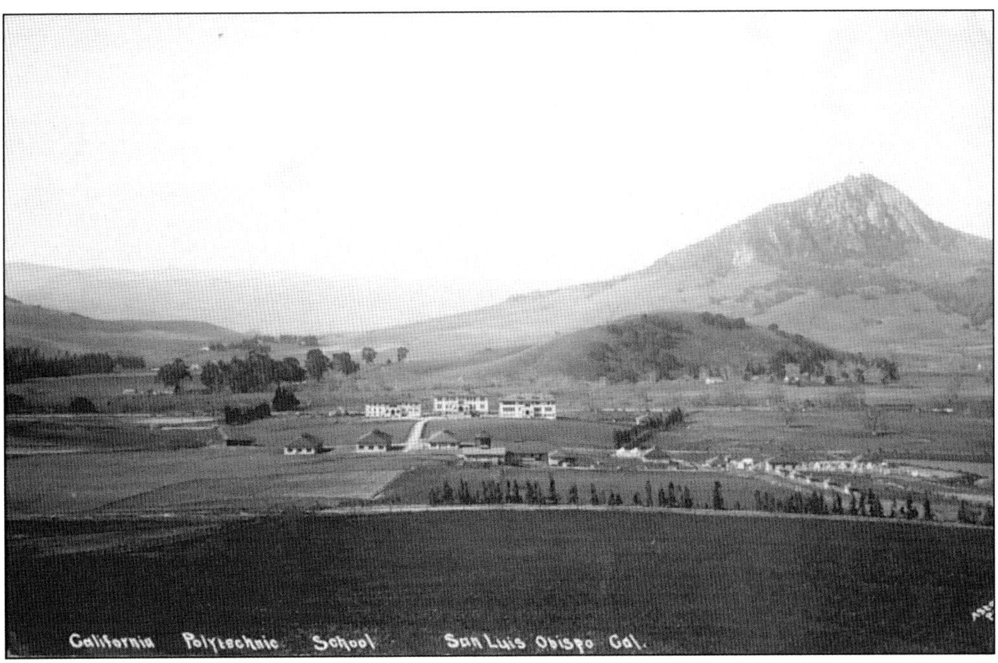
California Polytechnic School San Luis Obispo Cal.

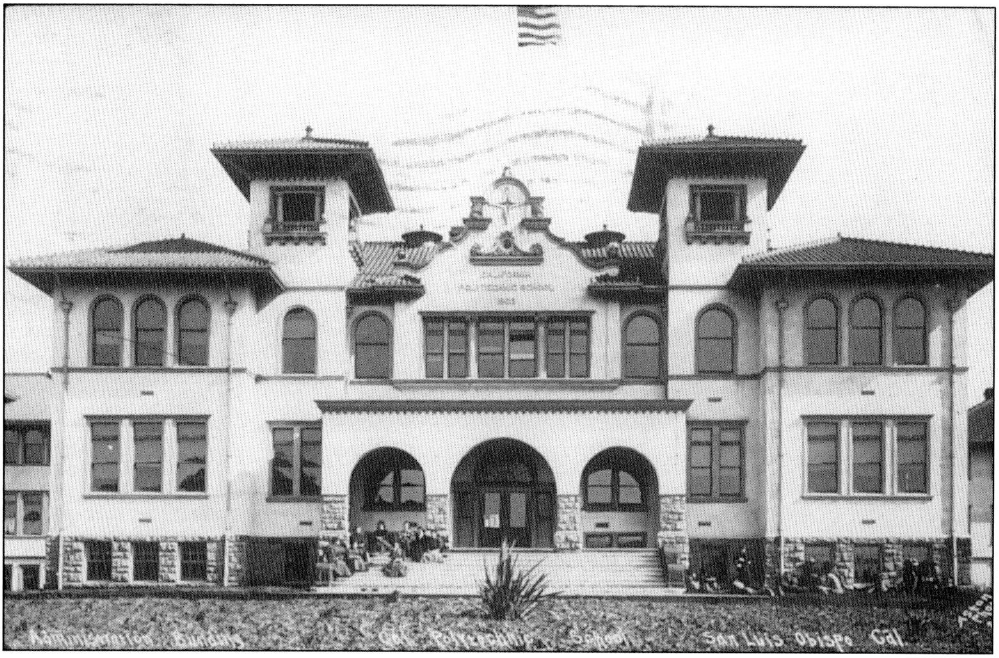

Pictured above is the Administration and Instruction Building, Cal Poly, 1903.

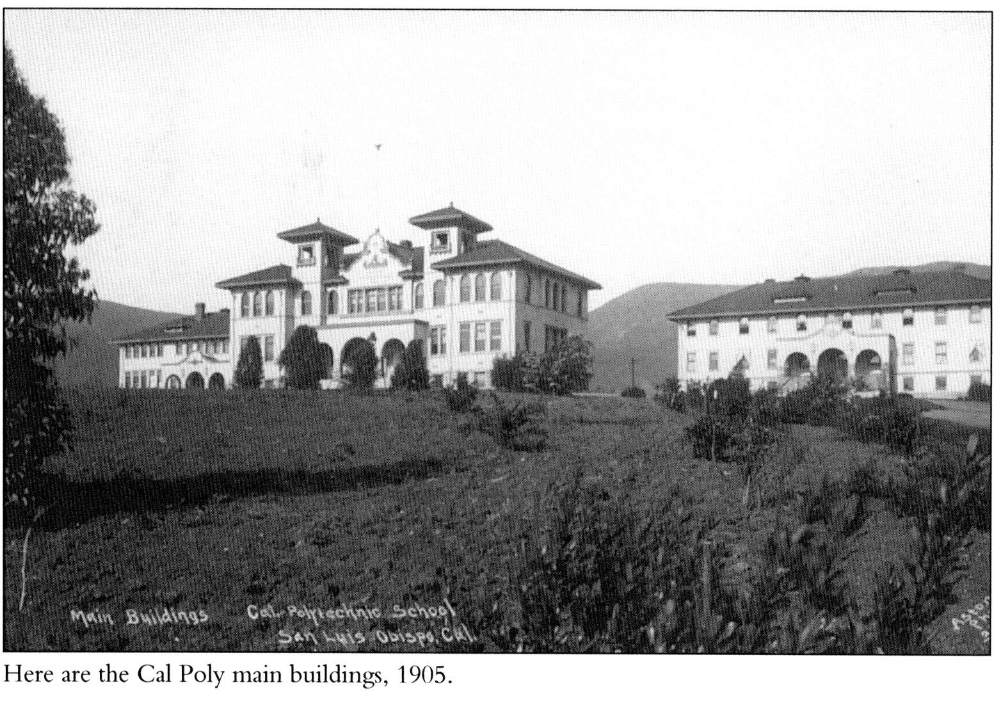

Here are the Cal Poly main buildings, 1905.

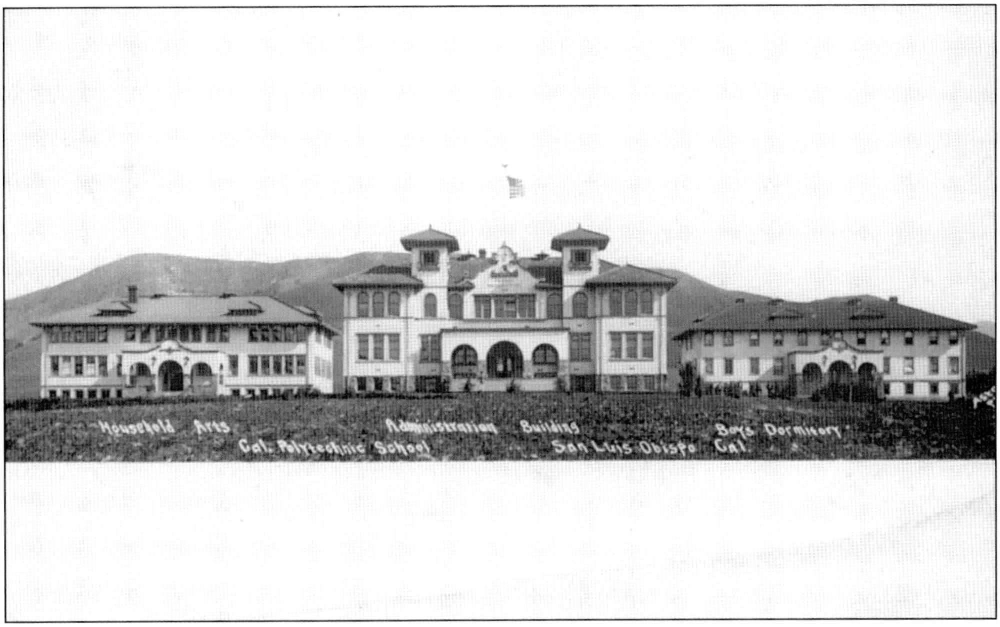

The education of the girls at Cal Poly generally took place in the Household Arts Building on the campus, which is the building to the far left in this postcard, 1905.

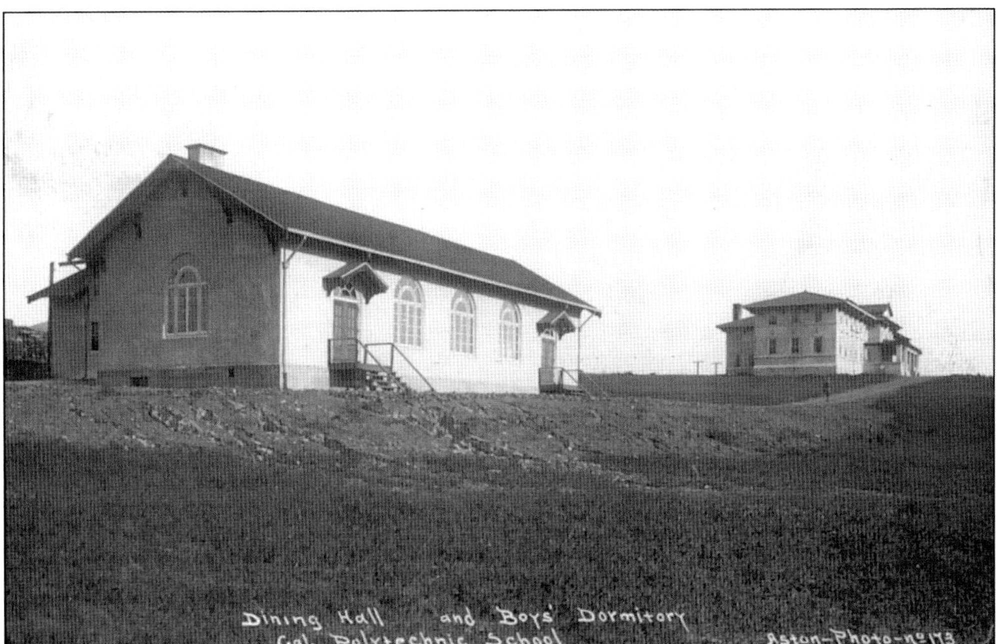

The girls were also responsible for preparing the meals that both they and the boys ate in the cafeteria.

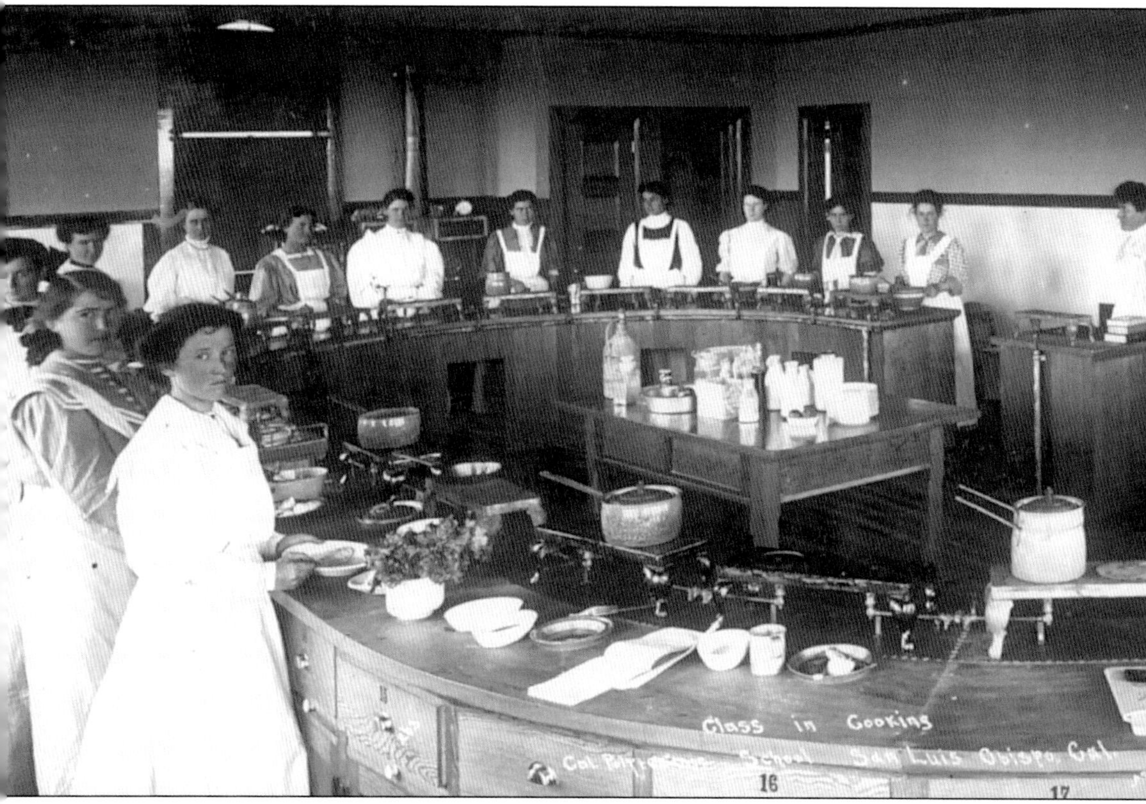

The training for food preparation in the cooking class took place in the Household Arts Building. Gwendolyn Stewart is giving instruction in this picture; she is on the far right side.

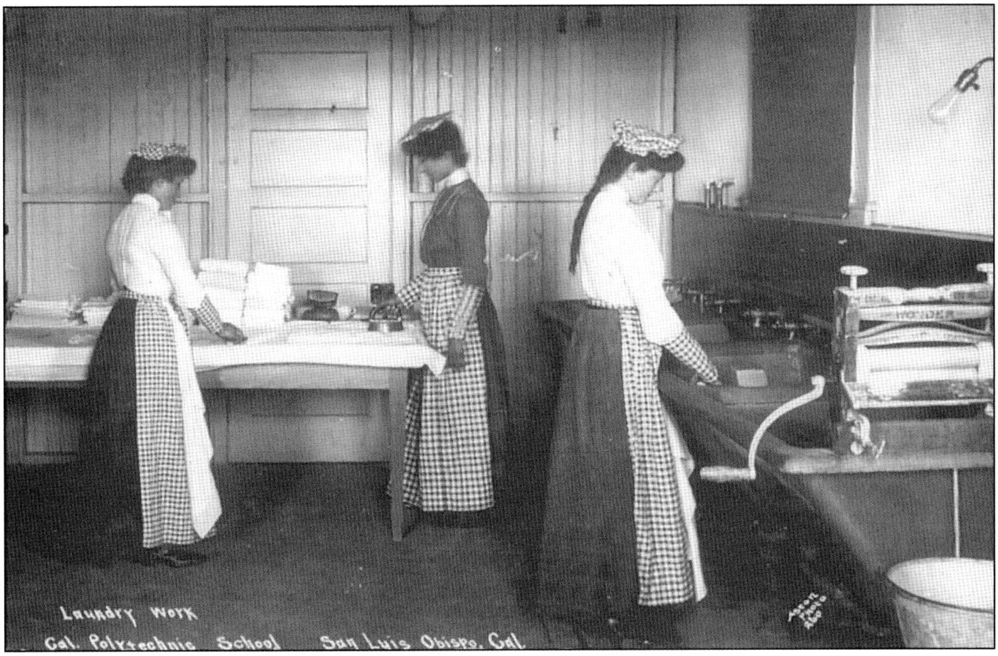

The laundry for the entire school was managed through the instruction of the girls, in the class aptly named "Laundry Work."

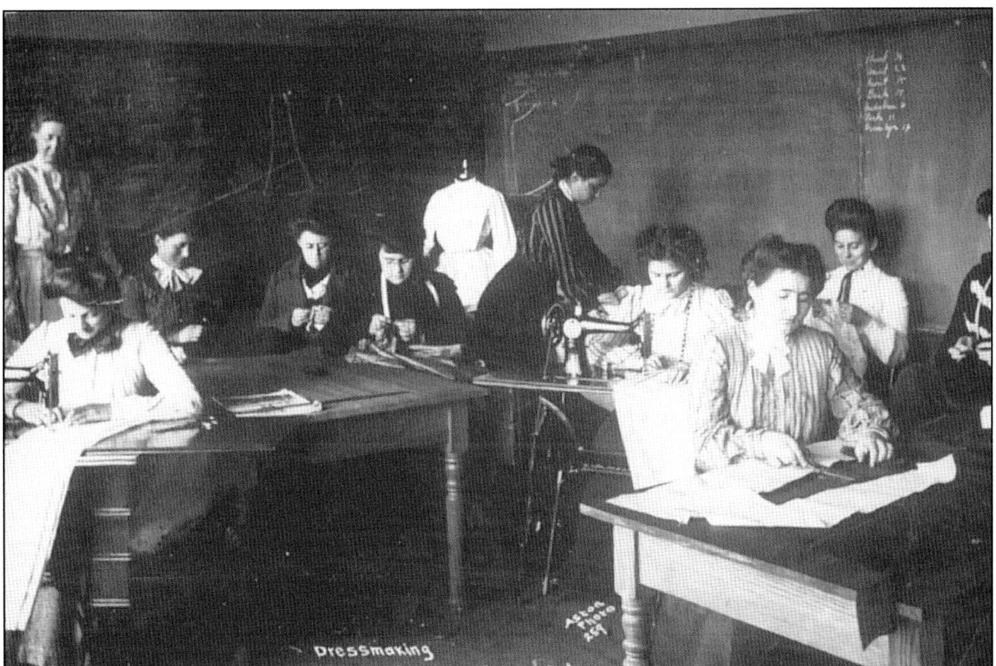

Dressmaking class was the consensus favorite with the female students. In the more advanced stages of this coursework each student was given the opportunity to design her own model, under the direction of Miss Stewart, *c.* 1906.

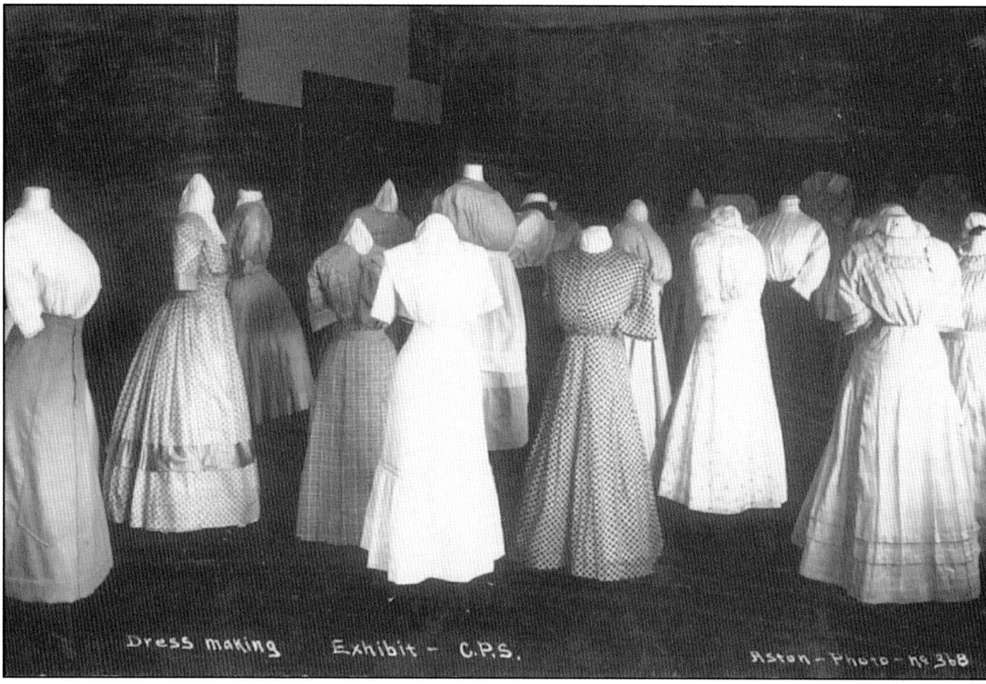

At the end of each term the completed dresses were placed on display for the entire San Luis Obispo community to review and purchase, as long as the designer agreed to display it. This is the 1907 review of the girls' latest fashions.

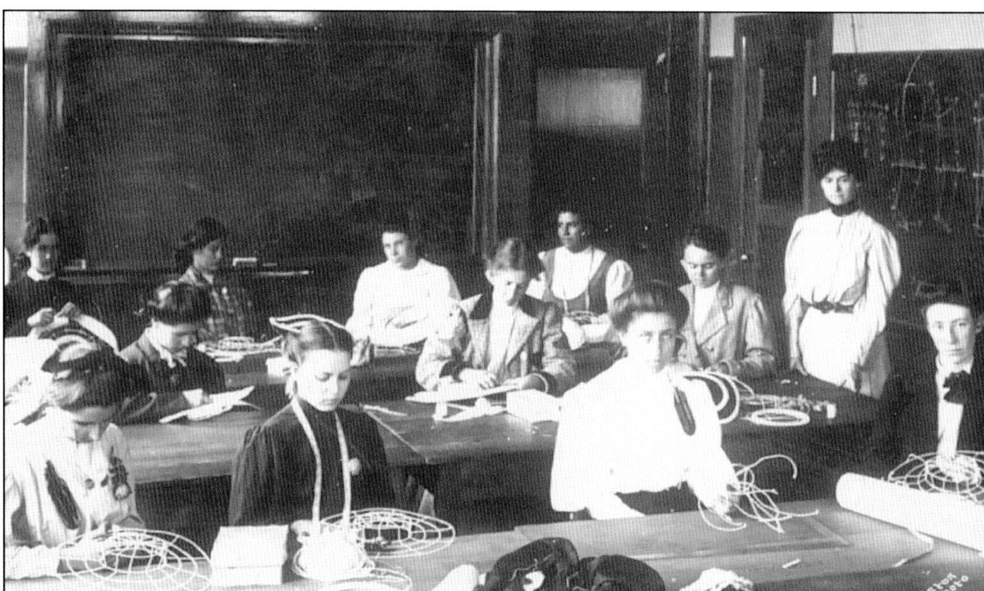

The milliner class was a necessity, as no young lady cared to be without a fine hat in those days. The hats the girls at Cal Poly produced were sold for a "nice profit" which benefited both the school and the students, 1904.

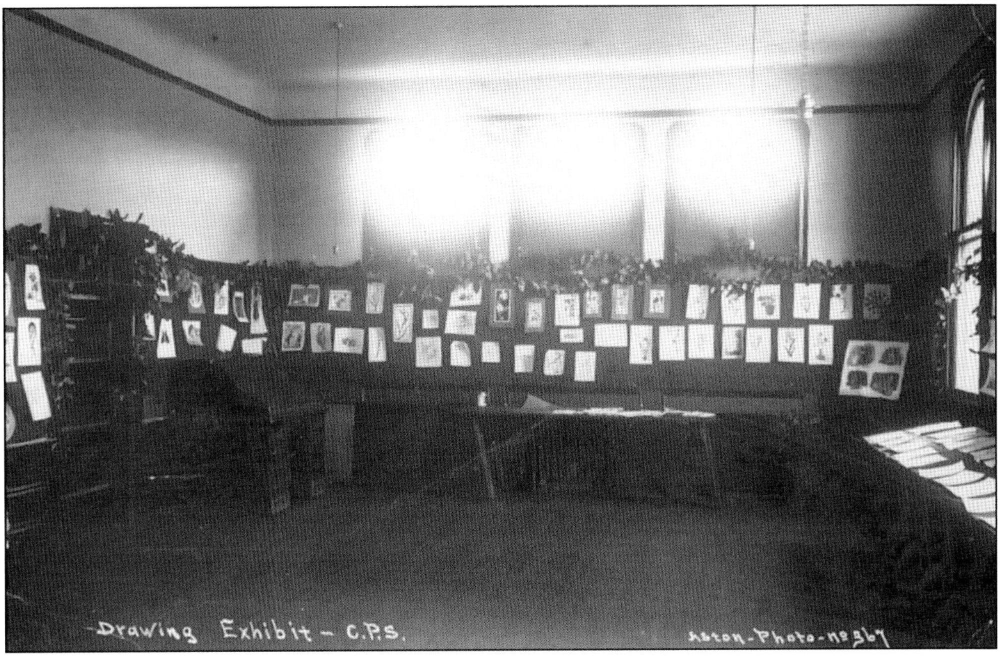

Painting and drawing was considered one of the essential components of the household arts. It was also a class that contained both boys and girls, and for this reason alone it was consistently one of the most popular offered at Cal Poly.

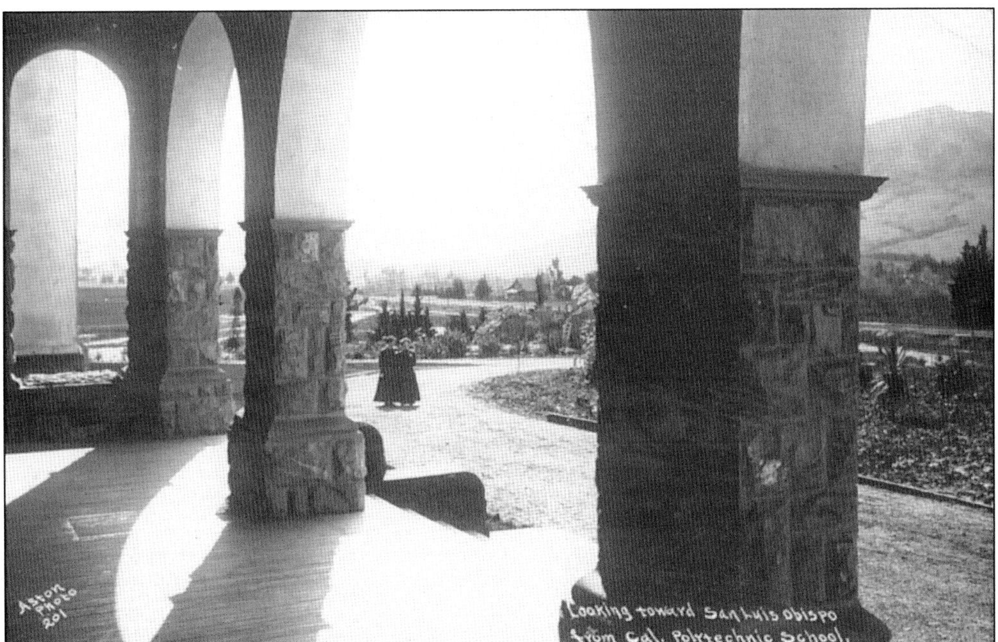

Two girls at the end of the school day at Cal Poly, October 1906. The day for the students began at 7:30 a.m., with academics concluding at 3:00 p.m. Generally all after-school activities terminated by 8:00 p.m., thus allowing for some additional study time or socializing. These early students of Cal Poly nonetheless had a busy daily routine.

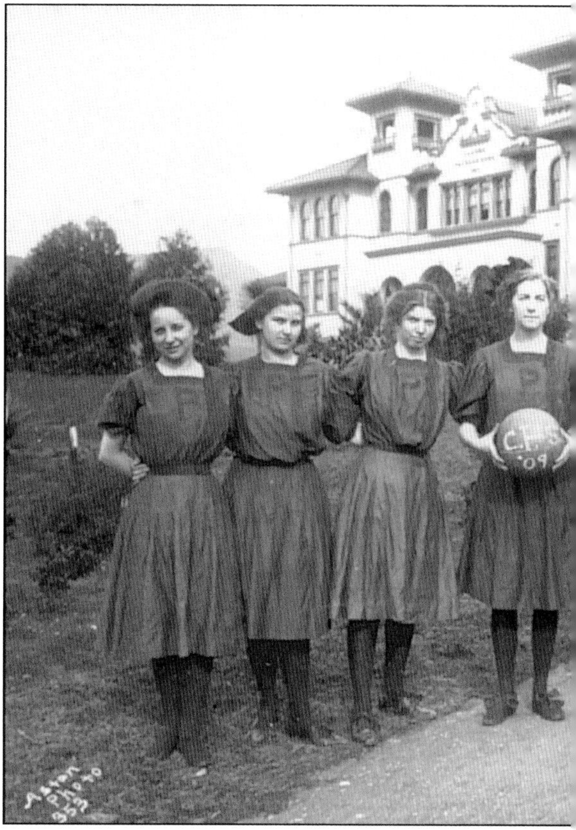

Athletics were also open for the female students at Cal Poly. Pictured here are the 1909 and 1911 girls basketball teams with Coach Evelyn Secrest, an alumnus of Cal Poly.

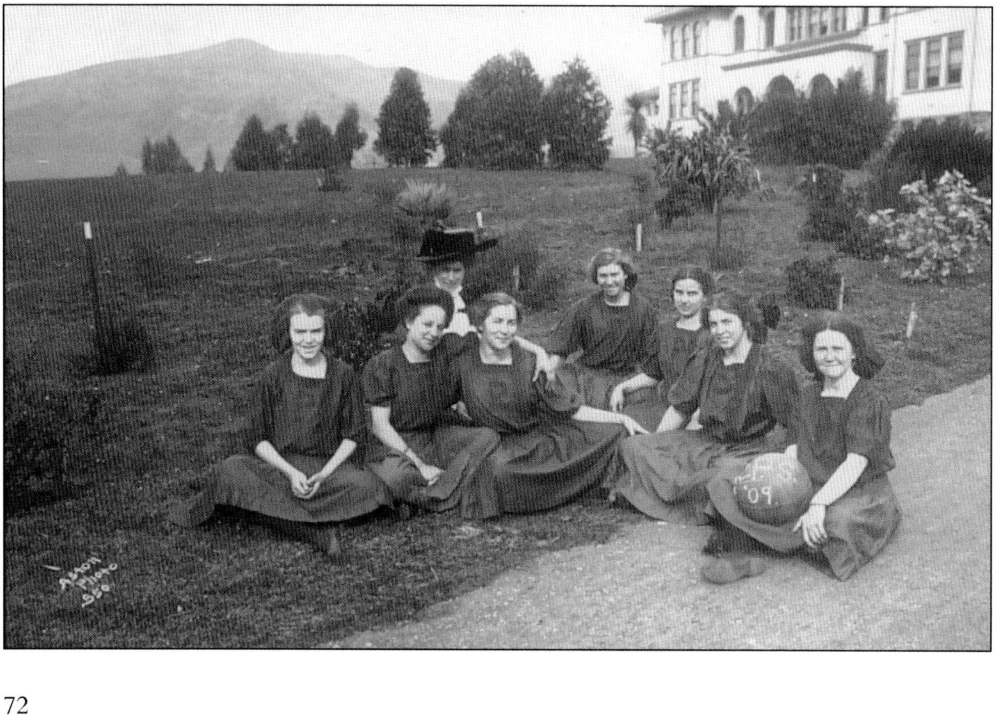

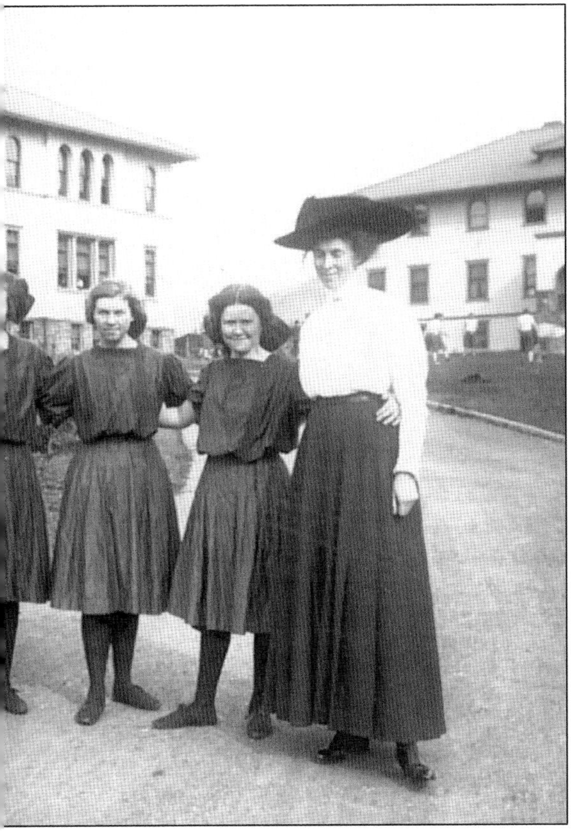

Note the bulky uniforms the athletes wore in comparison to those of the boys

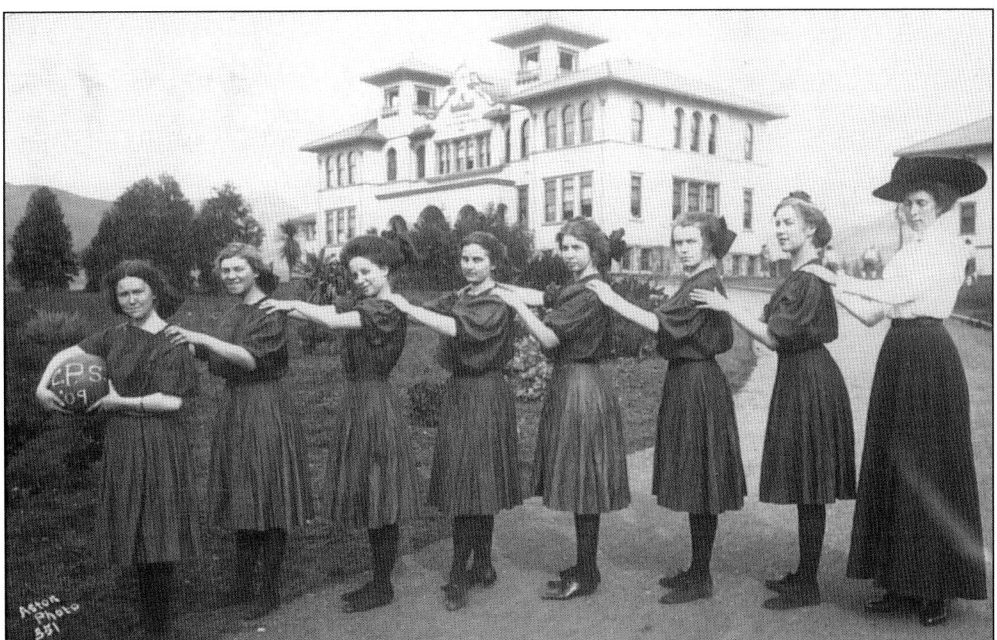

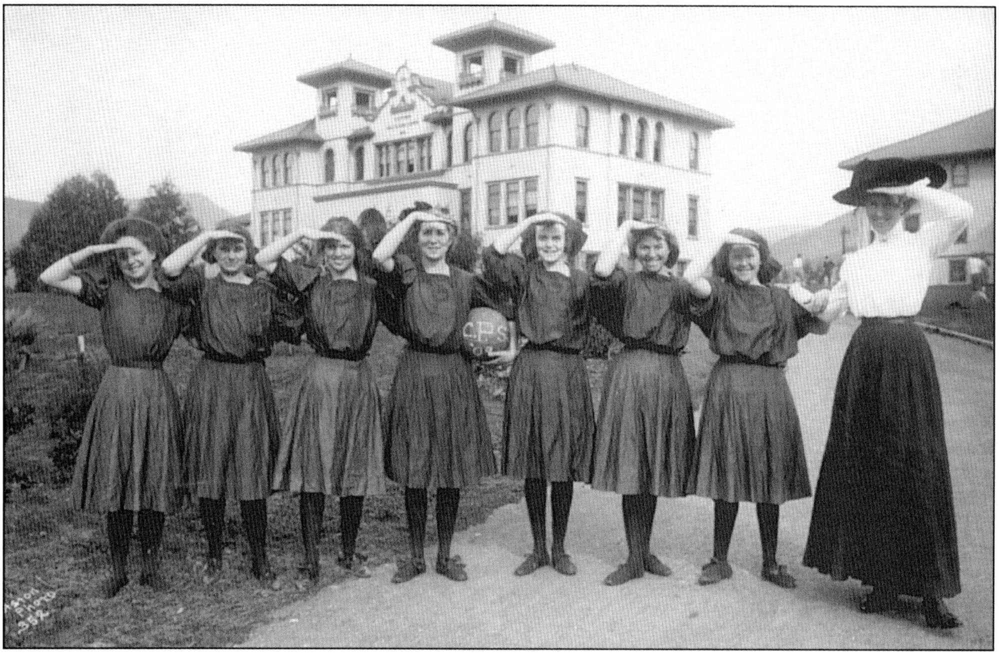

Although Cal Poly was a co-educational institution, the student population was heavily male during the first ten years. The students at Cal Poly came from all parts of California, from out of

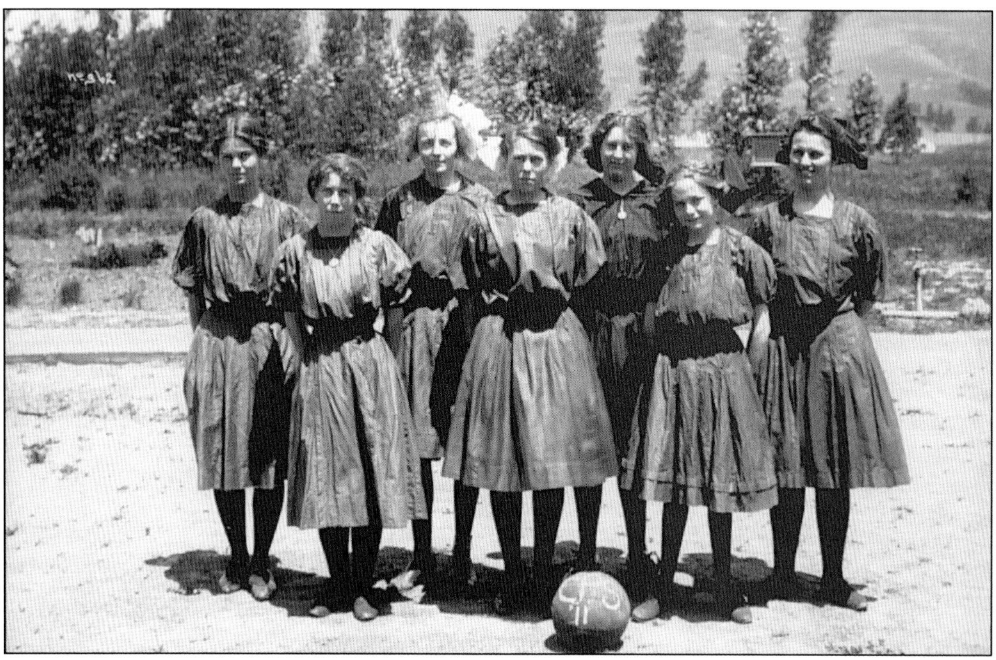

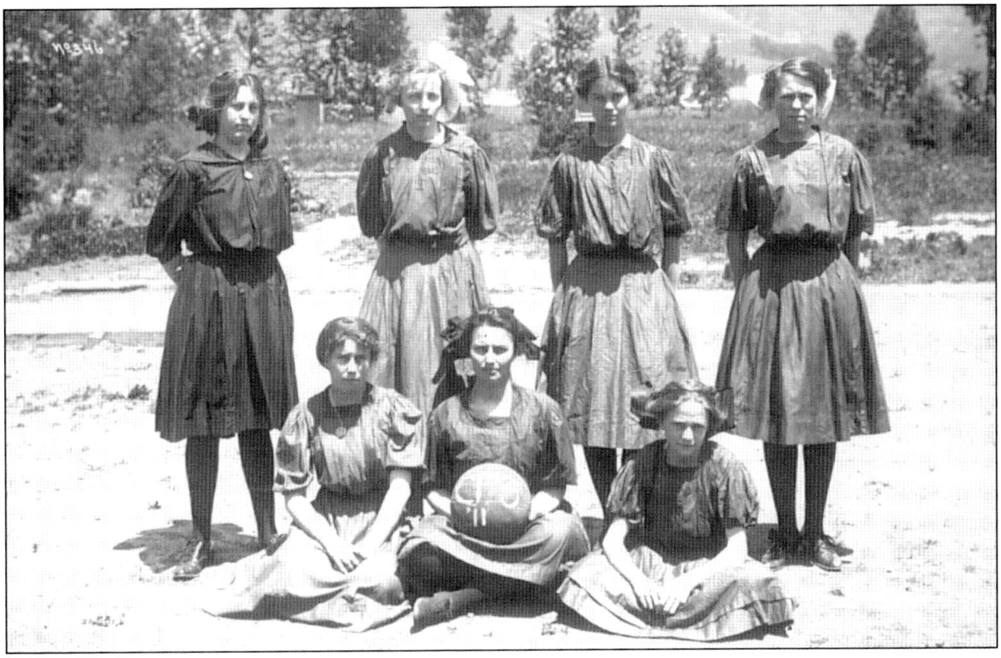

state, and from foreign lands, such as Japan. In 1910 a girls' dormitory was built, as the 79 female students could not all find situations in town.

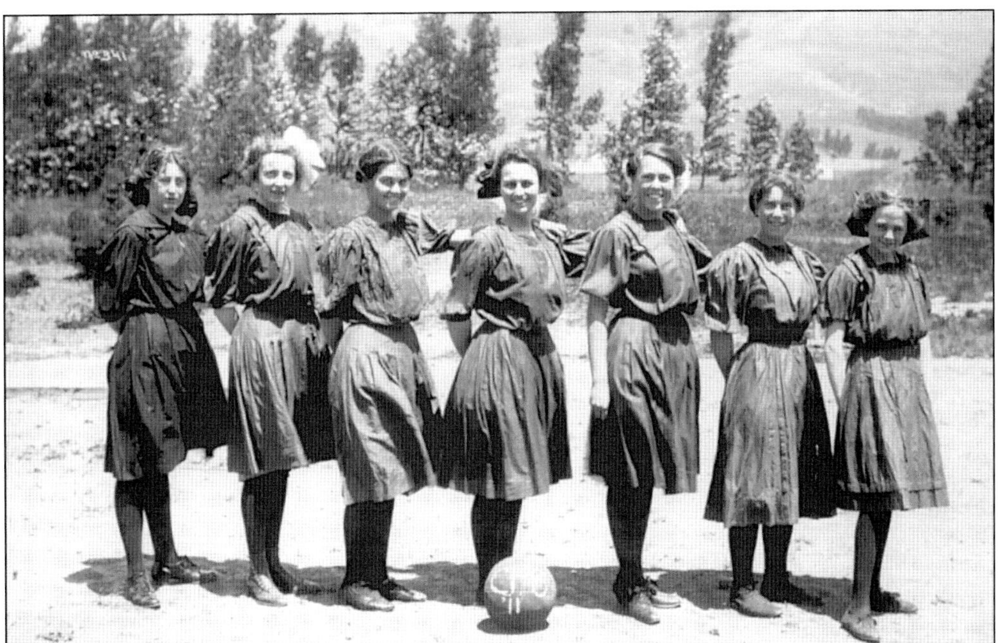

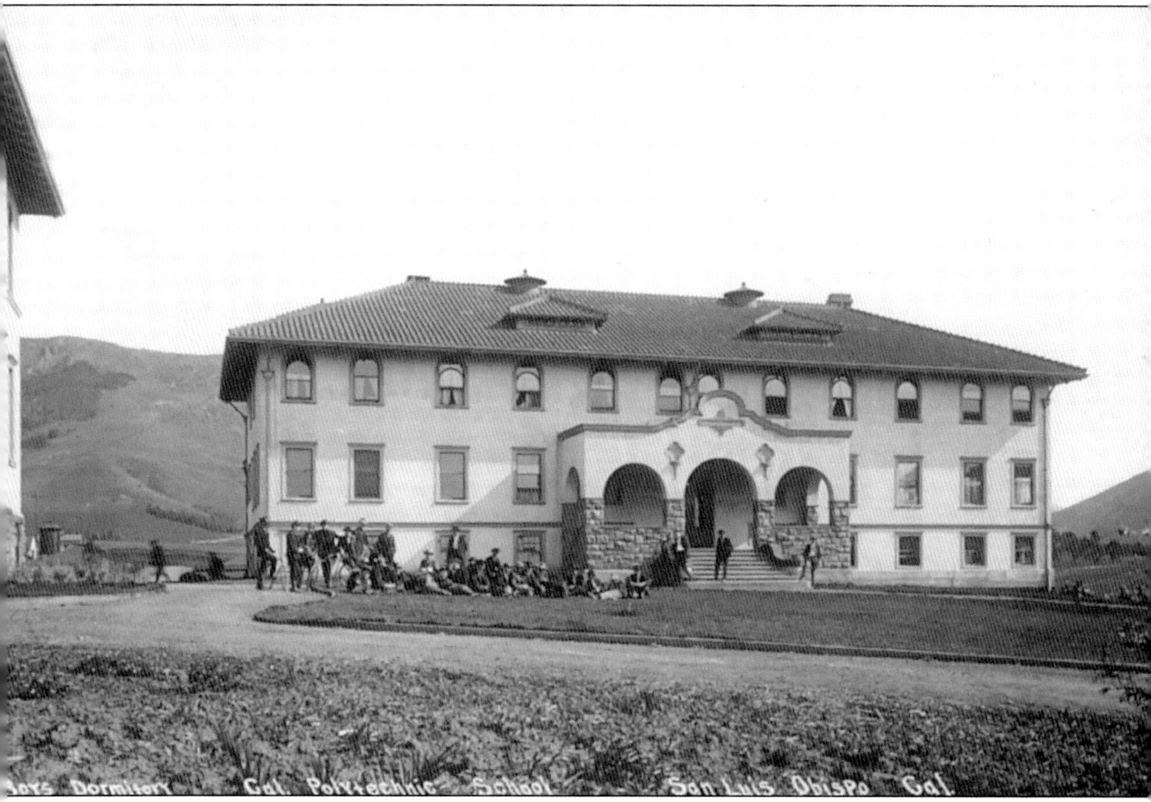

The boys' dormitory, one of the original buildings, housed 120 when this photo was taken in 1908.

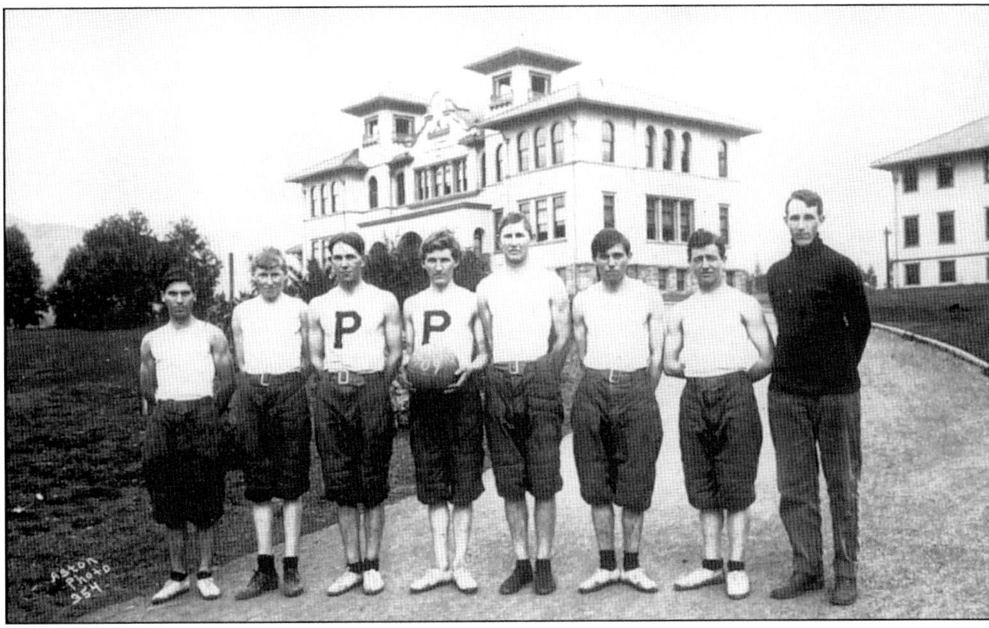

The 1909 boys varsity basketball team.

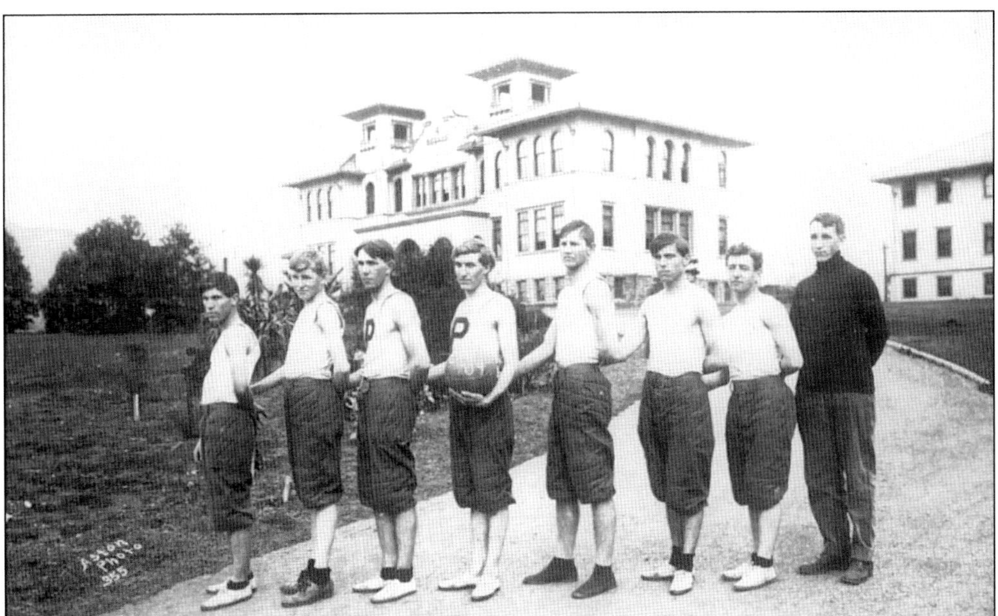

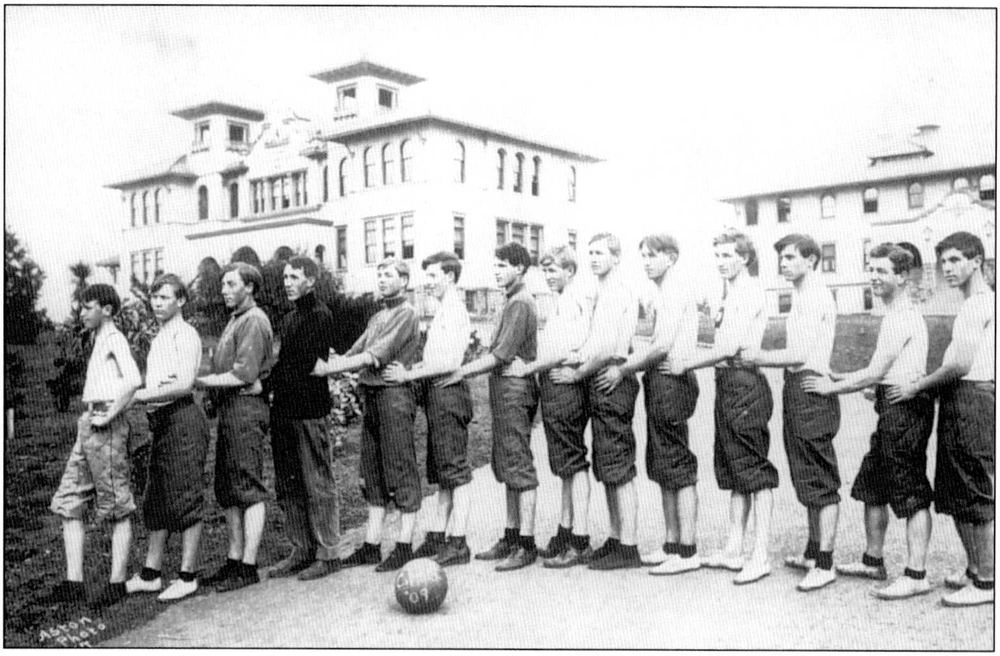

The 1909 boys varsity and reserve varsity basketball teams. The varsity and junior varsity teams more often than not played each other as the number of athletic teams in the area was not particularly high.

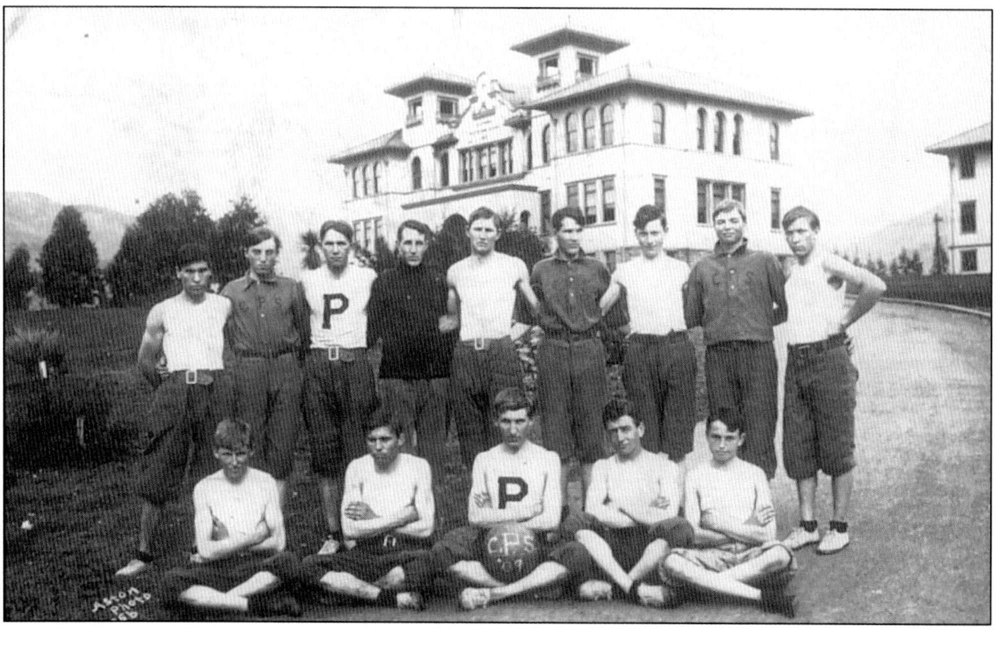

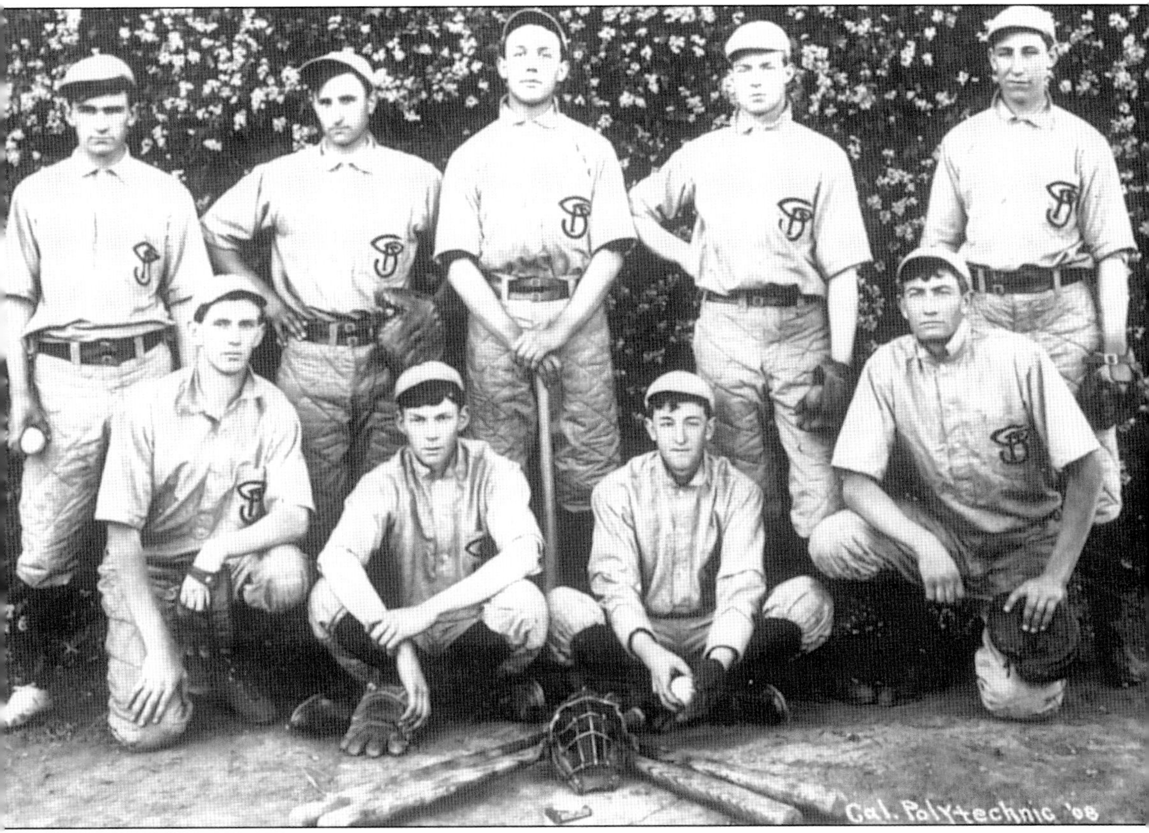

The 1908 boys' baseball team was the first sport to institute cuts due to the popularity of the sport amongst the boys. In 1908, 35 boys tried out for the team, with 14 of them successfully making the final cut. The junior varsity team did not cut any who tried out, but only had 11 official uniforms for the players.

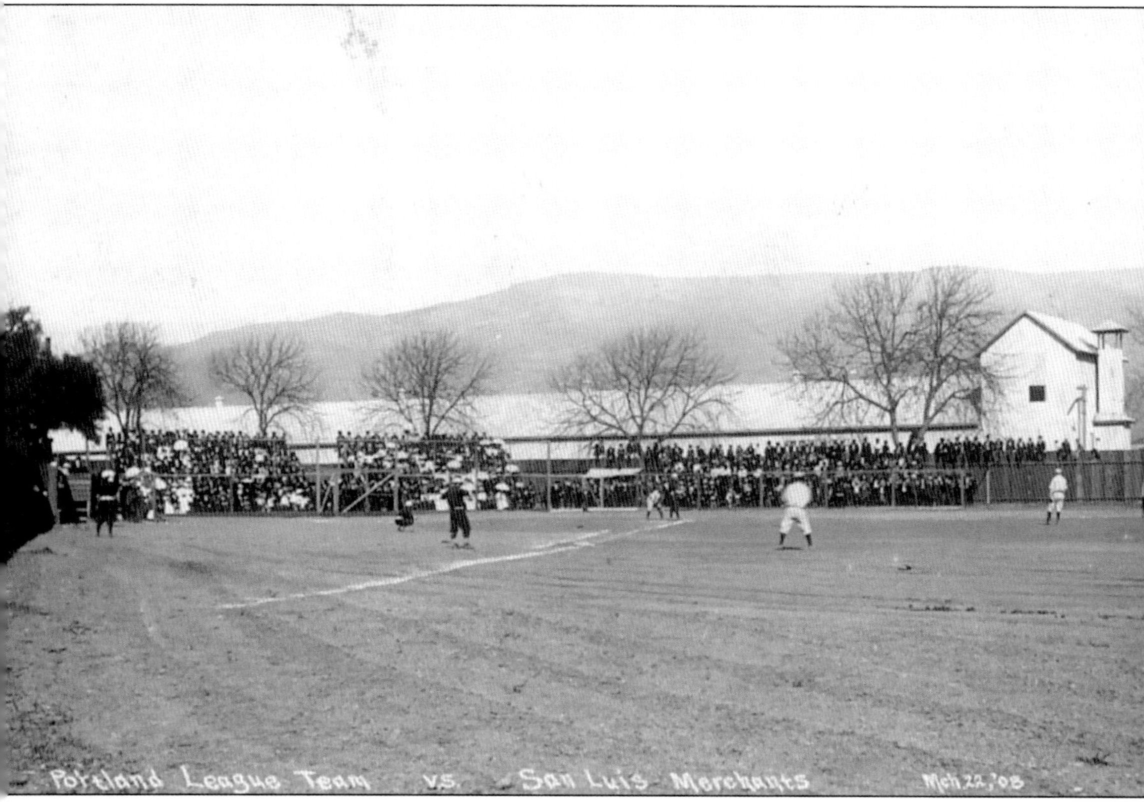

The 1908 boys' baseball team in action against the Portland team.

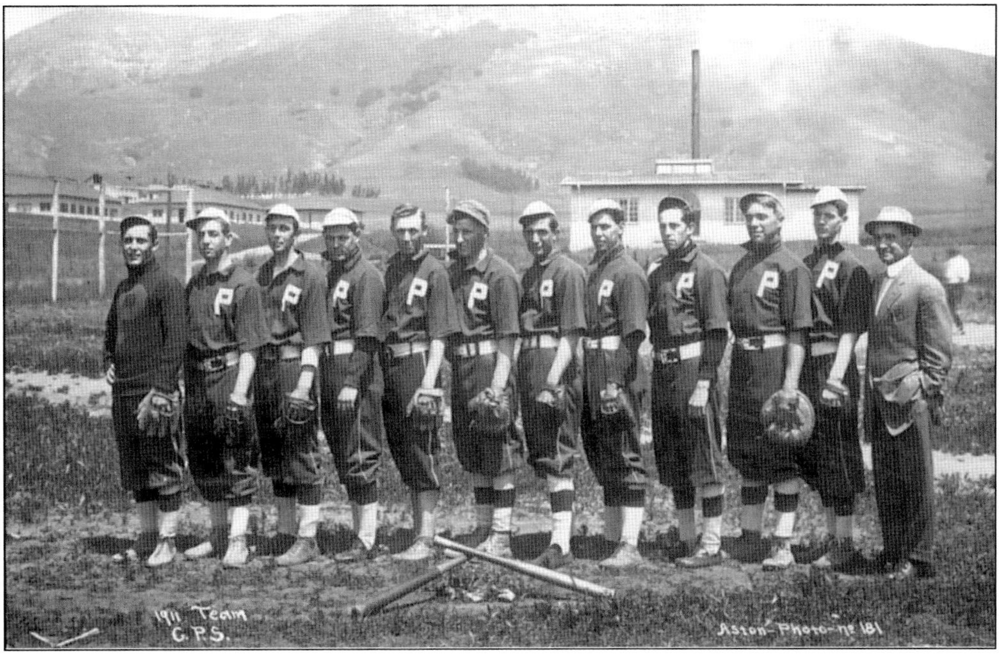

In 1911 Cal Poly became a member of the San Luis Bay Athletic Association for each of the girls and boys sports. Pictured is the boys baseball team, and is followed by the other boys' teams for the years of 1911–1912.

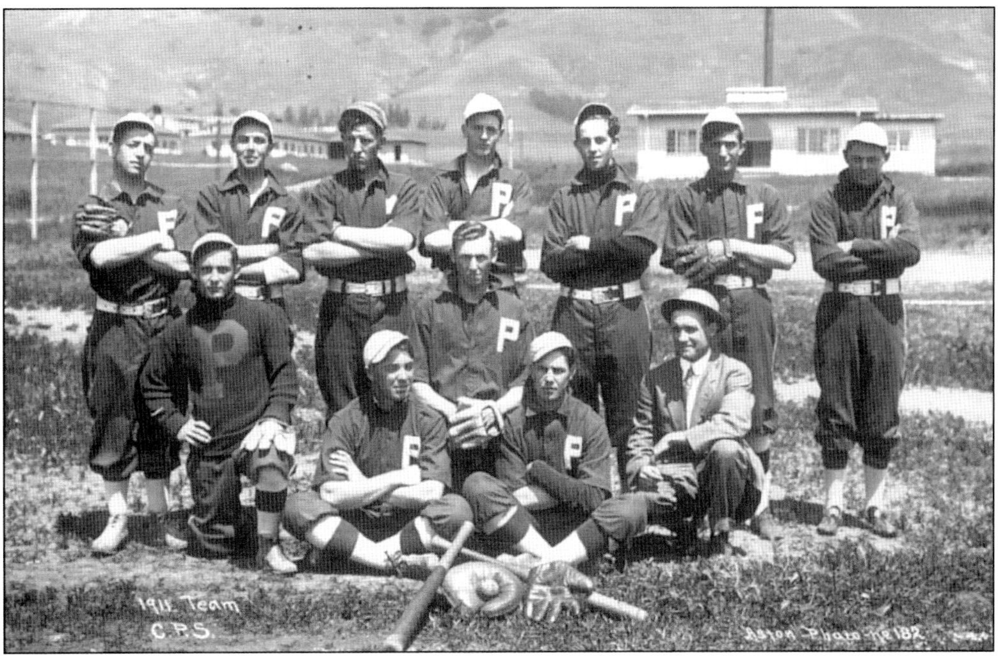

Baseball.

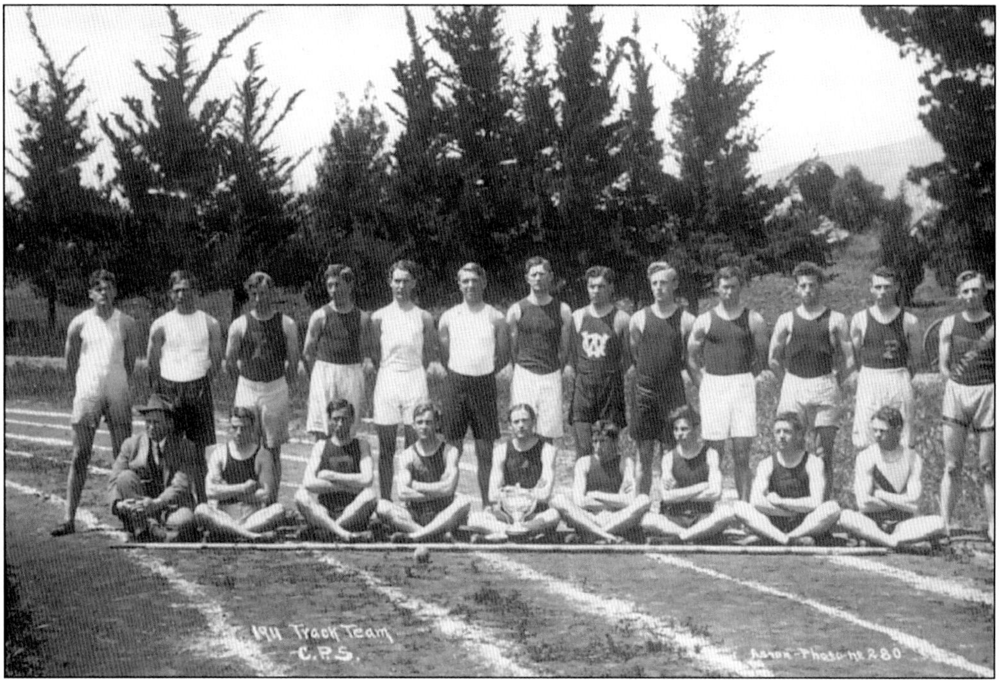

Track and Field.

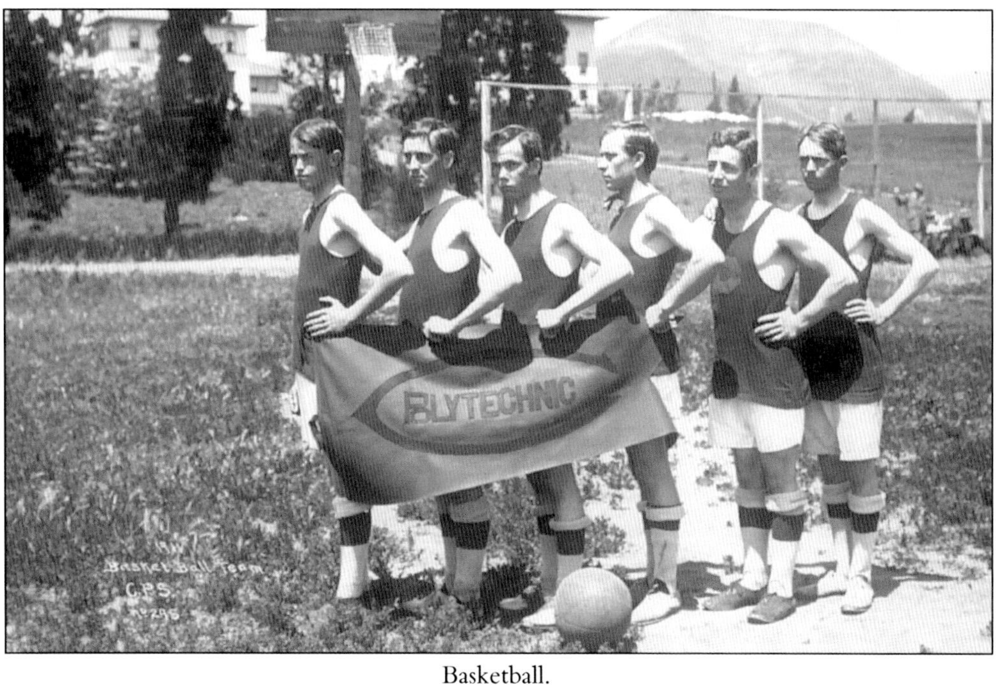

Basketball.

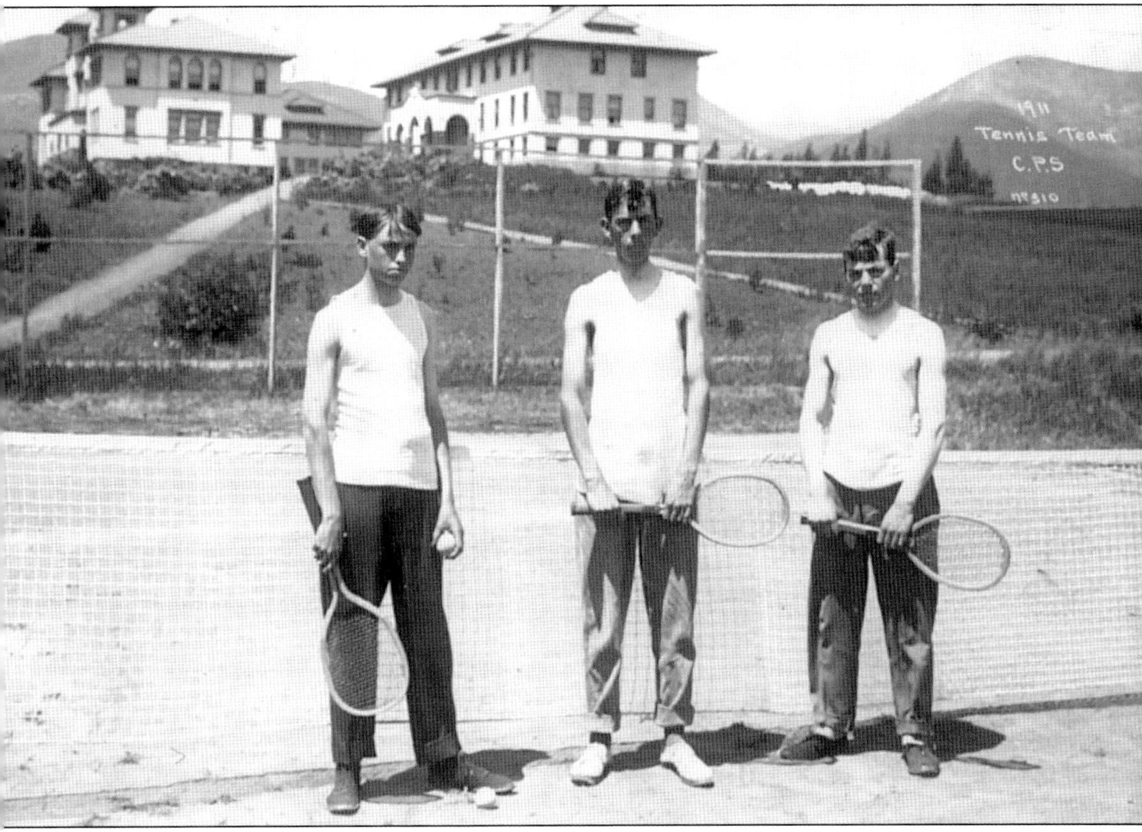

Tennis.

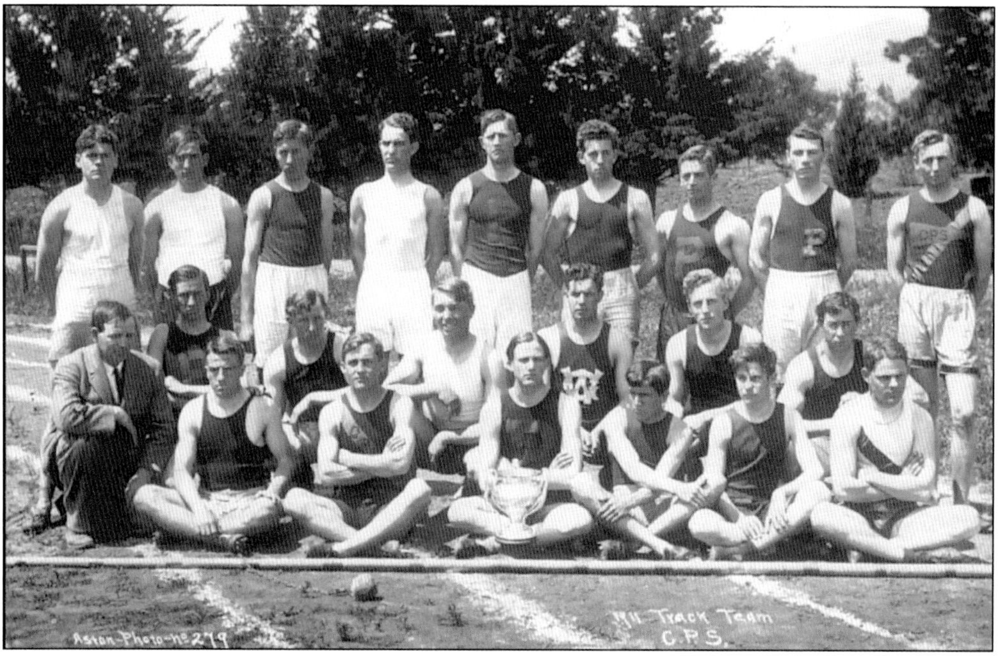

This 1911 team set many of the Cal Poly's track and field records. Track was the second most popular sport in the spring season behind baseball. Many of the baseball players also competed in track and field. Most notable was 1909 graduate Arthur Mason.

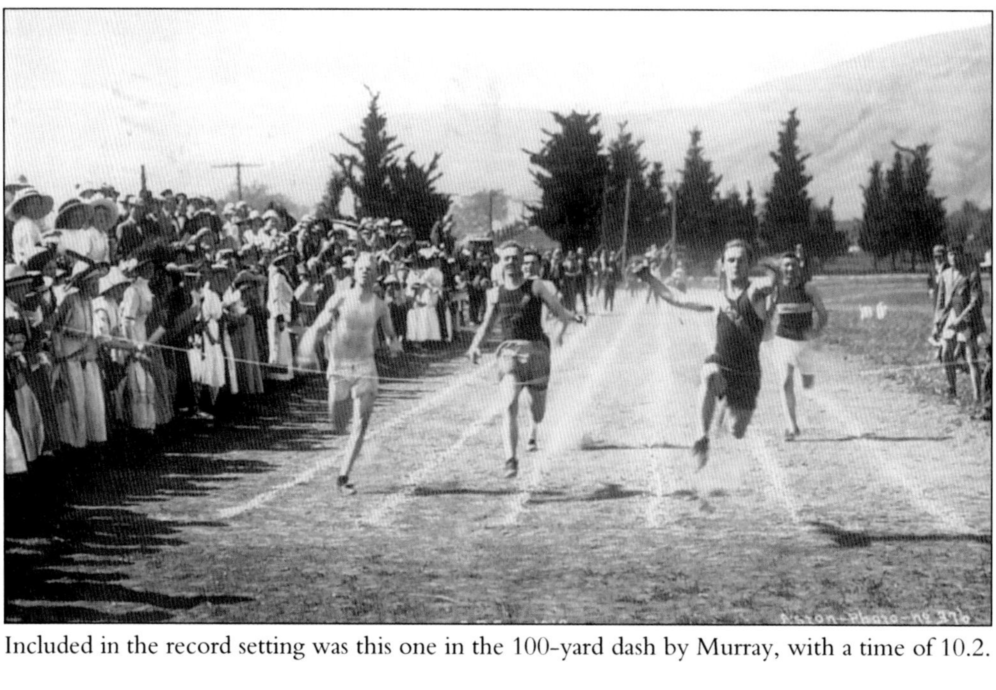

Included in the record setting was this one in the 100-yard dash by Murray, with a time of 10.2.

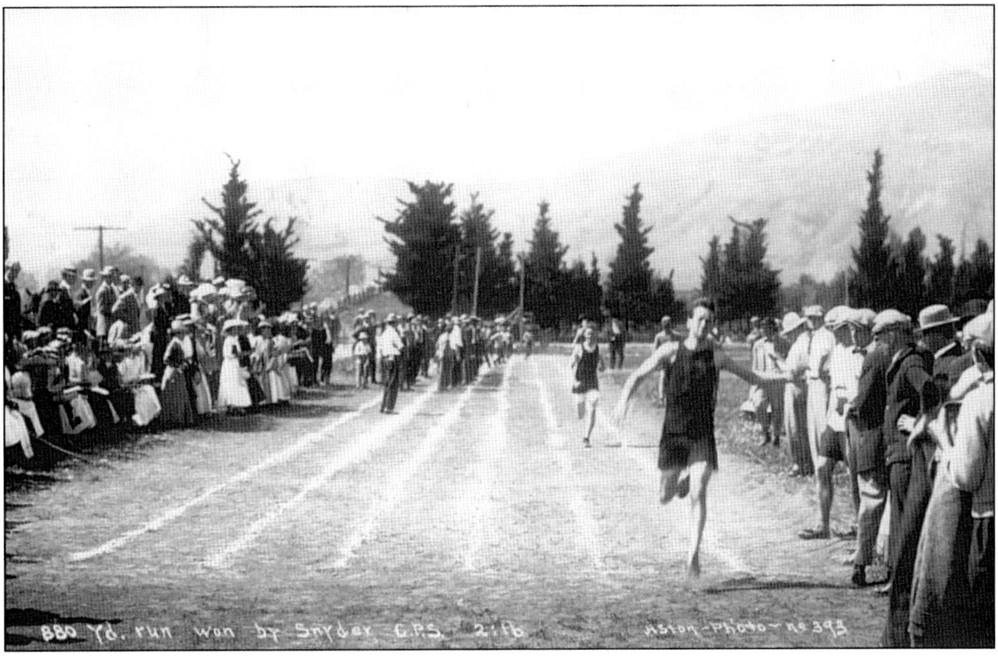

Snyder crosses the finish line for Cal Poly nearly 5 seconds ahead of the next competitor in 1911.

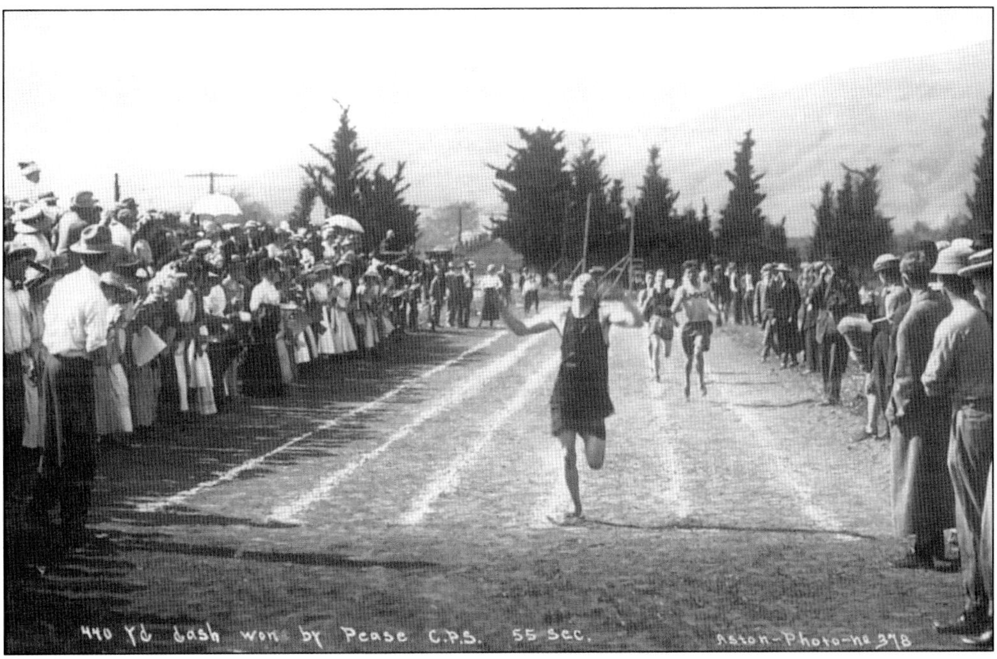

Pease wins the 440-yard dash in a record time of 55 seconds, well ahead of the second-place finisher from Santa Margarita, 1911.

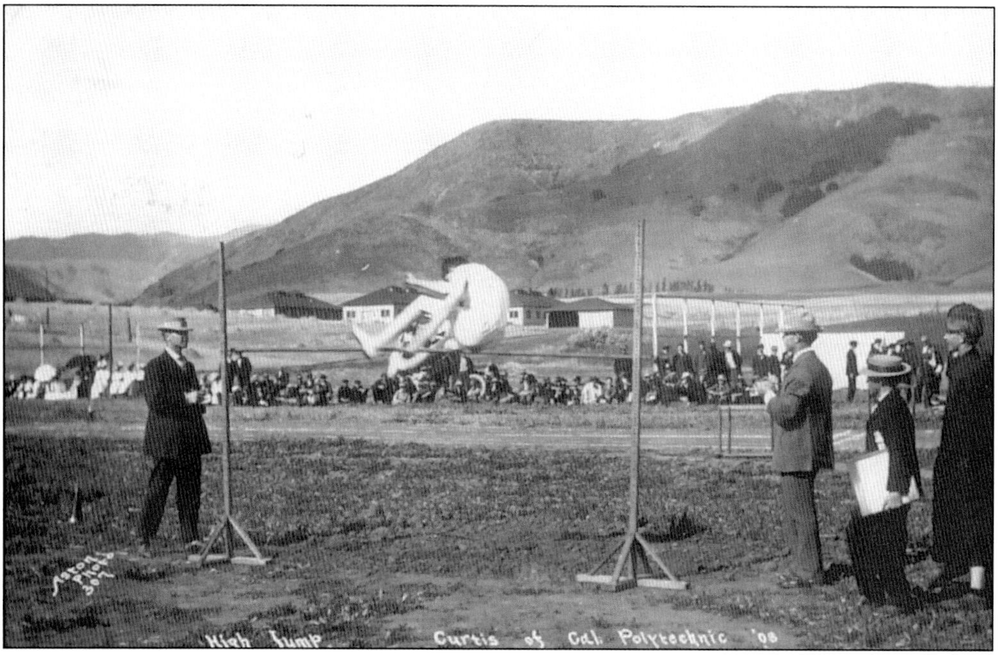

In 1908 Curtis and Hopkins of Cal Poly make their attempts at clearing the bar in the high jump.

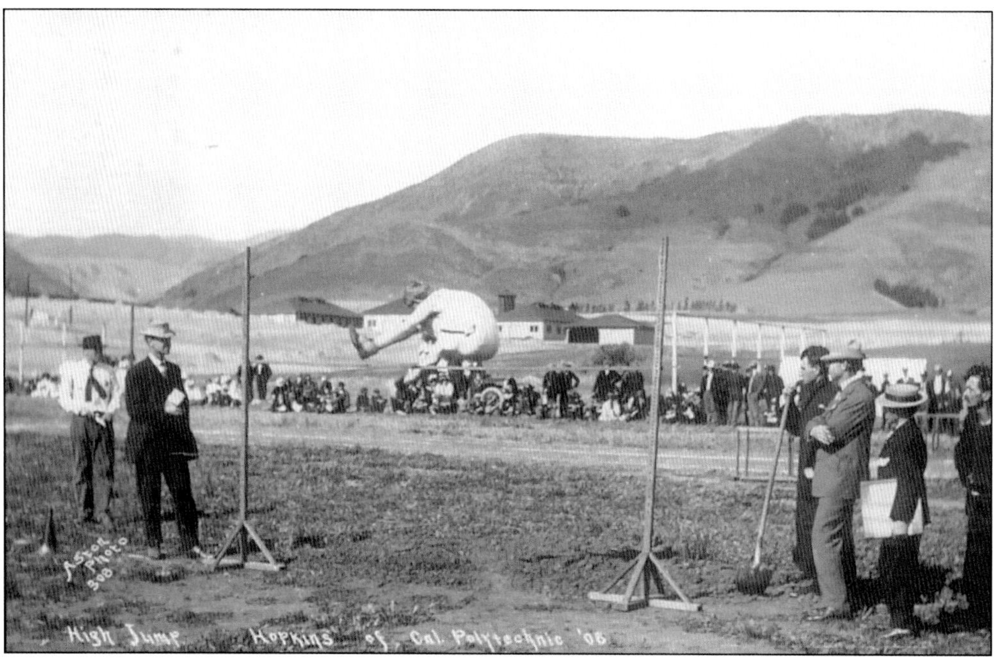

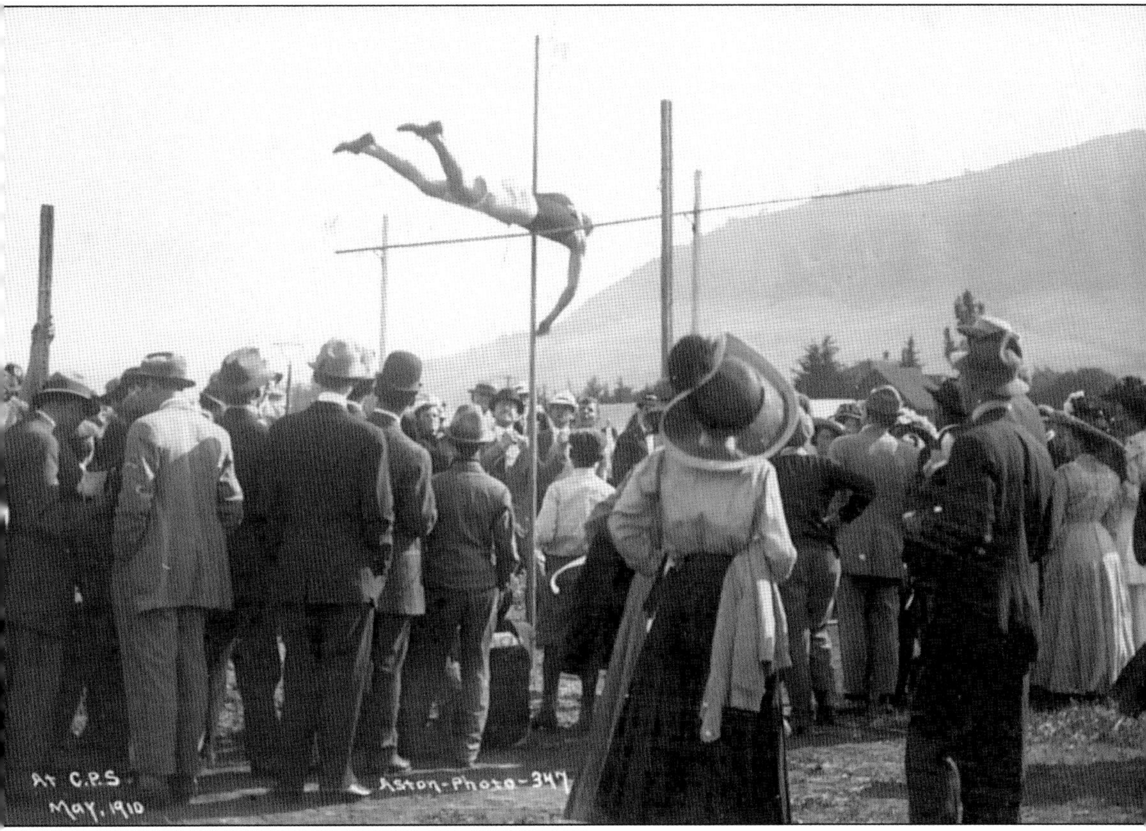

An unknown Cal Poly athlete clears the mark in the pole-vault event, 1910.

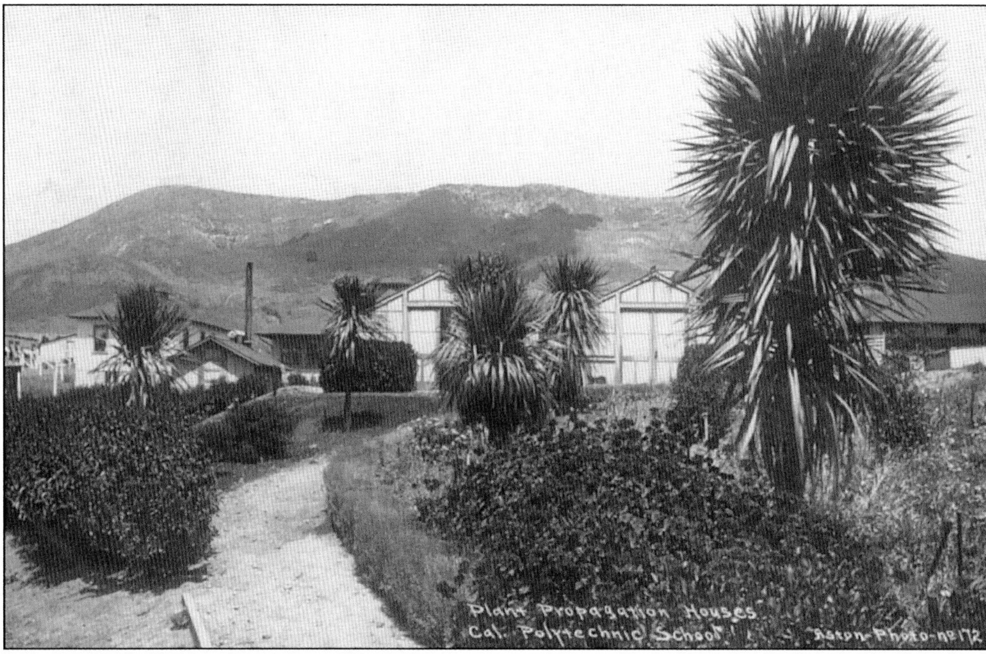

Above and below are the Plant Propagation Houses at Cal Poly, 1910.

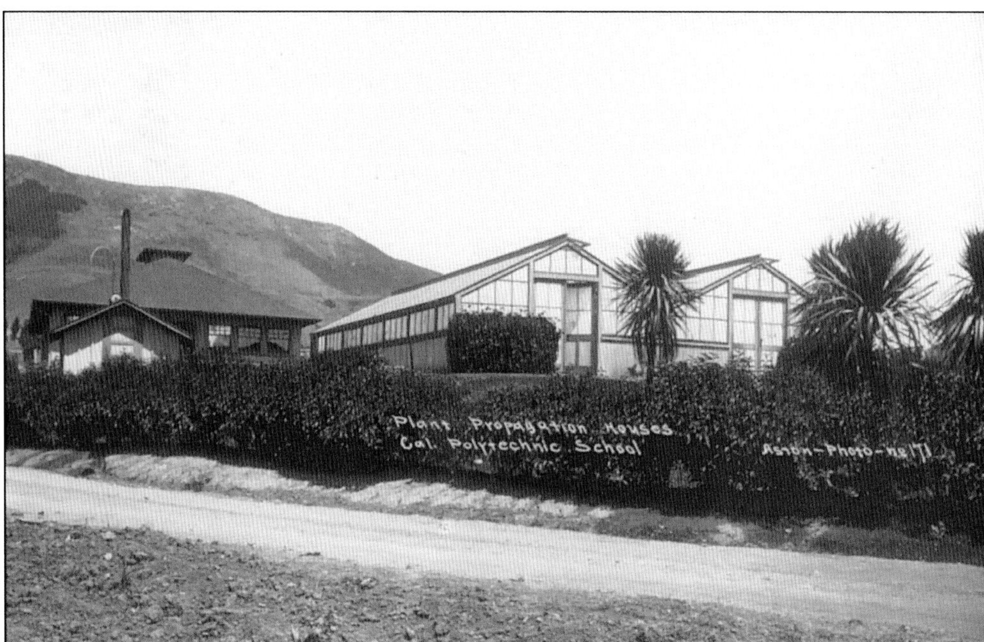

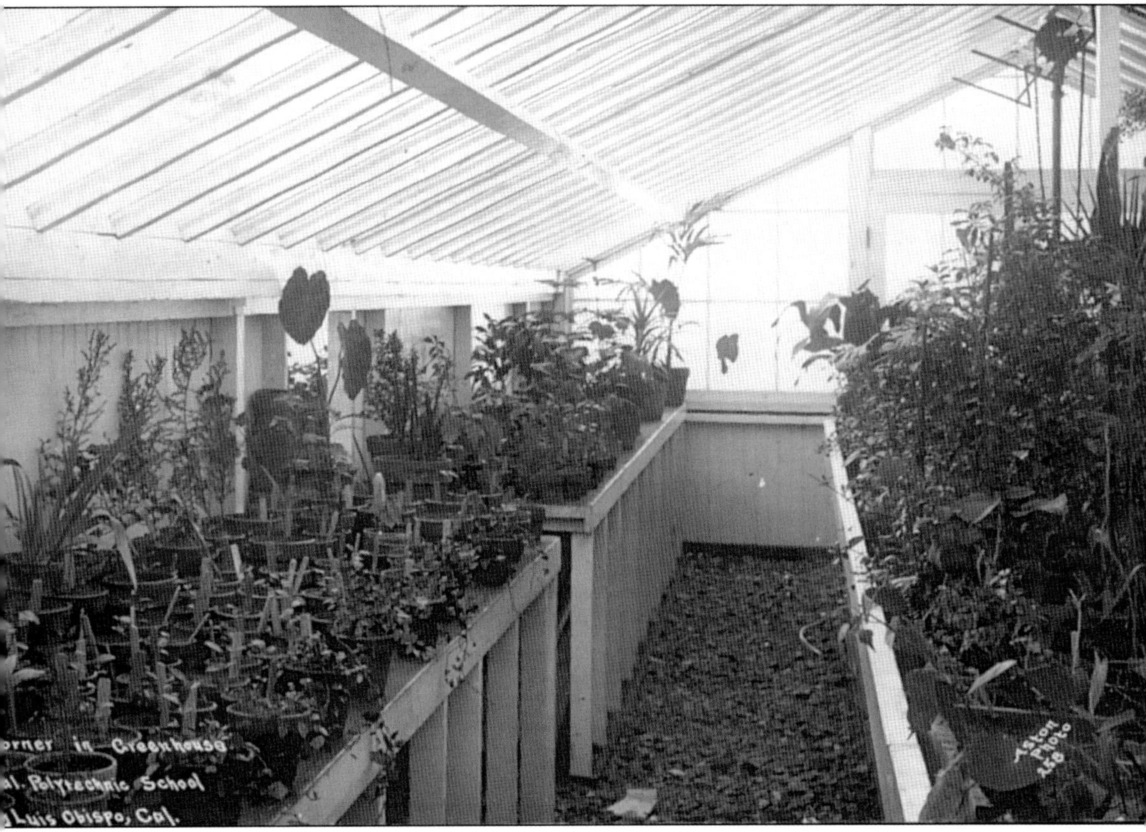

\Pictured above is the interior of one of the greenhouses at Cal Poly, 1908.

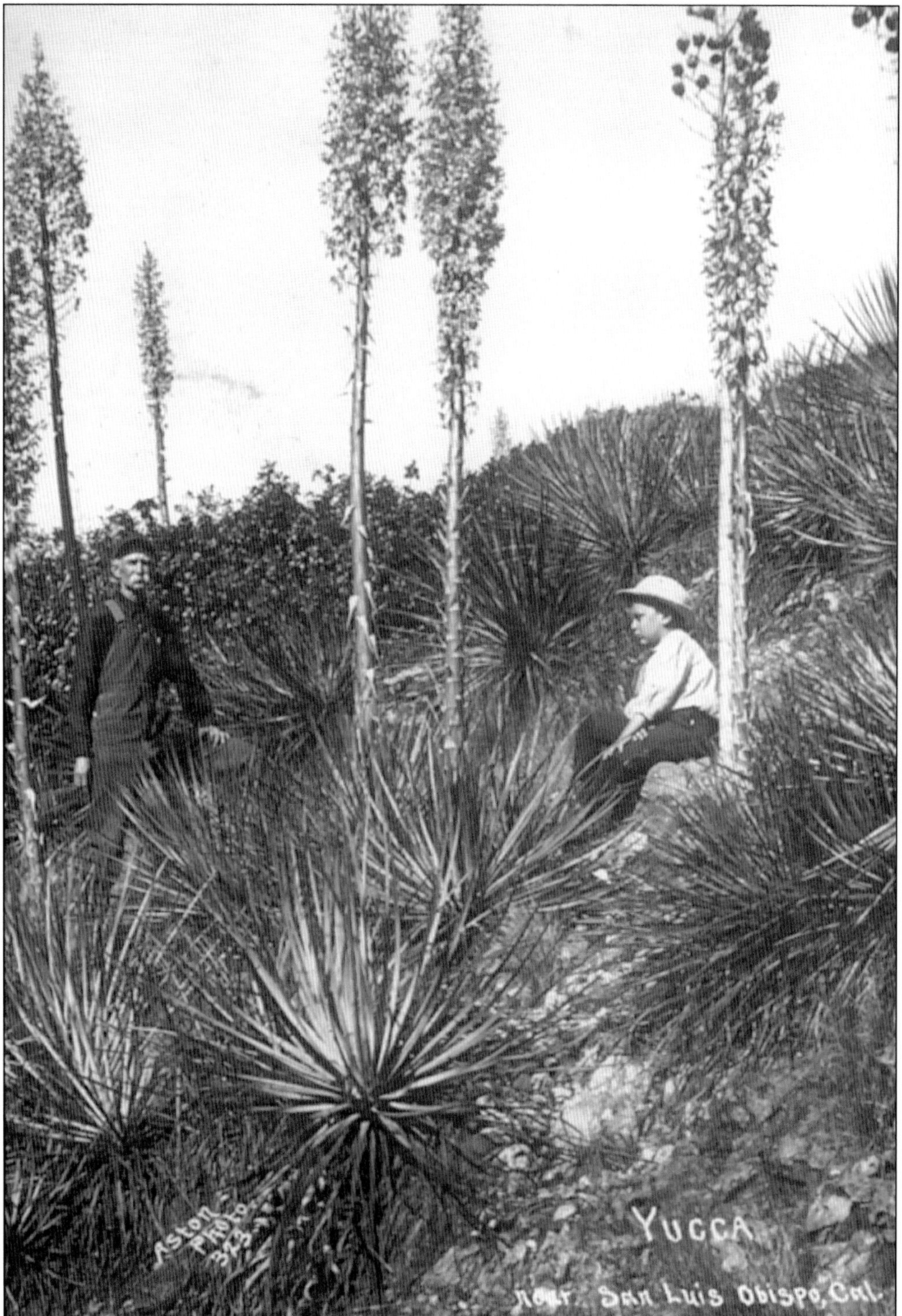

Here are some of the Yucca plants developed by Cal Poly, and planted near the school, 1910.

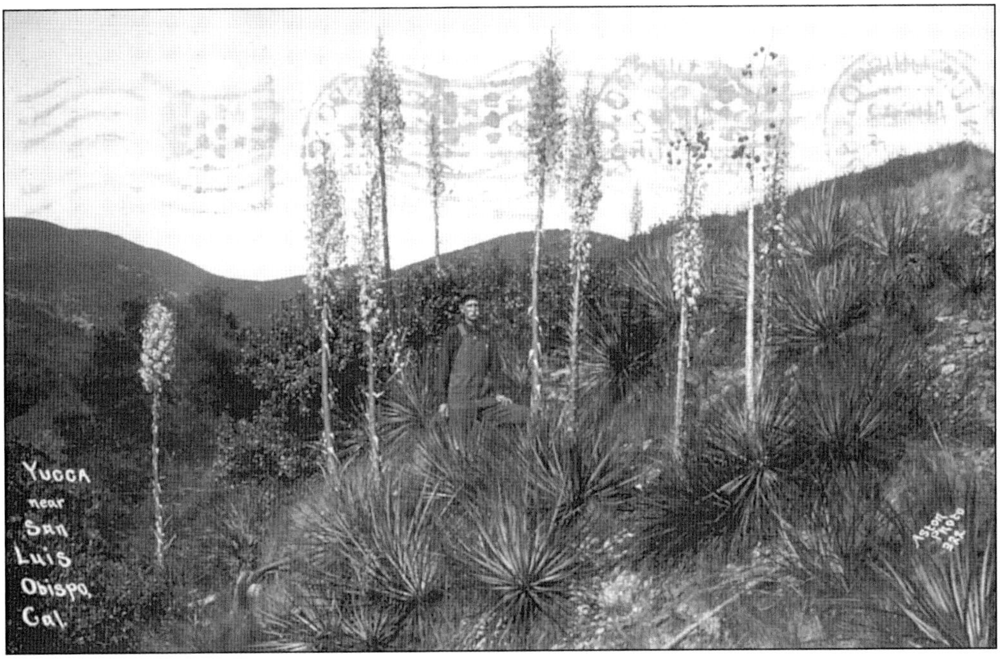

Pictured here are more Yucca plants.

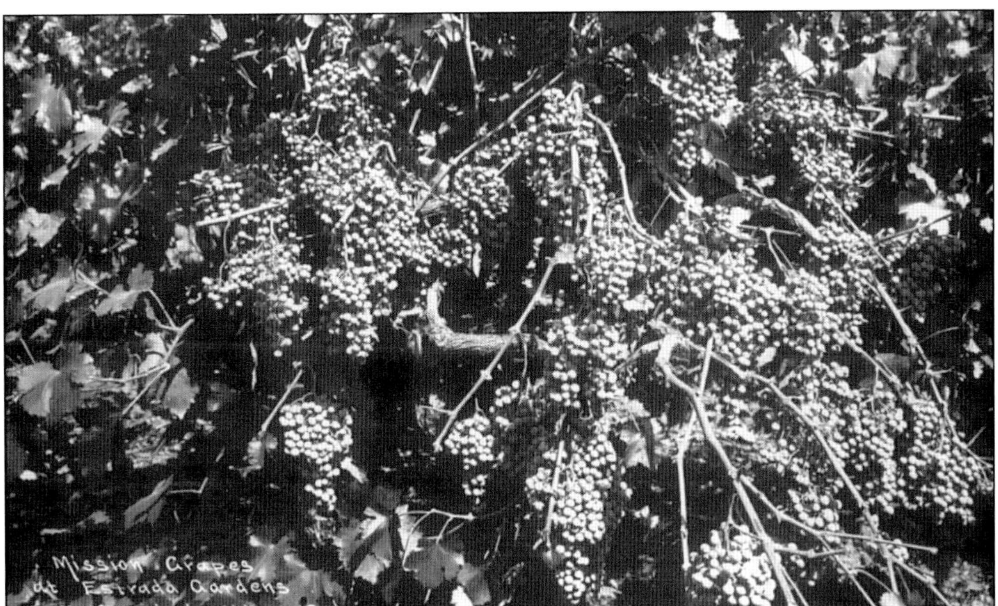

Pictured are grapes cultivated by students from Cal Poly at the Estrada Gardens. These particular grapes were considered outstanding, *c.* 1909.

The following two pages show the pear trees in the Estrada Gardens that were cared for by Cal Poly students, 1910.

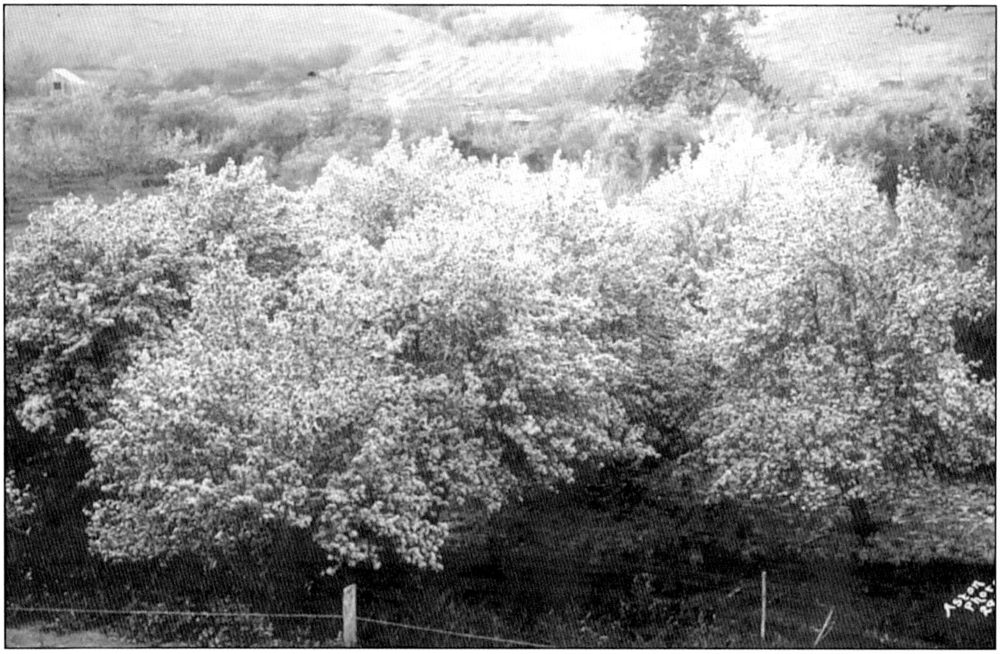

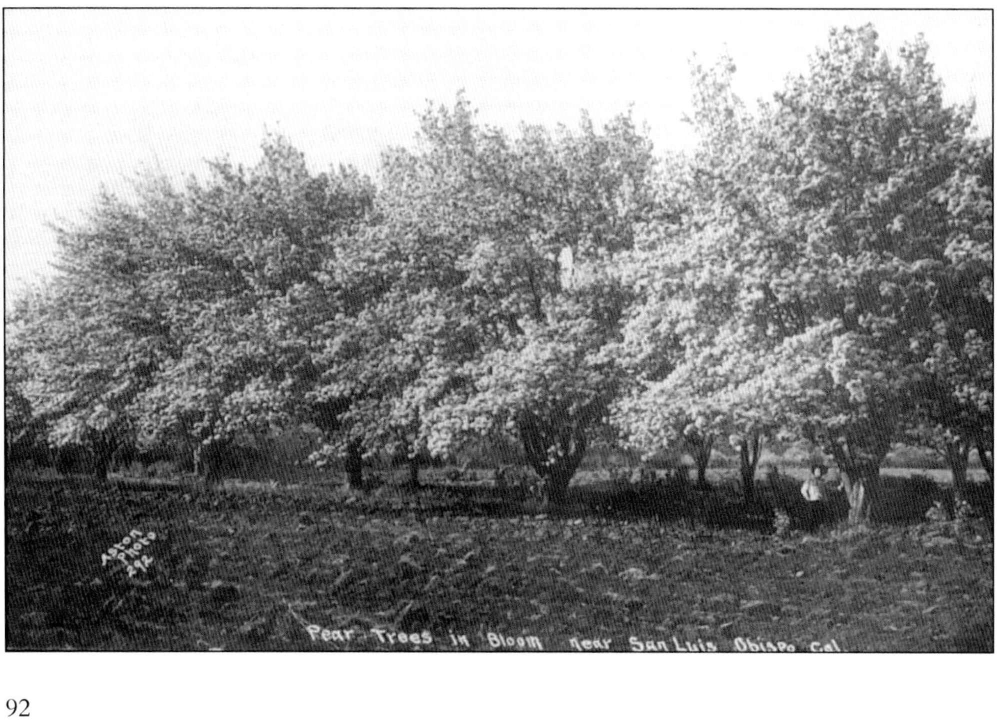

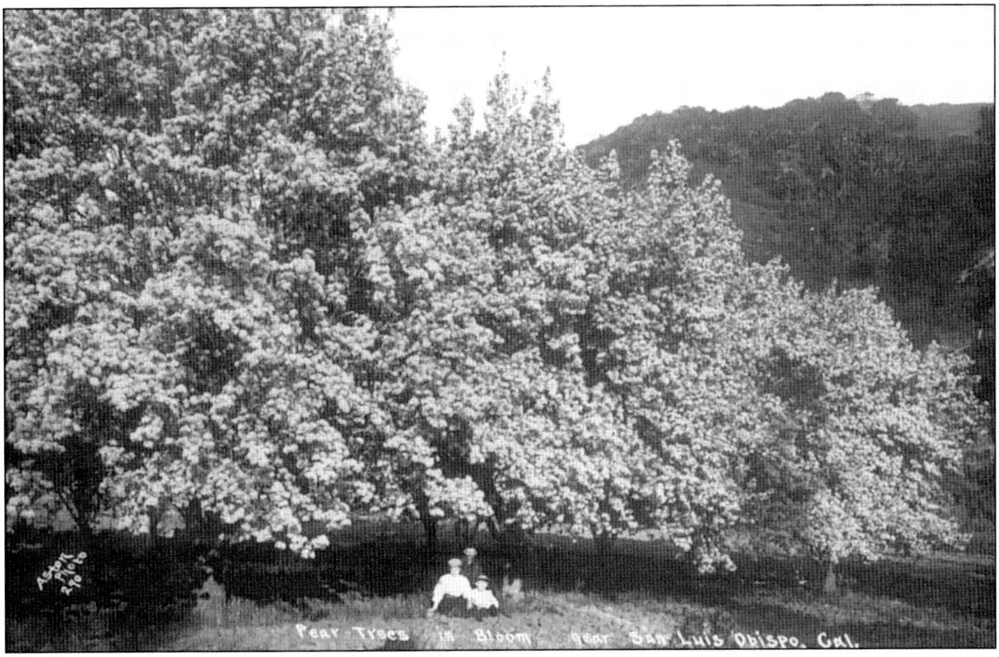
Aston Photo 290
Pear Trees in Bloom near San Luis Obispo, Cal.

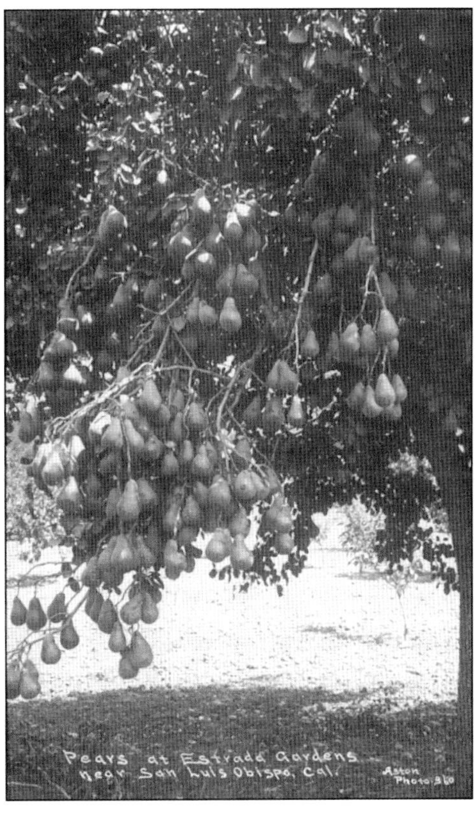
Pears at Estrada Gardens near San Luis Obispo, Cal.
Aston Photo 360

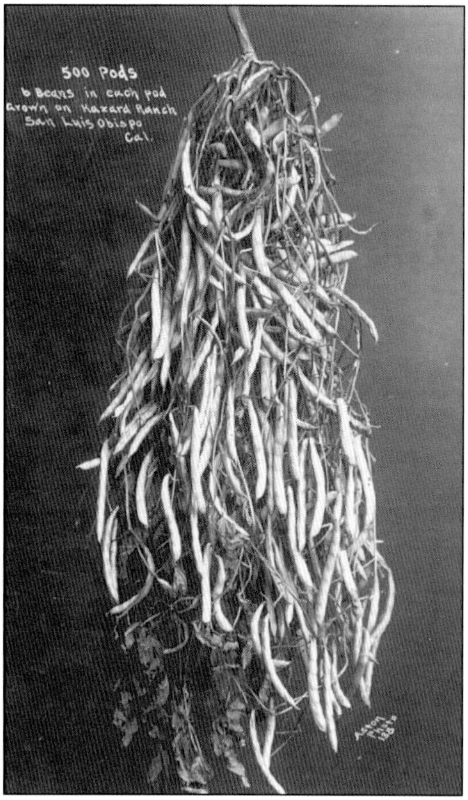

These 500 remarkable pods of beans were grown by an alumnus of Cal Poly in 1911, on Hazzard Ranch, San Luis Obispo.

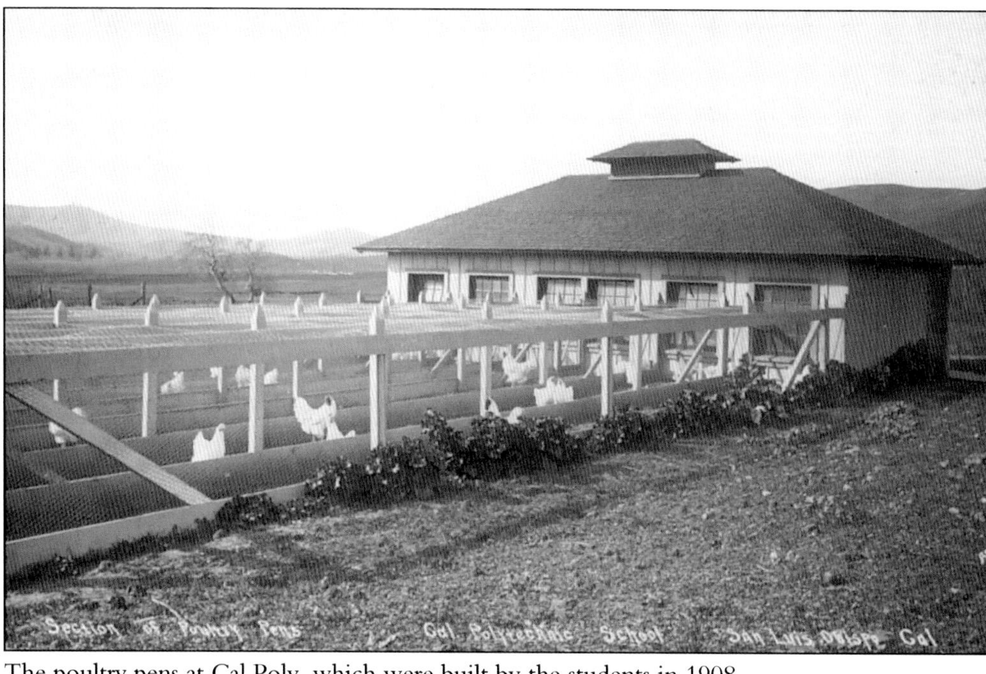

The poultry pens at Cal Poly, which were built by the students in 1908.

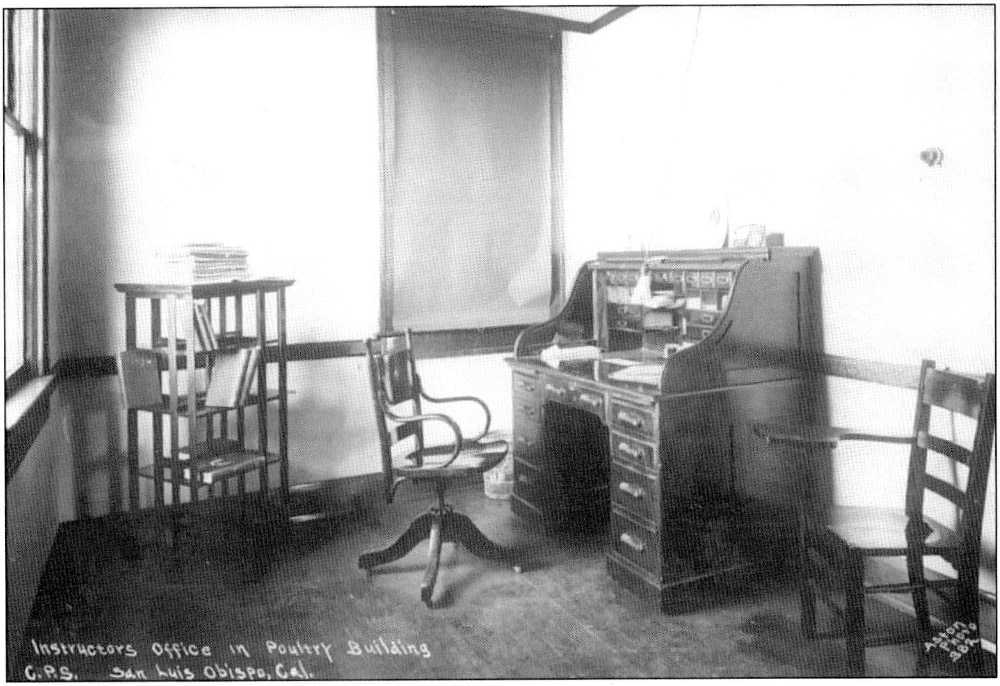

The Instructor's Office inside of the Poultry Building at Cal Poly, 1910.

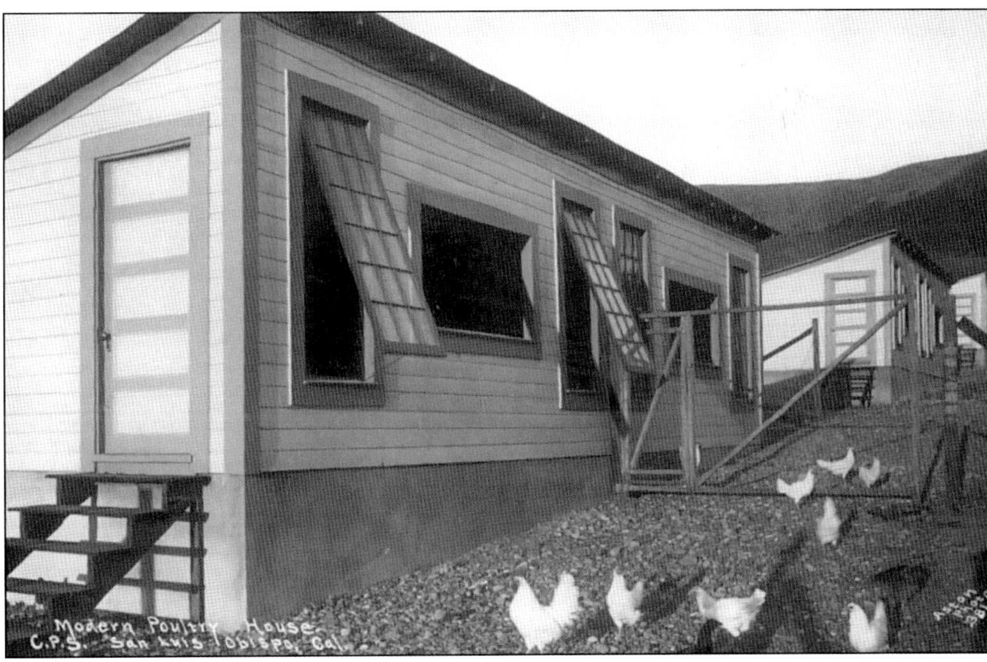

Exterior of the Modern Poultry Houses at Cal Poly, 1908. The chickens and their eggs were sold at the Cal Poly market and the Farmers Market in San Luis Obispo, thus emphasizing the entrepreneurial spirit that Dr. Anderson sought to instill in the student body.

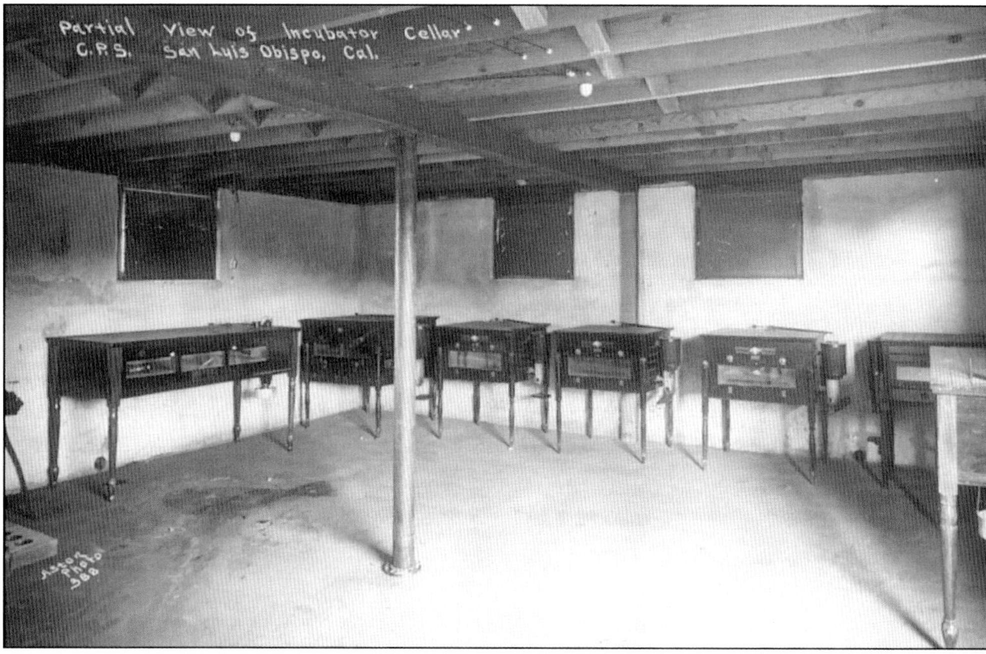

Above and below are the incubator cellar at the Poultry Houses at Cal Poly, 1909.

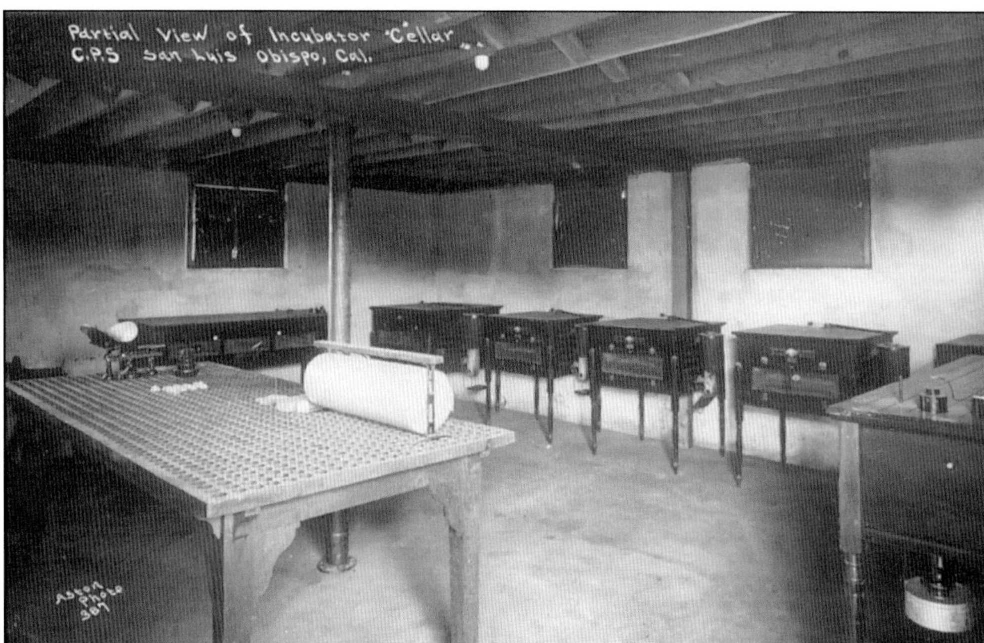

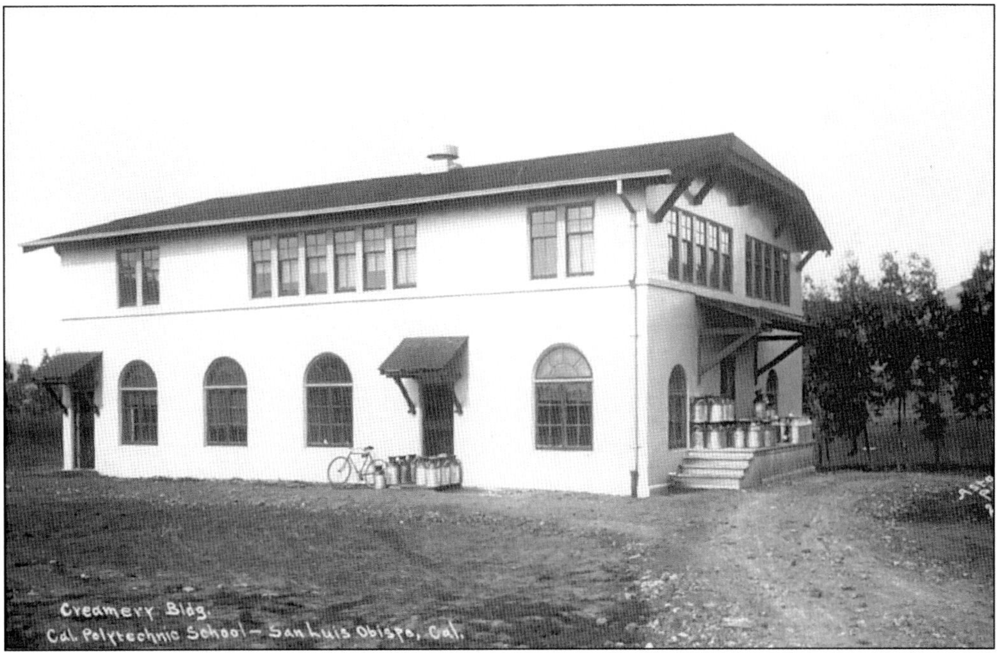

The Creamery at Cal Poly was fashioned in the "modern method of dairy farming." The intent was to not only introduce the young agricultural students to the latest techniques, but also instruct those boys interested in machine maintenance and engineering with this technology, *c.* 1906.

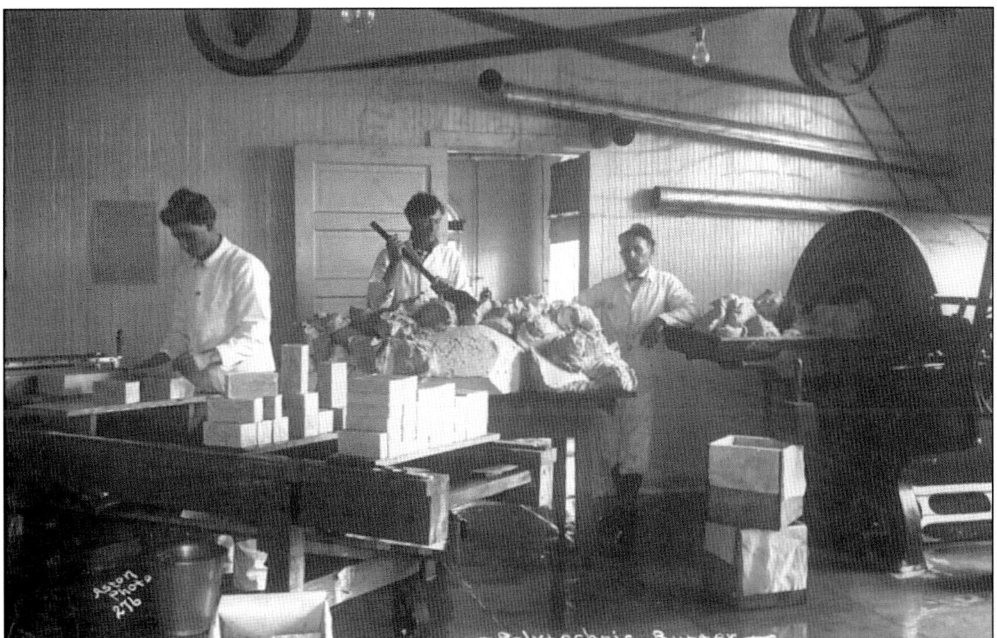

The butter produced at Cal Poly by the students under the label of Polytechnic Butter was distributed throughout the San Luis Obispo greater area, beginning in 1905. This postcard captures the students in action in 1908.

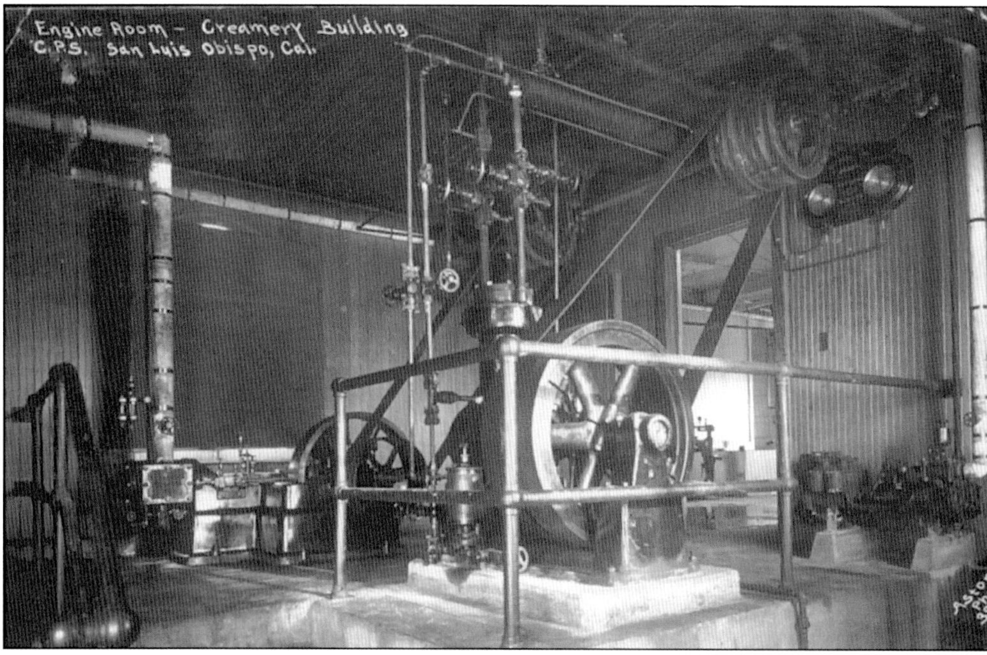

The Creamery contained the latest and greatest machinery that could be found at the dawn of the 20th century. These images are from 1908.

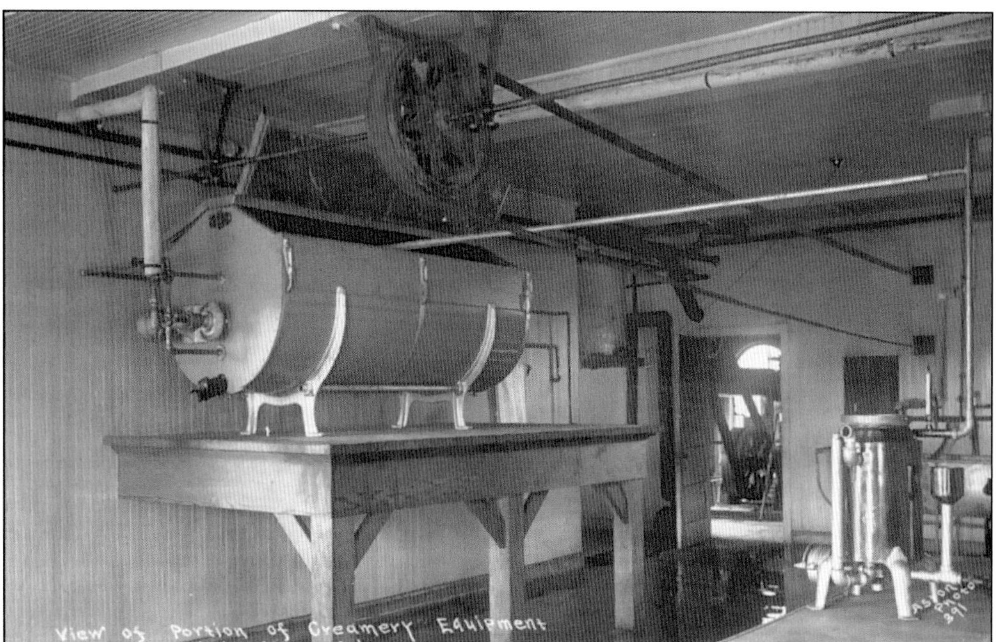

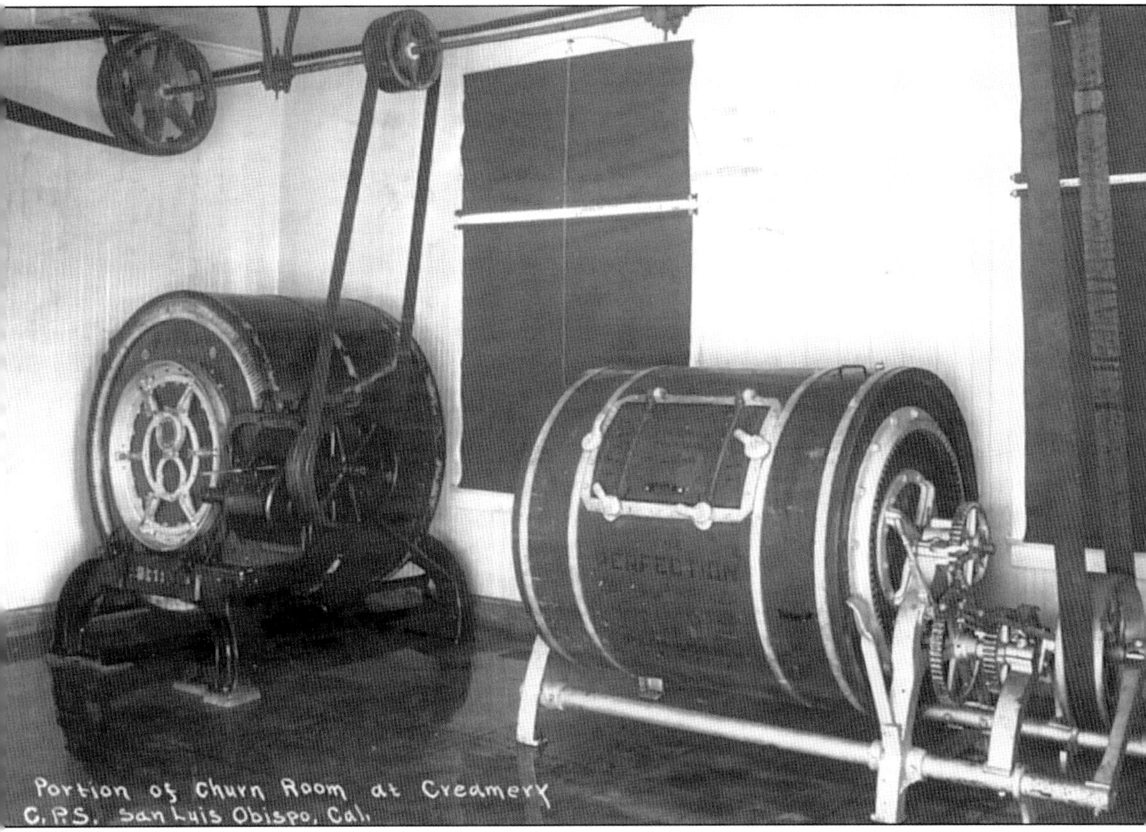

The mechanized butter churn not only freed up man hours, but also created a more consistent butter much appreciated by consumers, 1908.

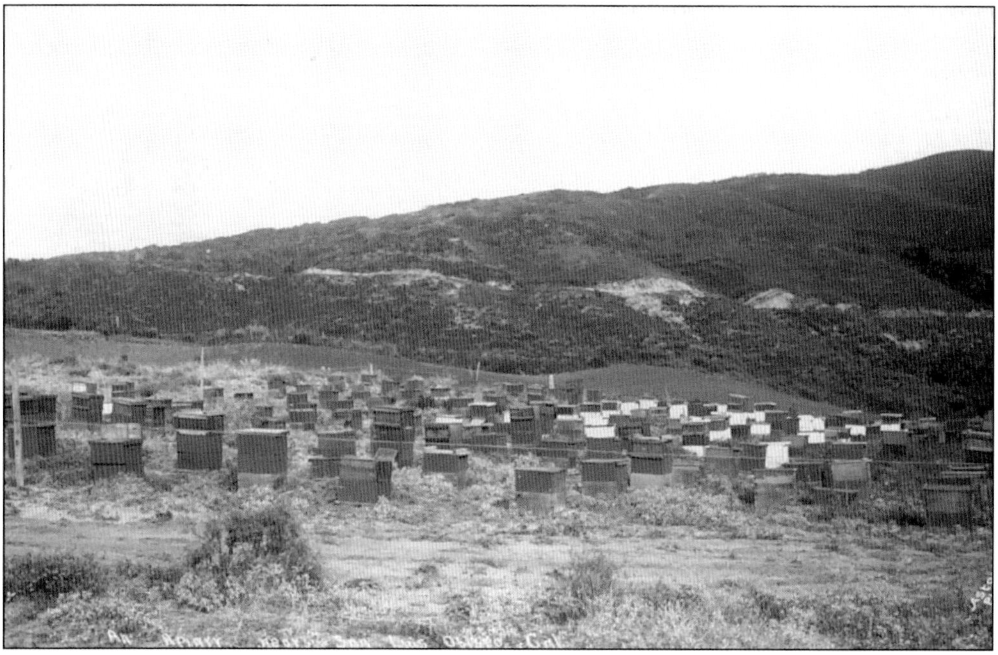

These two apiaries were maintained by students of Cal Poly, 1910.

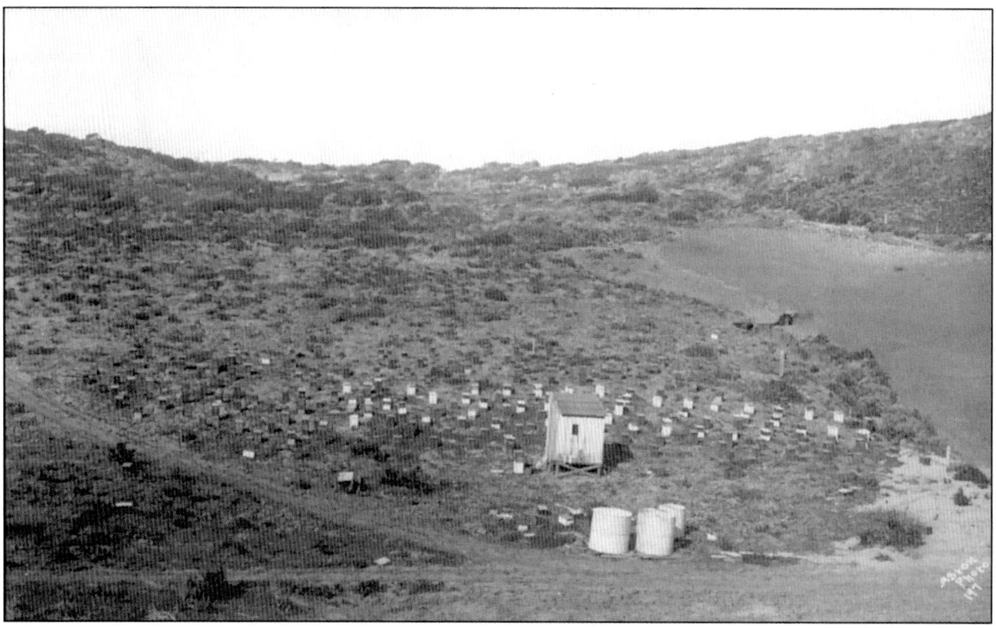

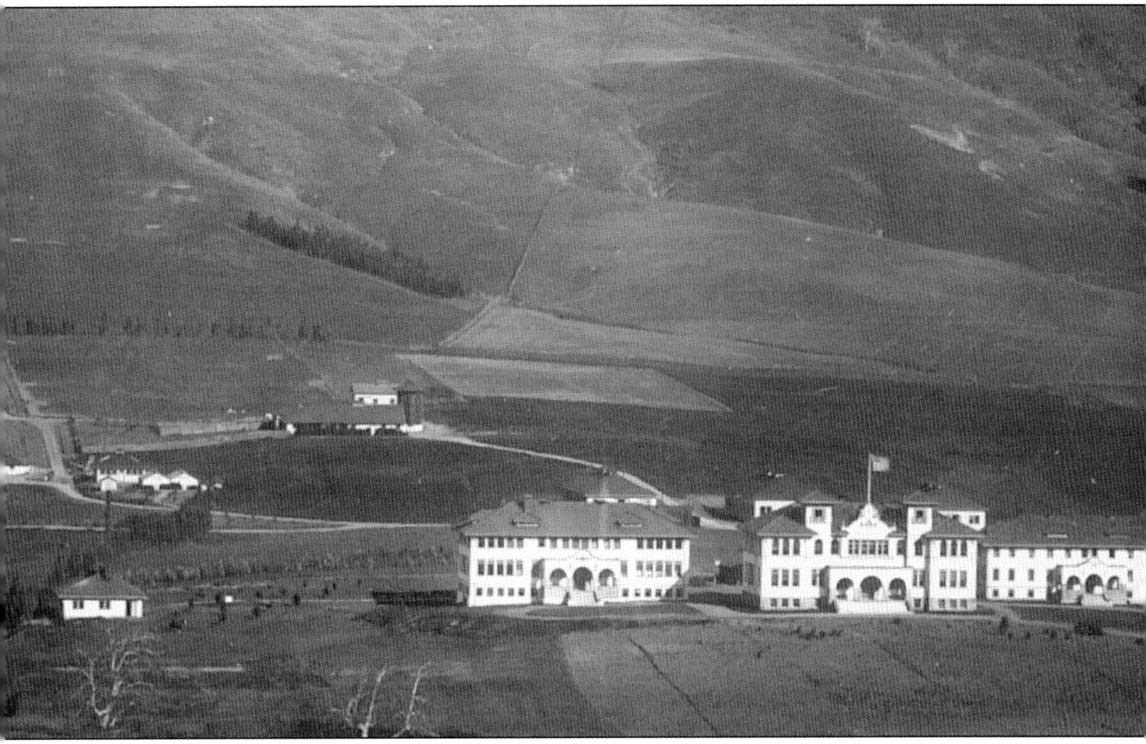

In the machine shop at Cal Poly the students were able to gain practical hands-on experience. The machine shop is located directly behind the main administration building in this 1910 photo.

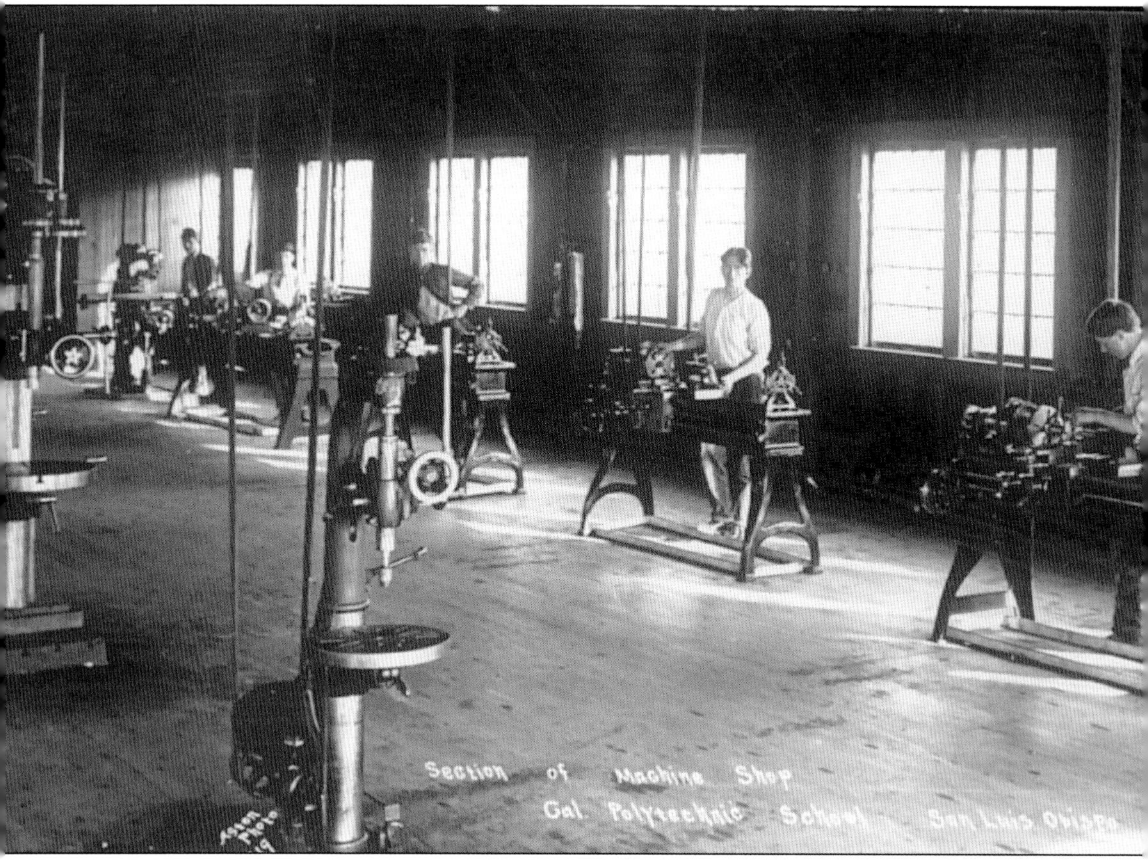

Various views inside the machine shop at Cal Poly, 1910. The photographer, Frank Aston, notes that the students did not generally wear ties inside the shops. Their wardrobe reflects the staging of this photographic event.

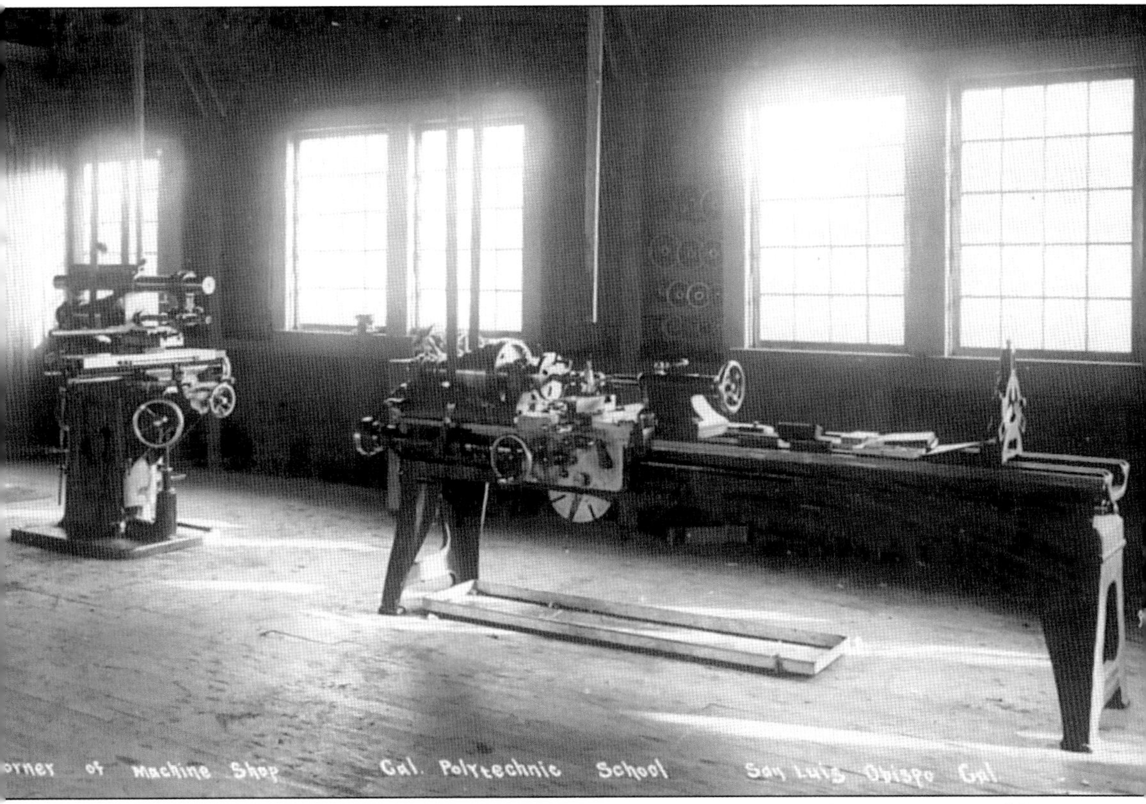

The lathe, as one student pointed out to photographer Frank Aston, was the centerpiece of the woodshop. The truly gifted craftsman could produce, among other things, a fine billiard cue stick, for a weekends folly.

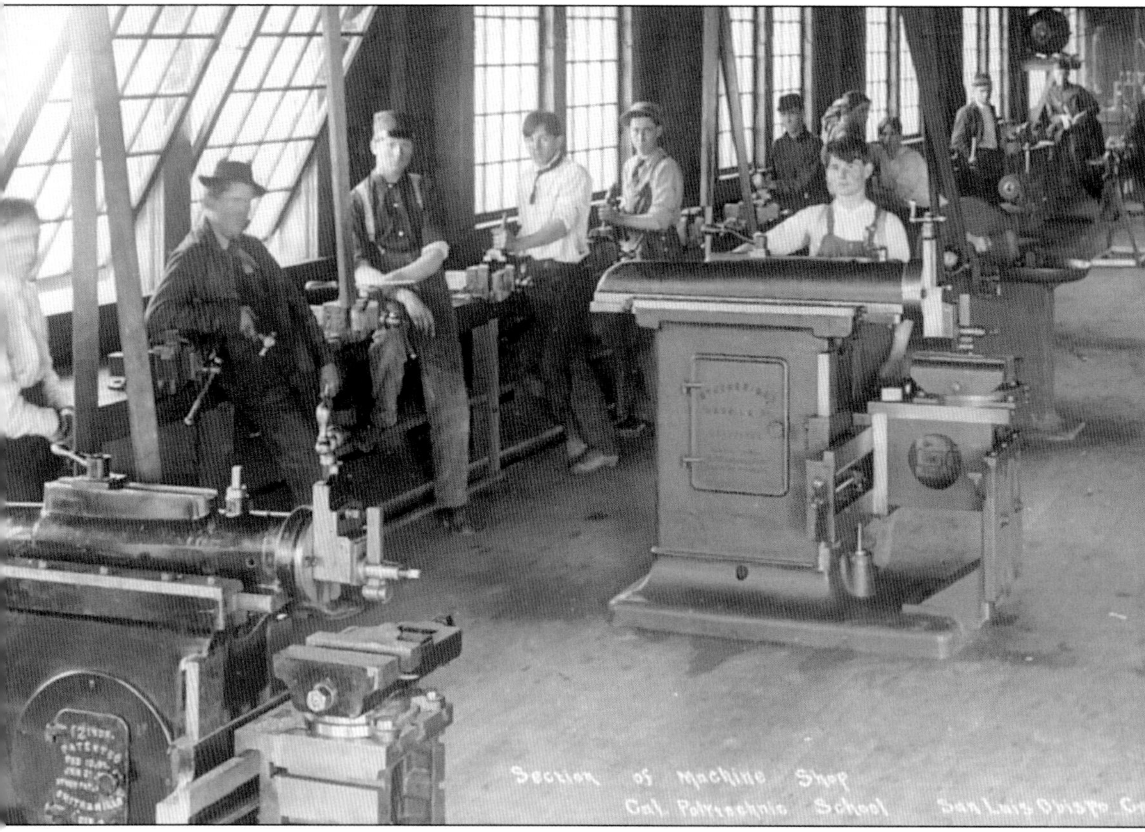

Here is the machine shop, Cal Poly.

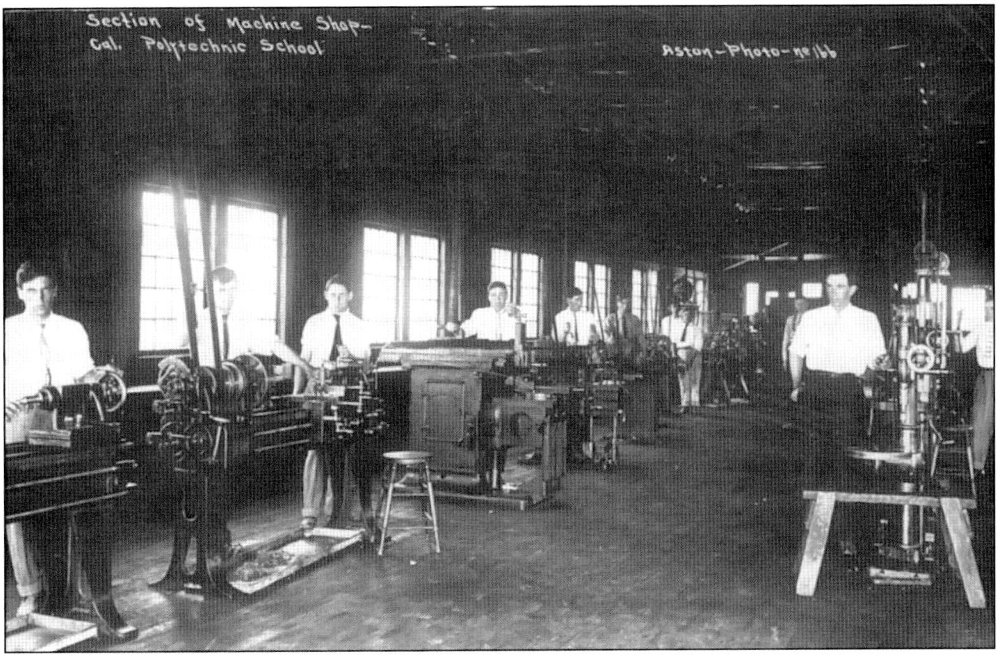

It is still possible for collectors to find furniture pieces assembled by Cal Poly students during this period at the antique shops around San Luis Obispo County. There have even been sightings of Cal Poly craftsmanship in eastern cities such as Albany, Atlanta, and Boston.

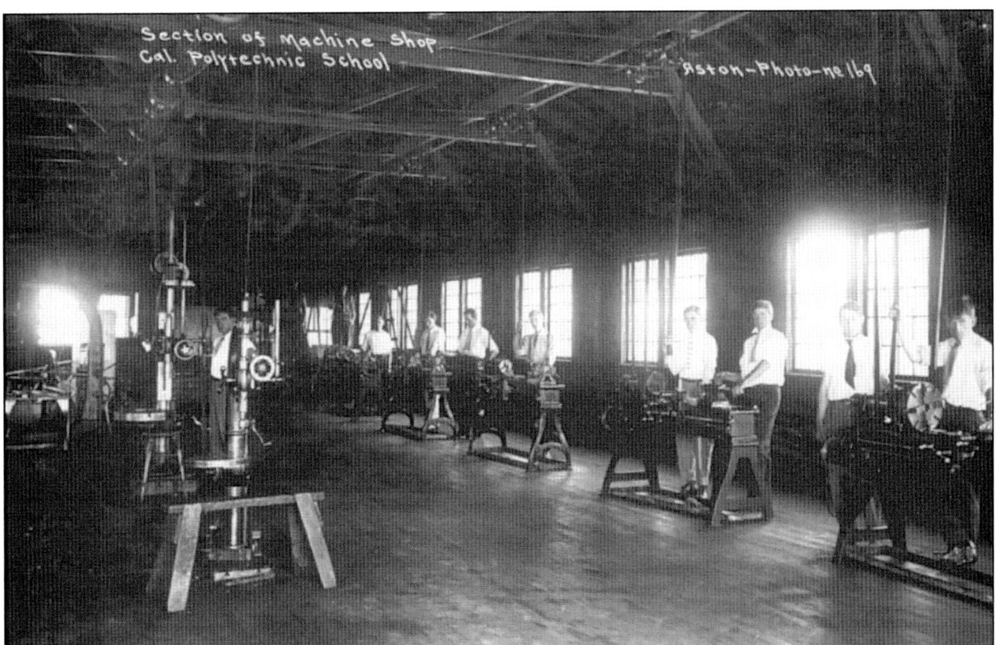

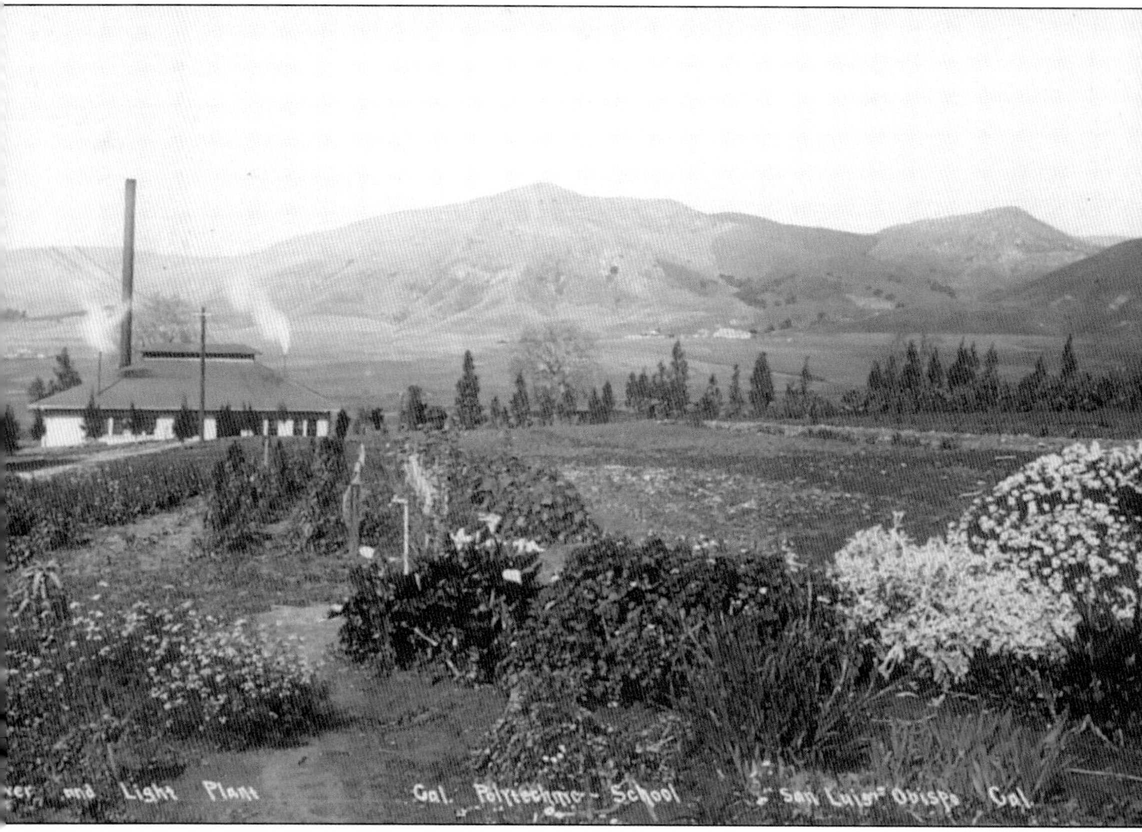

Above is the Power and Light Plant at Cal Poly, 1906.

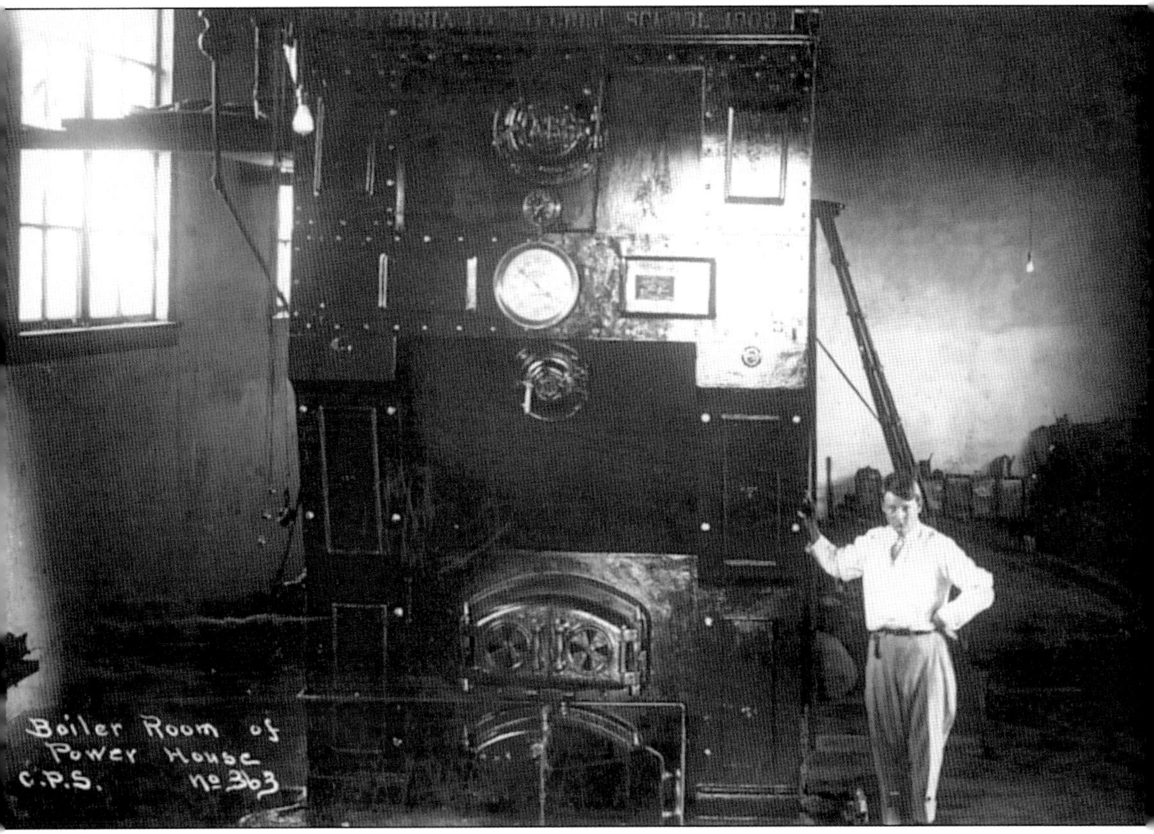

The 1909, 50-horsepower, return-tubular boiler—the center of the self-contained campuses power generation ability—is pictured with a student proudly standing in front of it.

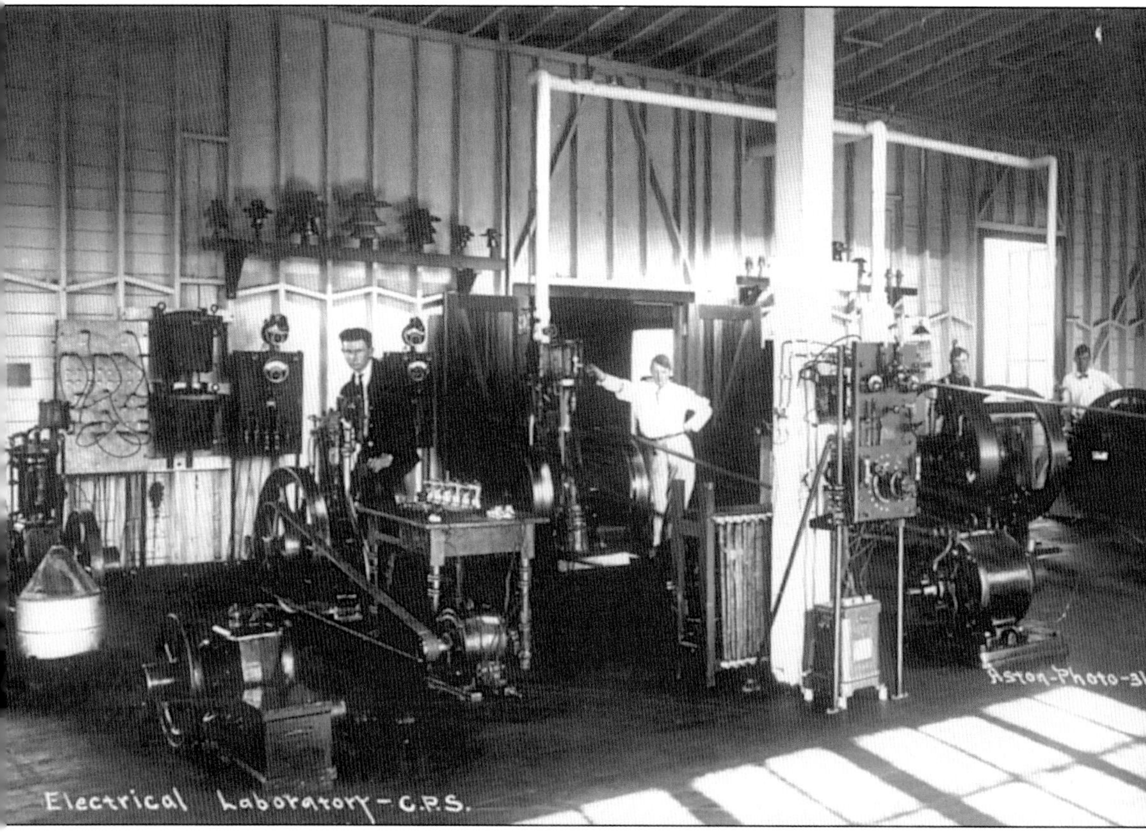

Pictured here is the electrical lab in the power plant at Cal Poly, 1909.

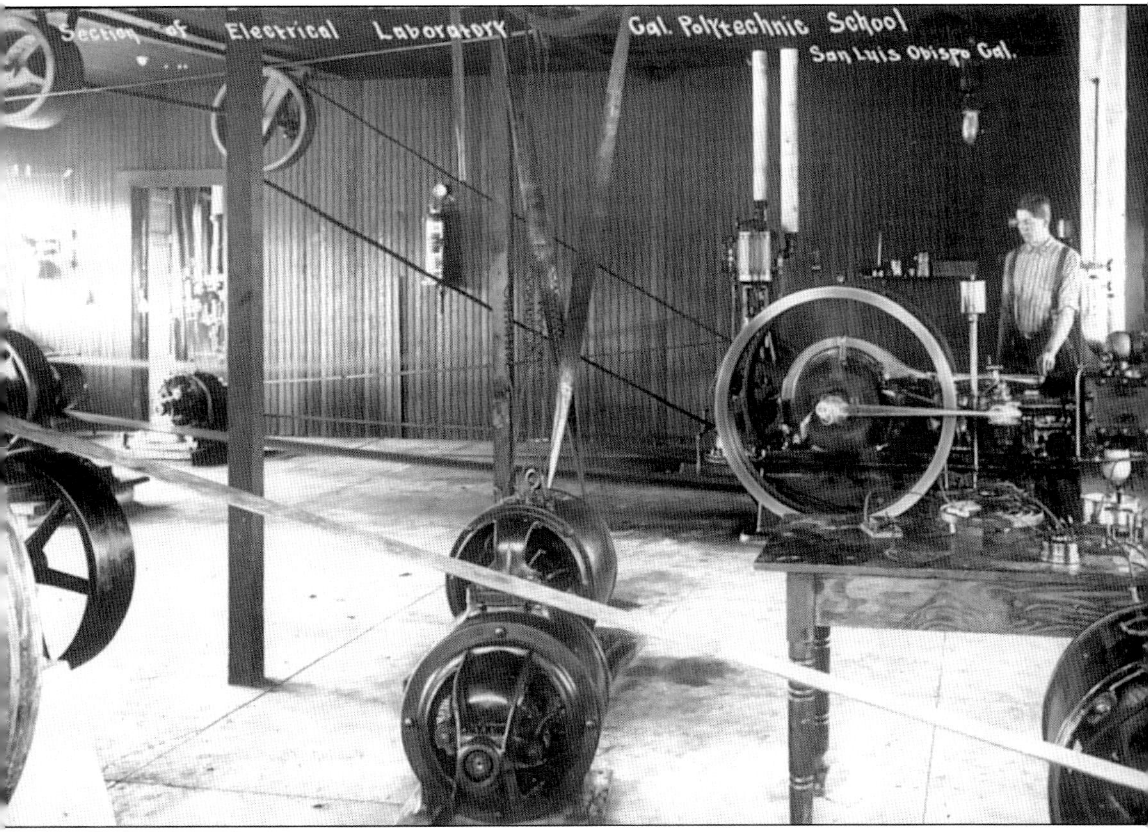

Pictured are students monitoring the various electrical engines in the electrical lab in the power plant at Cal Poly, 1909.

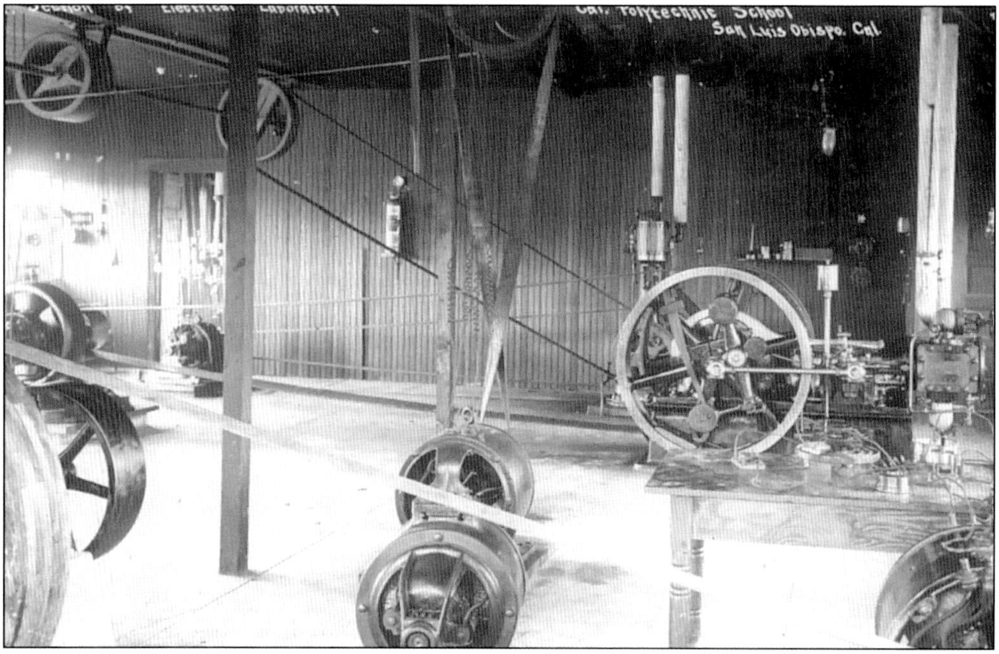

Above and below are images of the Electrical Lab, Cal Poly.

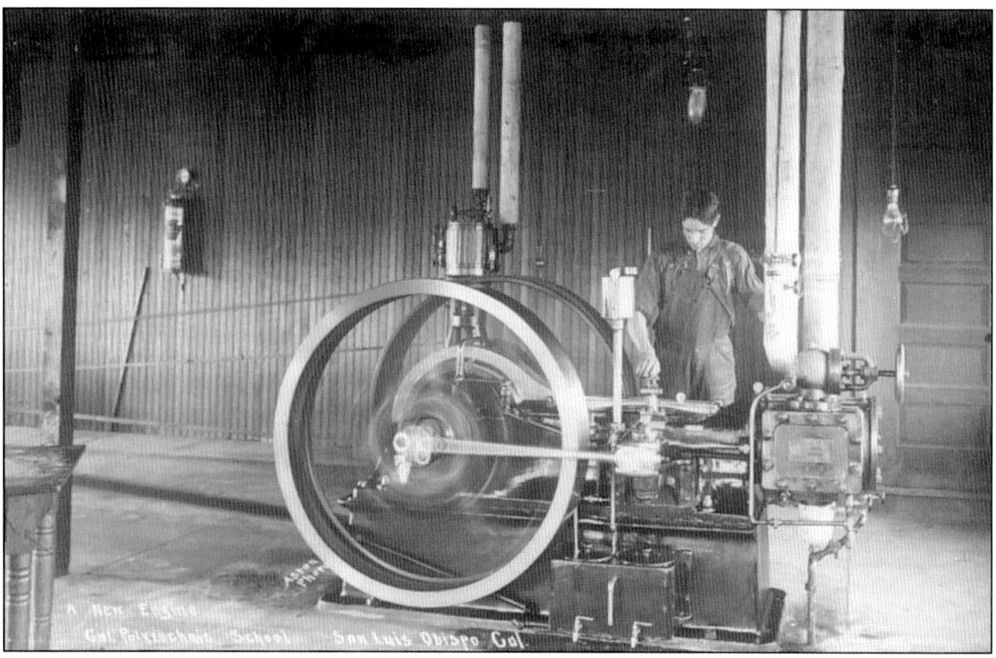

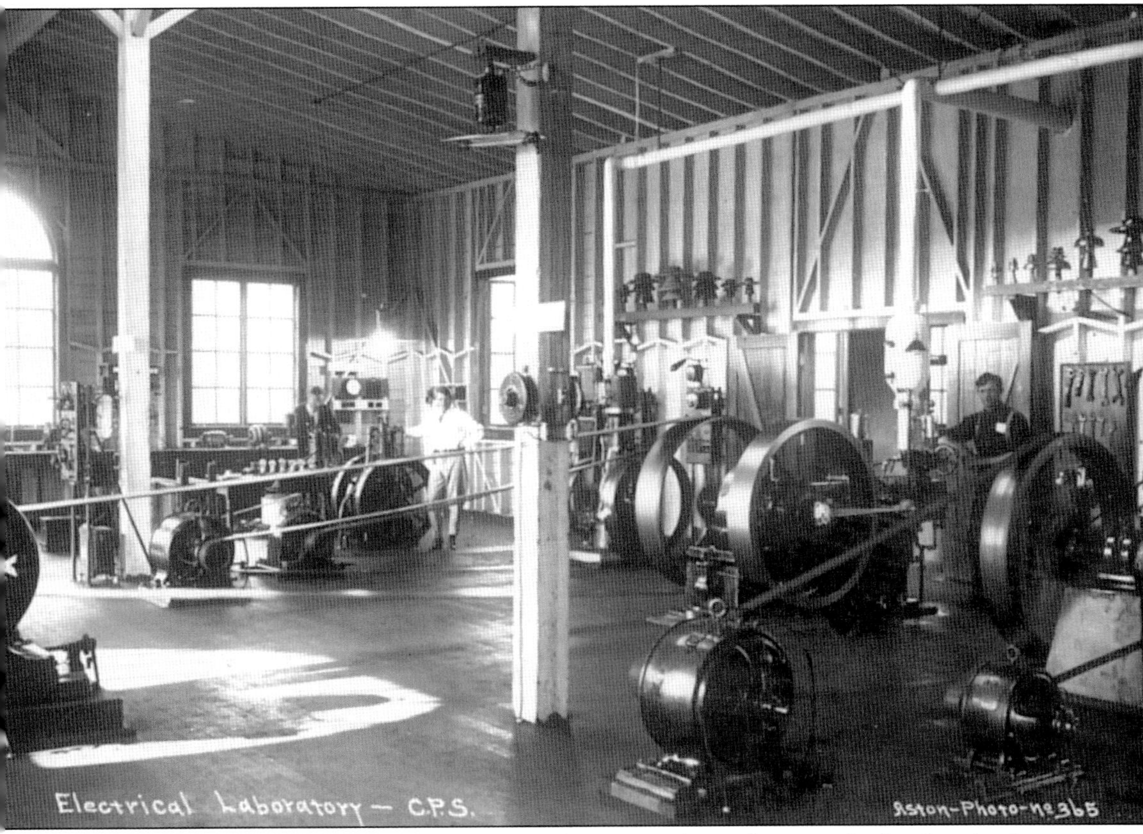

This image of the Electrical Laboratory at Cal Poly in 1908 shows the necessity for the school to have more than a few belts on reserve. Notice the well-seasoned students who have learned to tuck their ties inside of their shirts while working alongside these fast moving machine parts.

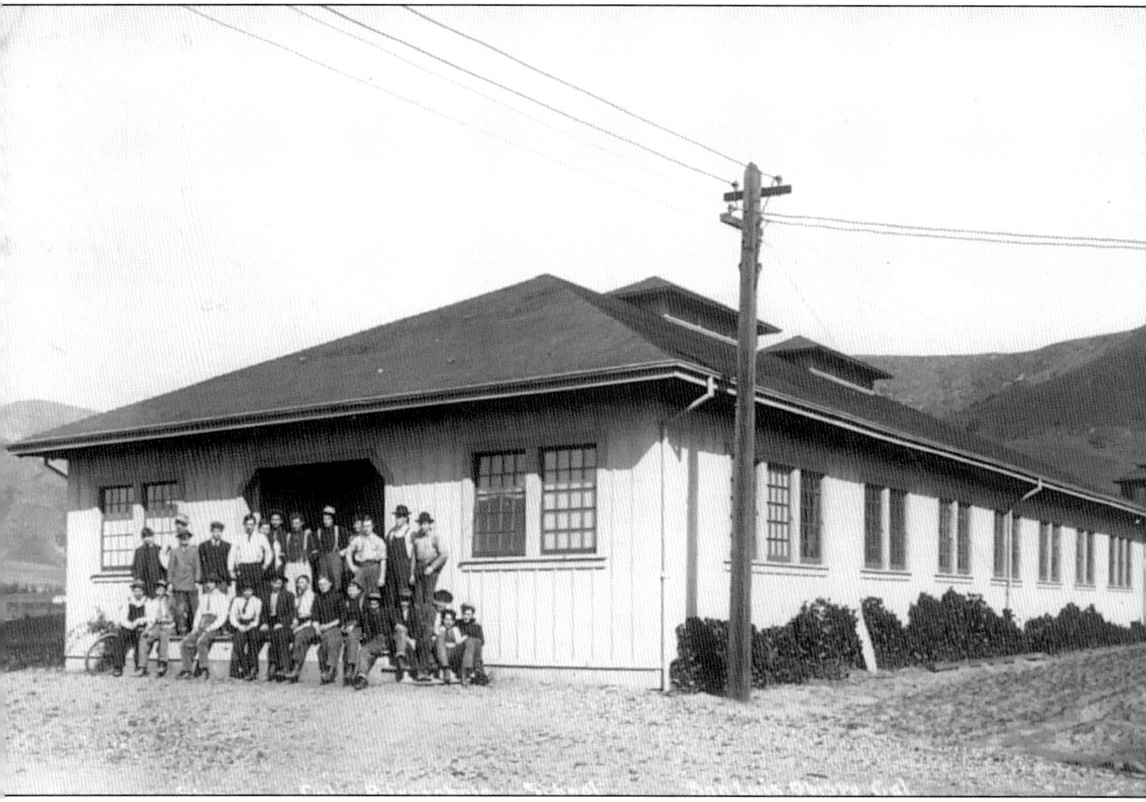

Pictured are carpentry students in front of their classrooms and labs at the carpentry shop at Cal Poly, 1907.

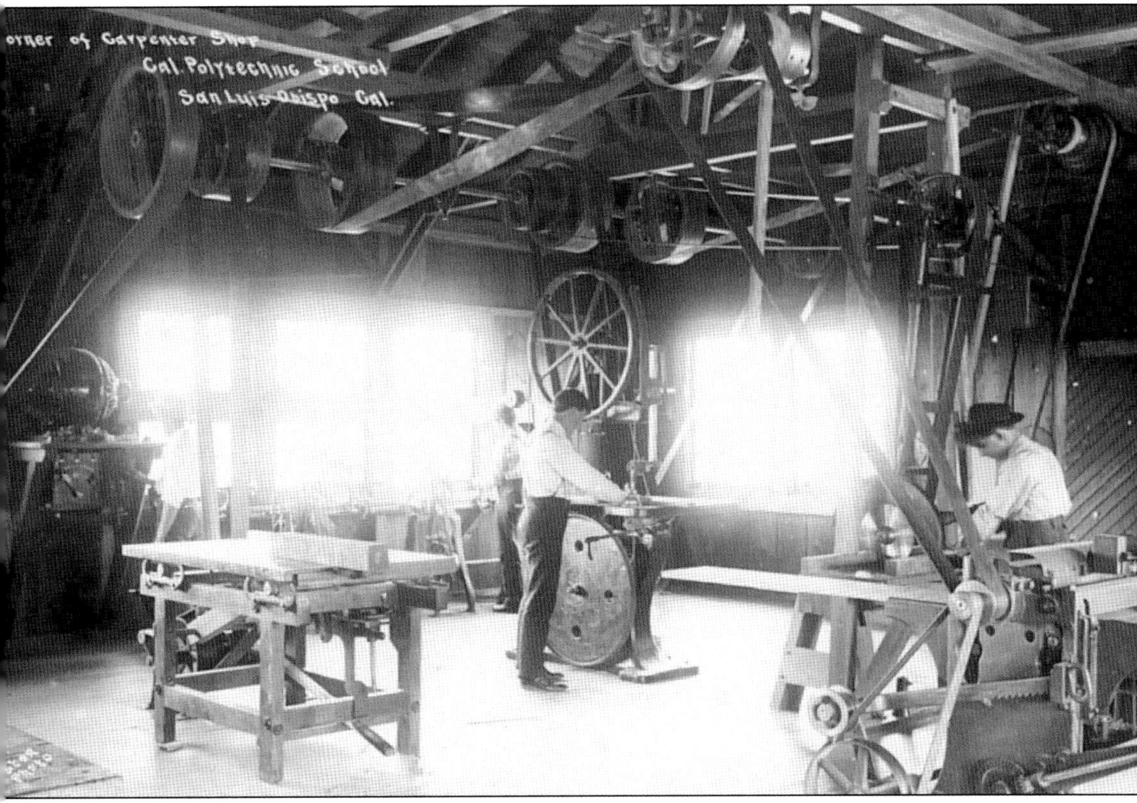

Students were responsible for the construction of all wood wares that the school needed. From new buildings to chairs and tables that filled their classrooms. Additionally, the young carpenters were able to sell their goods, which were quite often constructed to fill purchase orders by local businesses. These photos were taken in 1908.

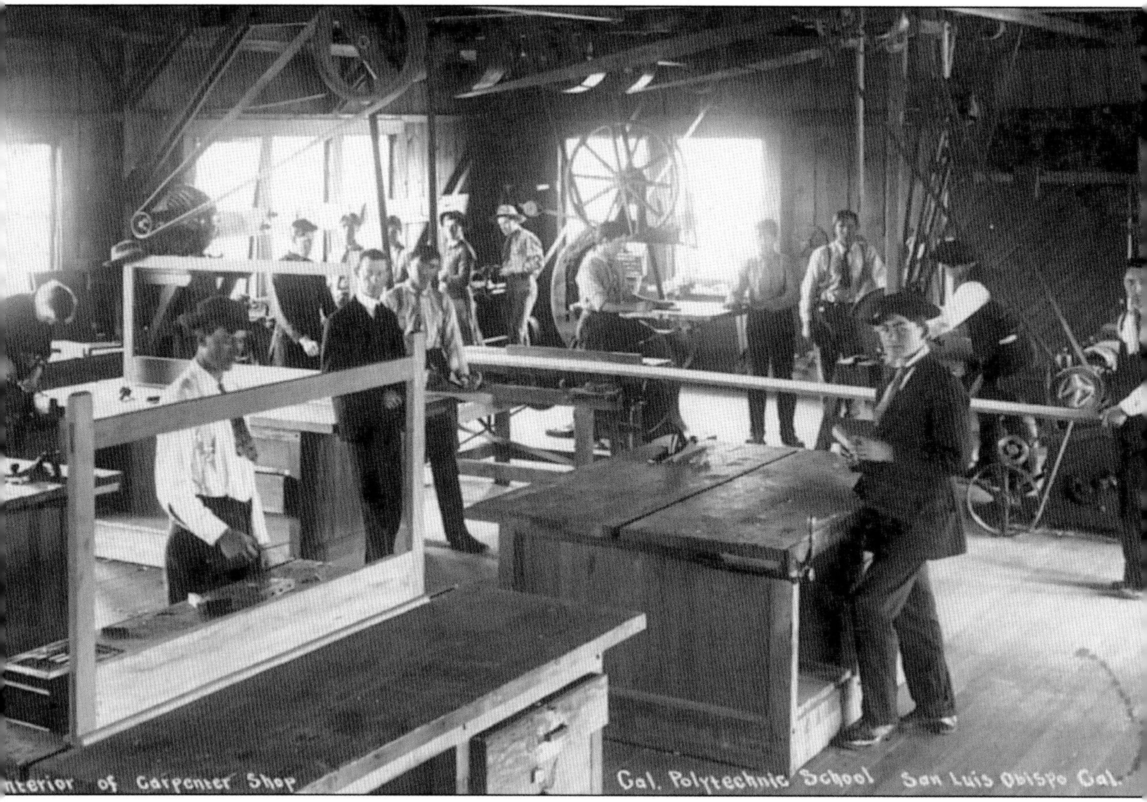

The Carpenter Shop was not simply the traditional classroom, as students worked diligently in teams, which assembled the "Modern Poultry Houses" at Cal Poly in 1910. Each six-man team was responsible for cutting the wood and constructing their own poultry house, under supervision, and all the while not just concerned with whether the chickens would come home to roost—there was the small factor of the grades!

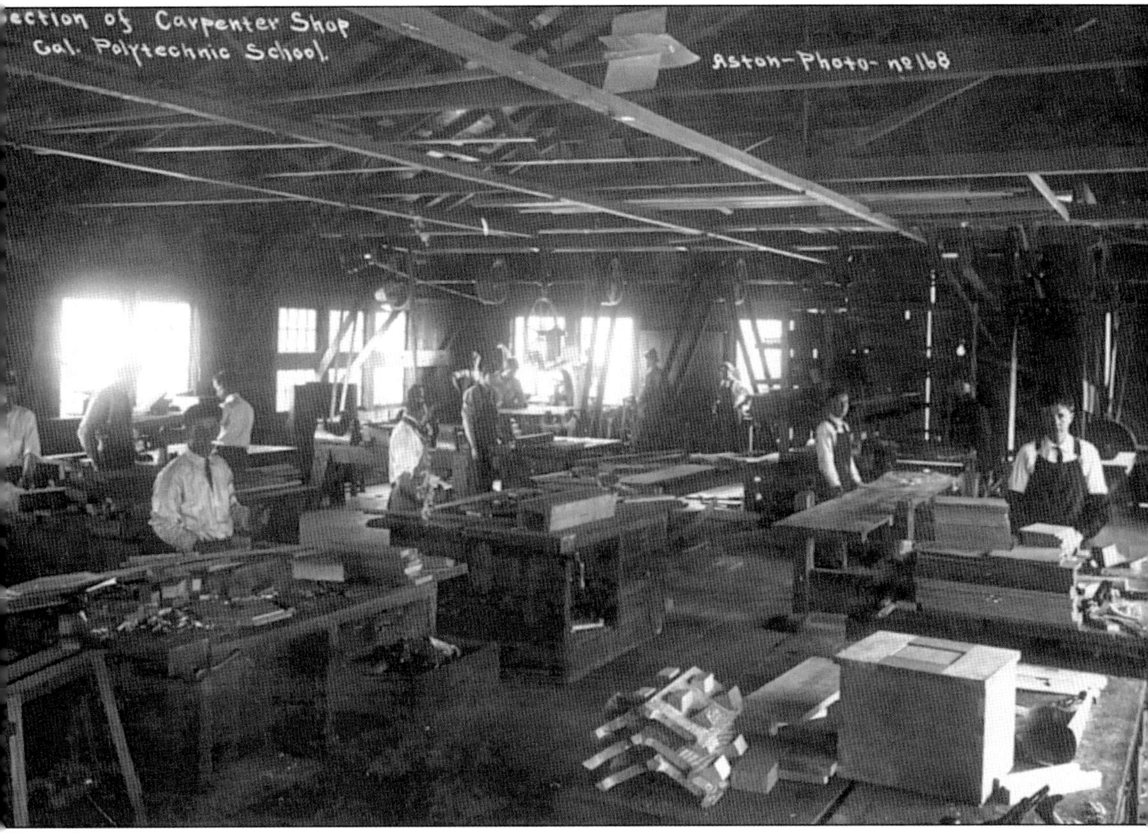

The students in the carpentry classes worked with wood at all stages of construction. From filling orders for planks to the manufacturing of completed pieces of furniture, the Cal Poly students were able to fit the bill.

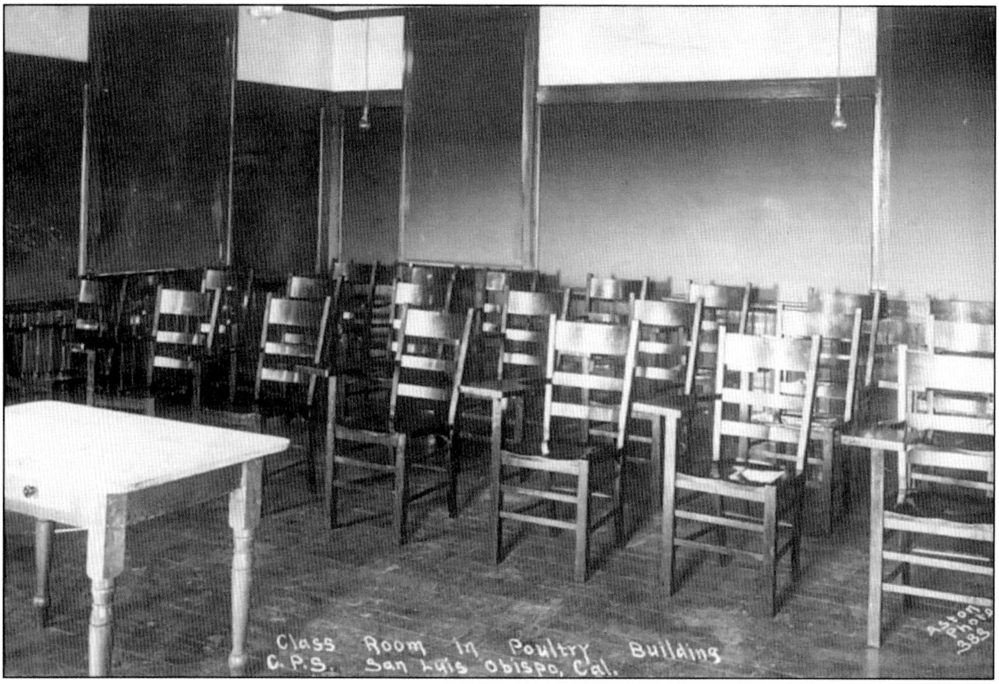

All of the chairs and tables in these two classrooms were constructed from "raw materials" and made into the finished product that allowed a class to operate, by Cal Poly students in 1909. The Poultry Building itself was left to professional construction companies, though surely the students would have liked to build their classrooms as well.

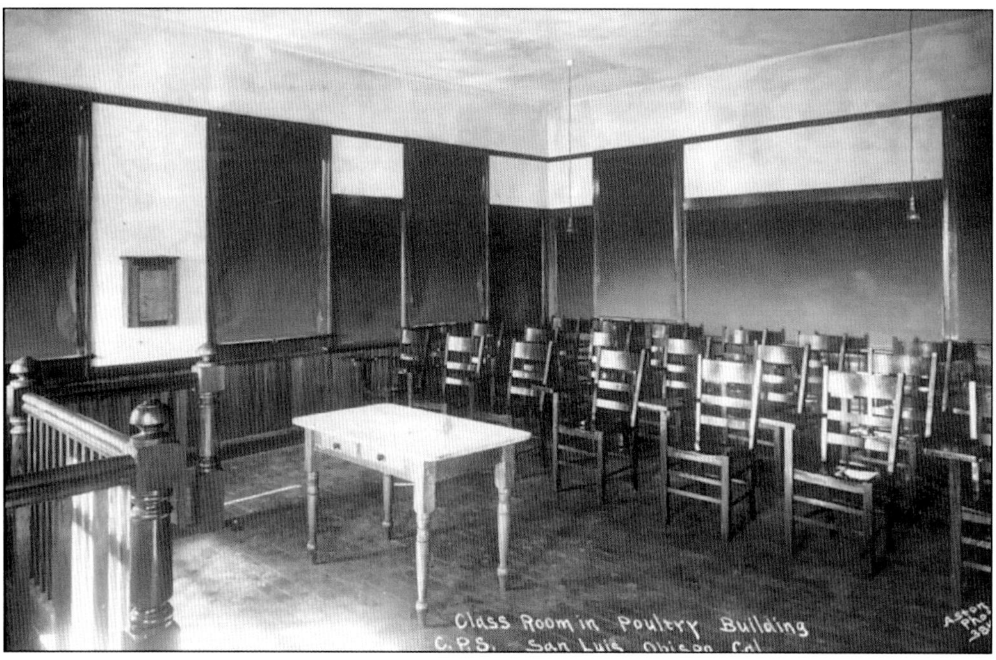

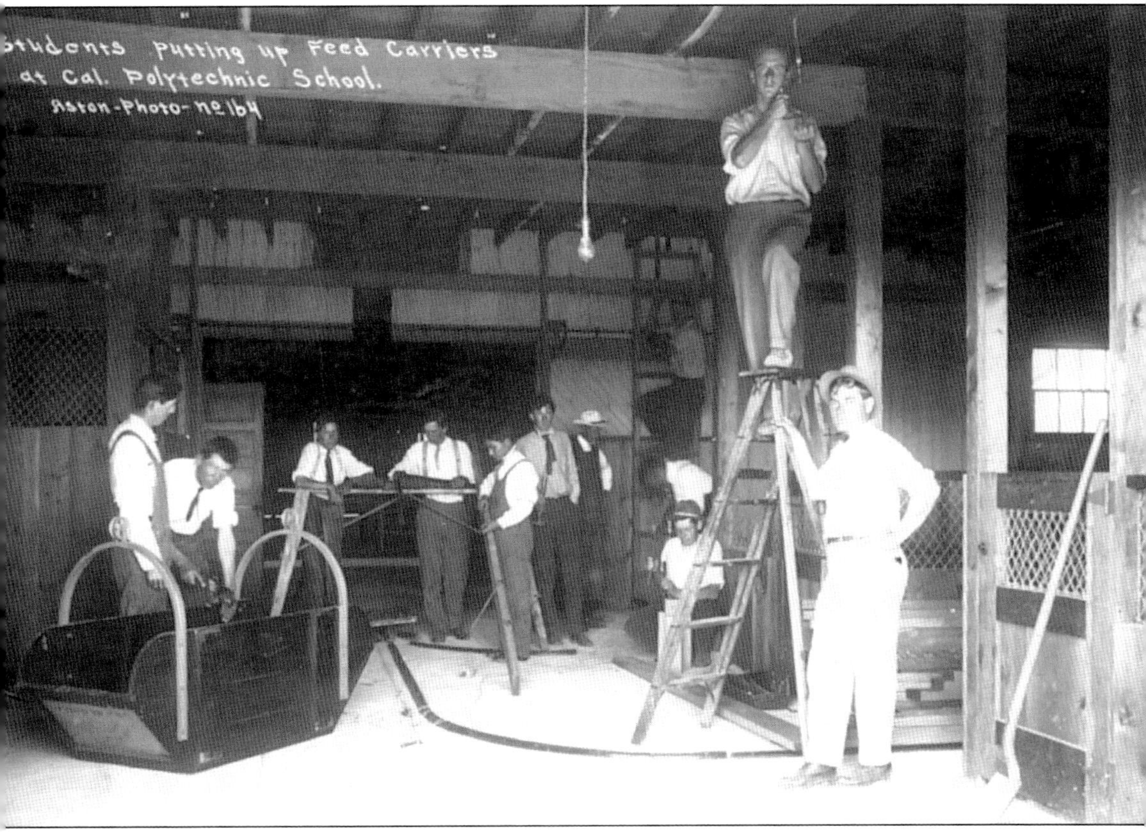

No need to call for outside help when something broke at Cal Poly. These students are building the new feed carriers for the stables in 1909.

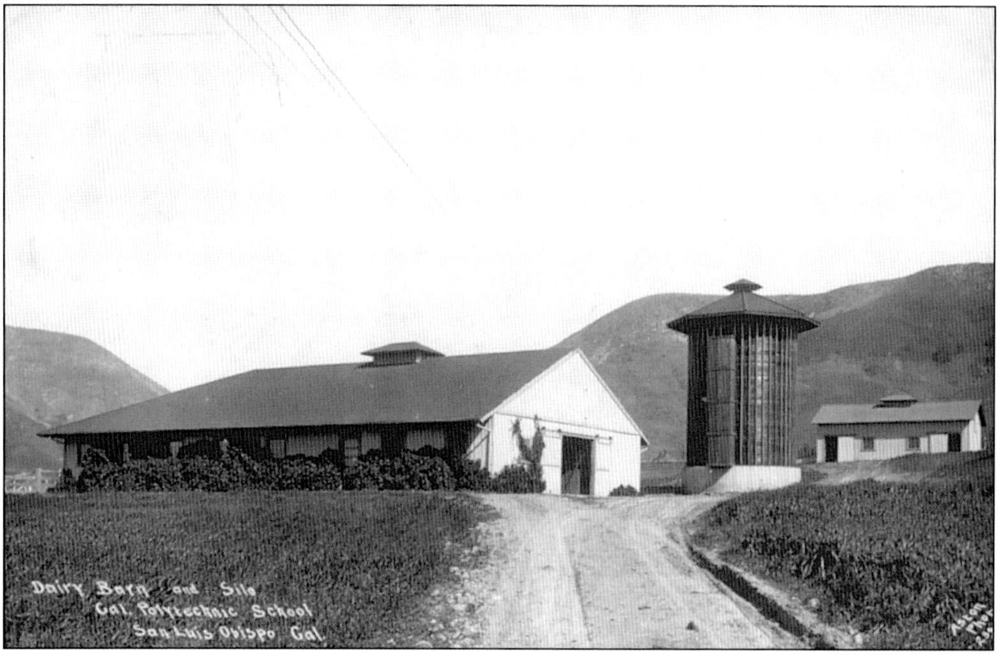

The dairy barn not only contained pigs and cows, but also the workhorses at Cal Poly. Students in the dairy arts were also instructed in the fine art of animal husbandry, 1908.

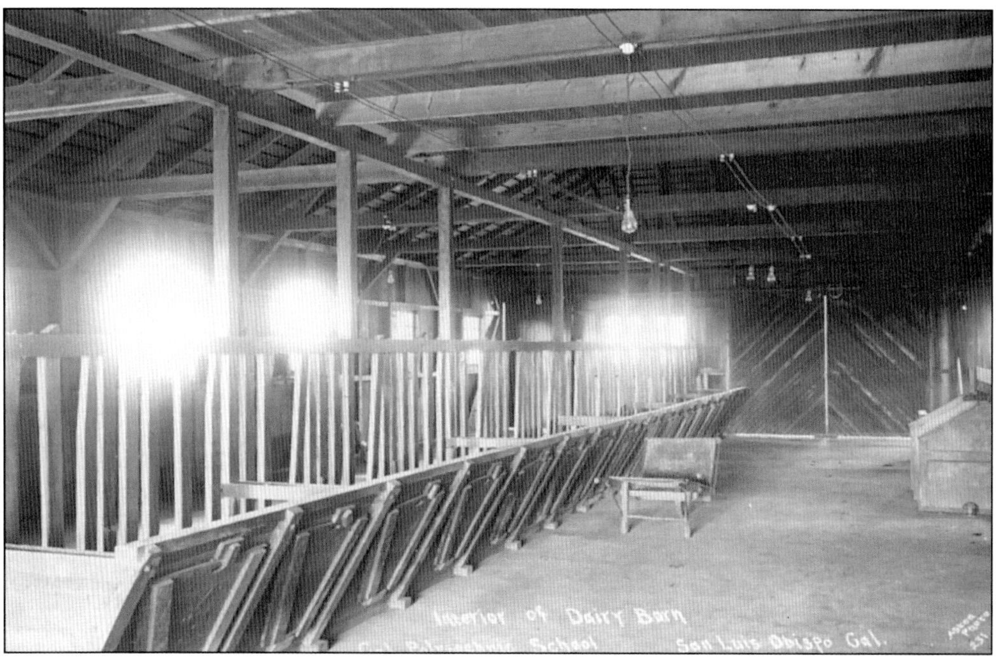

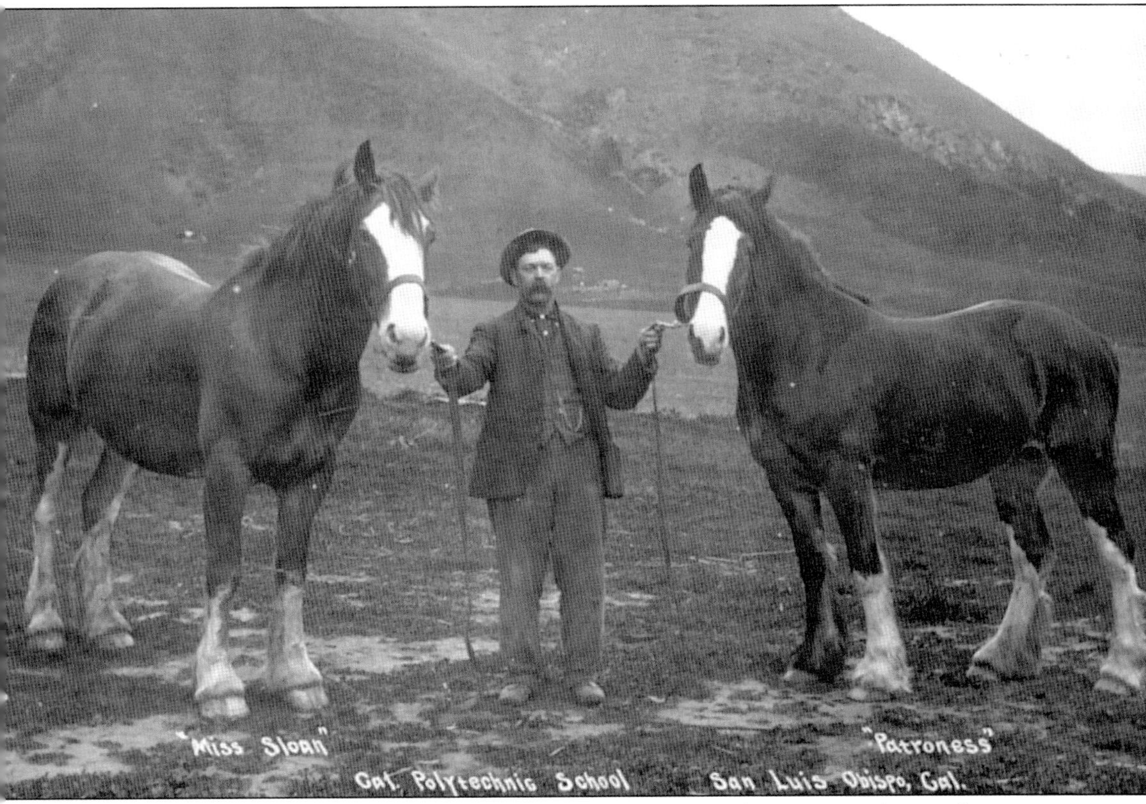

These images were taken in 1908. The man standing with the two horses, Miss Sloan and Patroness, is Dr. Anderson.

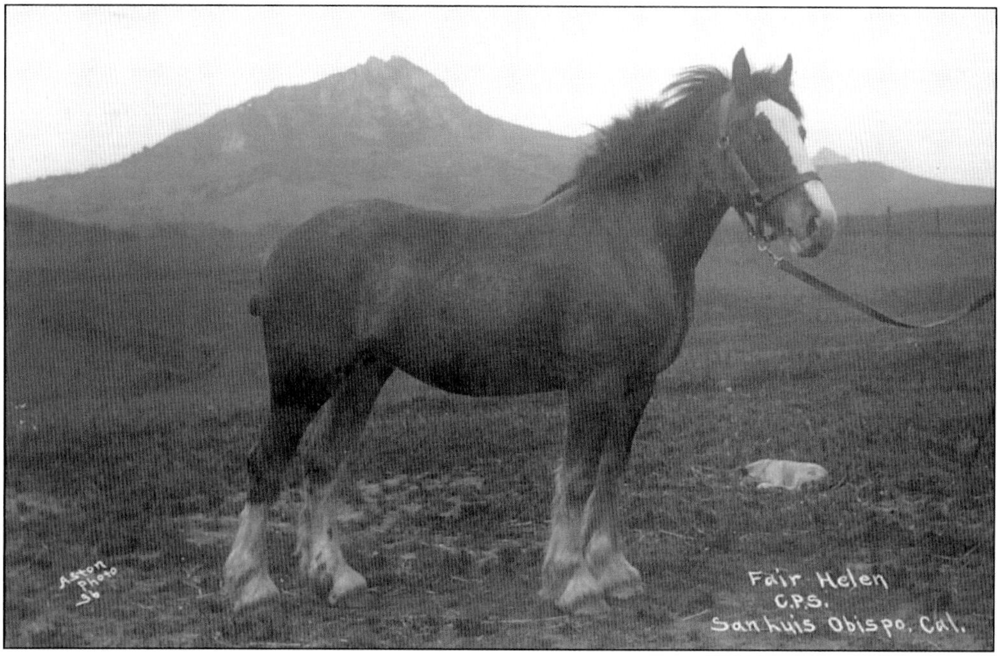

The University of California sent three heavy draft horses to Cal Poly as a gift in 1908. Two of the horses were Clydesdales, which was a relatively new breed of horse at the beginning of the 20th century. This Scottish breed of draft horse dates back to the 1830s, with an official Clydesdale Horse Society not forming until 1877. Clydesdales were bred with the intent of developing an active breed of workhorse—just what the young Cal Poly needed. Fair Helen, pictured above, measured just 14 hands in this picture, and Patroness measured 13 hands. In 1910, two years after these photos were taken, each horse measured 17 hands!

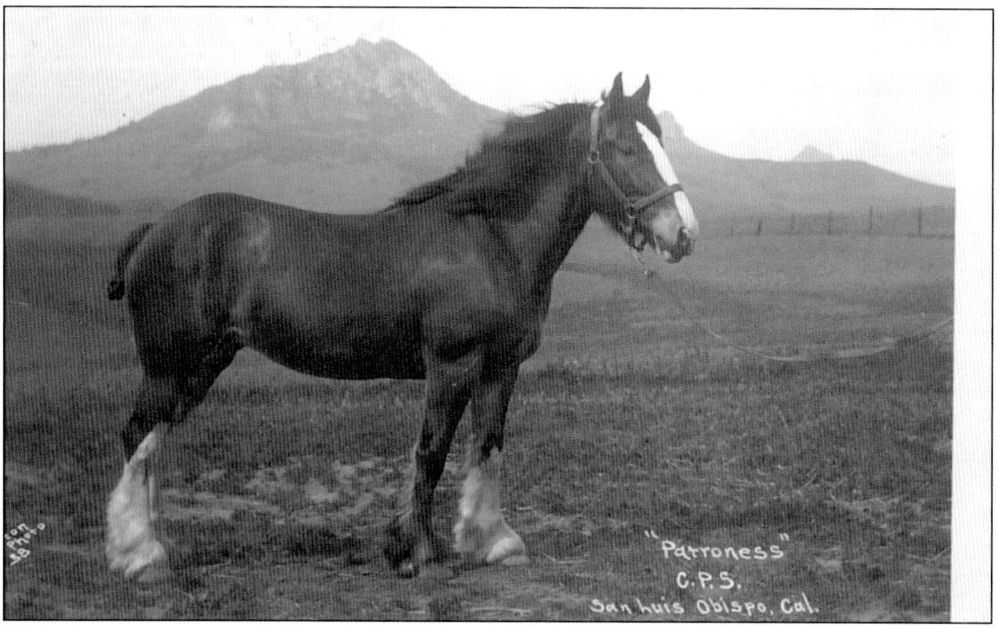

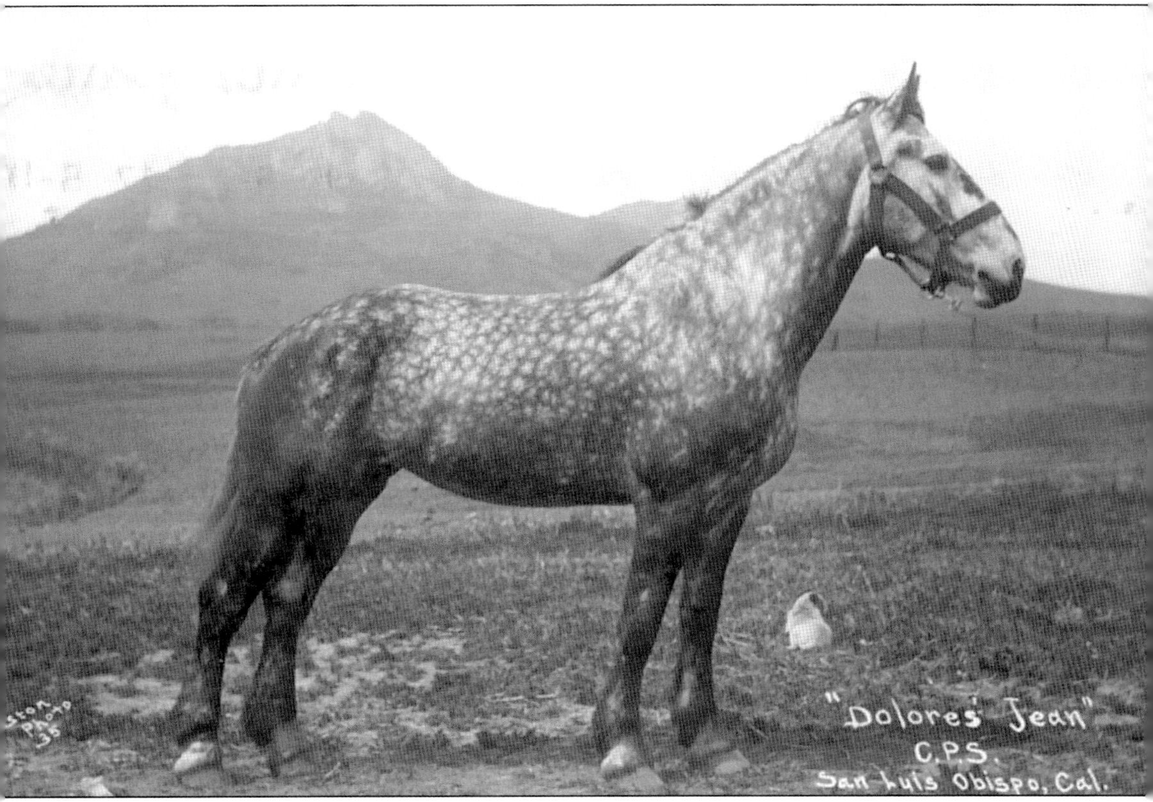

The third horse that was donated by the University of California along with the two Clydesdales in 1908 was this Kladruber, affectionately known as Dolores Jean. The Kladruber breed of horse, although a workhorse, was more of a harness horse than a heavy draft horse. This breed has its origin in the 16th century, with the Holy Roman Emperor, the Hapsburg Maximilian II, developing what he considered to be a favorable coach horse for pulling the ceremonial Royal carriage, "Tall, Strong, Fast, and Beautiful" were the criteria, and the Kladruber was the result. When she arrived at Cal Poly Dolores Jean measured 15 hands in this 1908 picture, by 1910 she measured 17.5 hands.

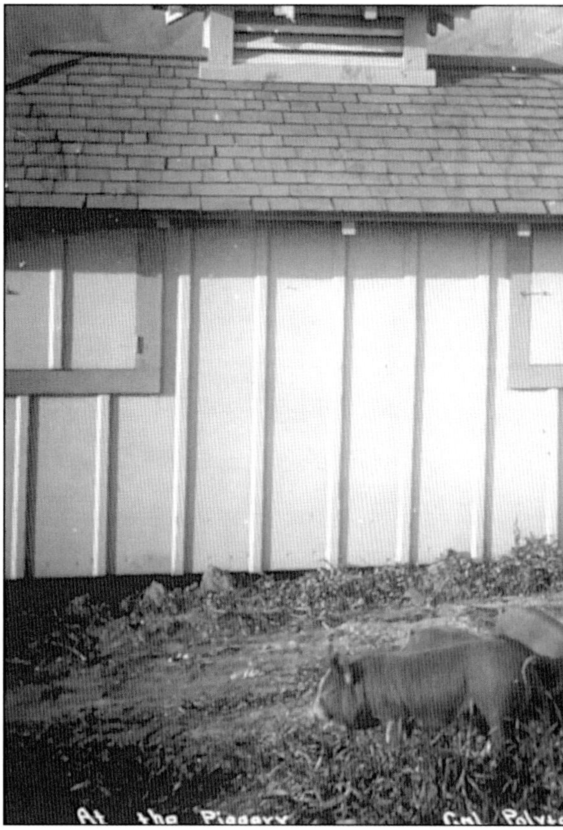

The dark cows in the background of this picture are Swedish Red cows, a breed of cow well known for its lactating potential. A great deal of Polytechnic Butter in the early stage here!

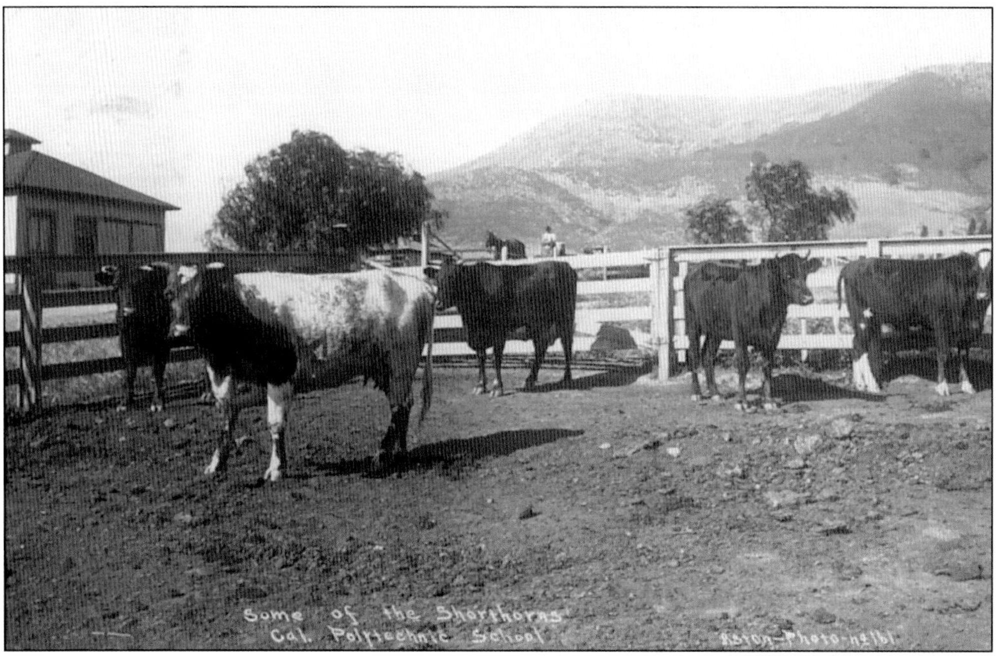

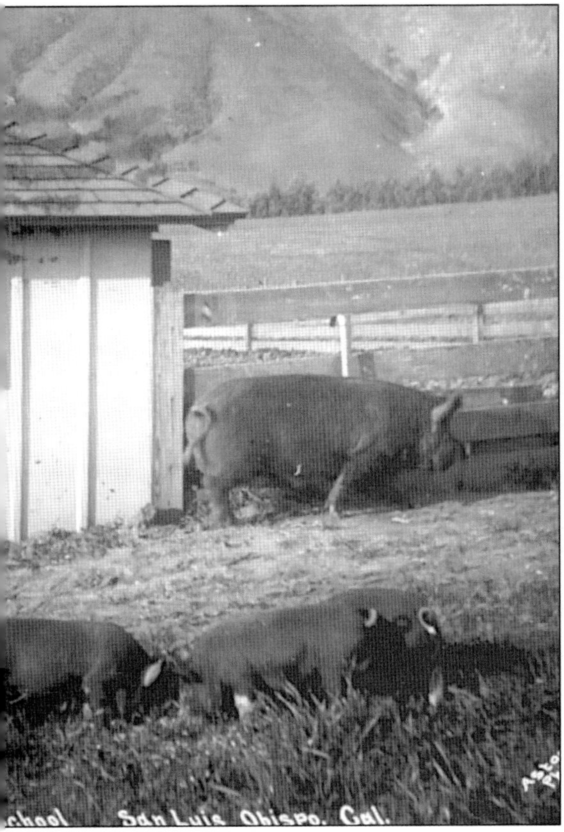

This Danish Jersey cow was one of several breeds of cattle that the students at Cal Poly were managing in the areas of dairy production and animal husbandry. The Danish Jersey cows have traditionally been known for their higher than average butterfat content in their milk. This particular Danish Jersey cow recorded nearly 2 percent of fat in her milk in 1909, which was the record at Cal Poly that year for the Danish Jerseys.

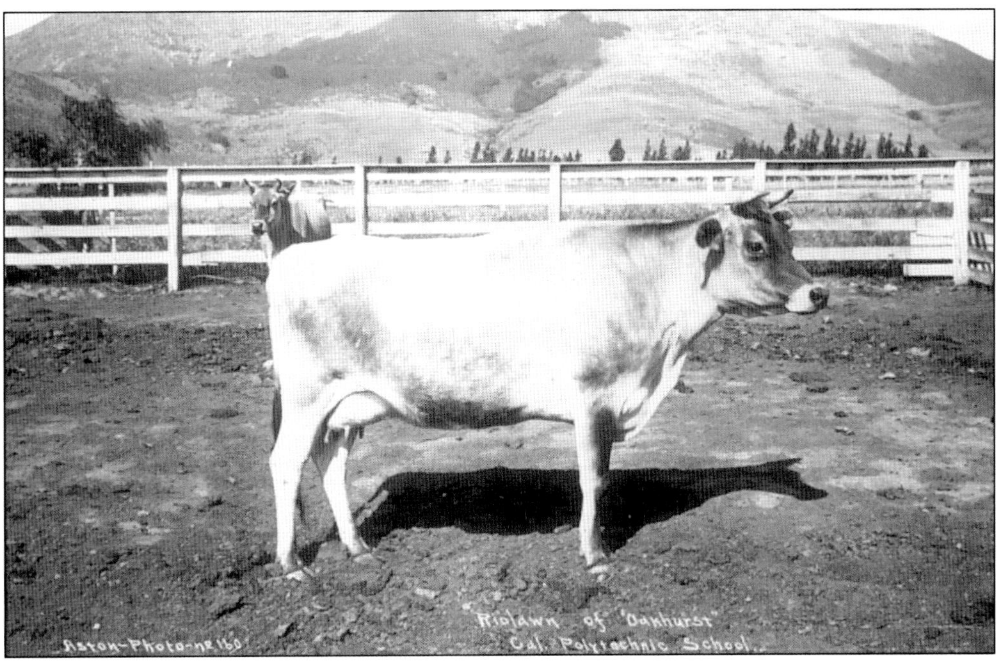

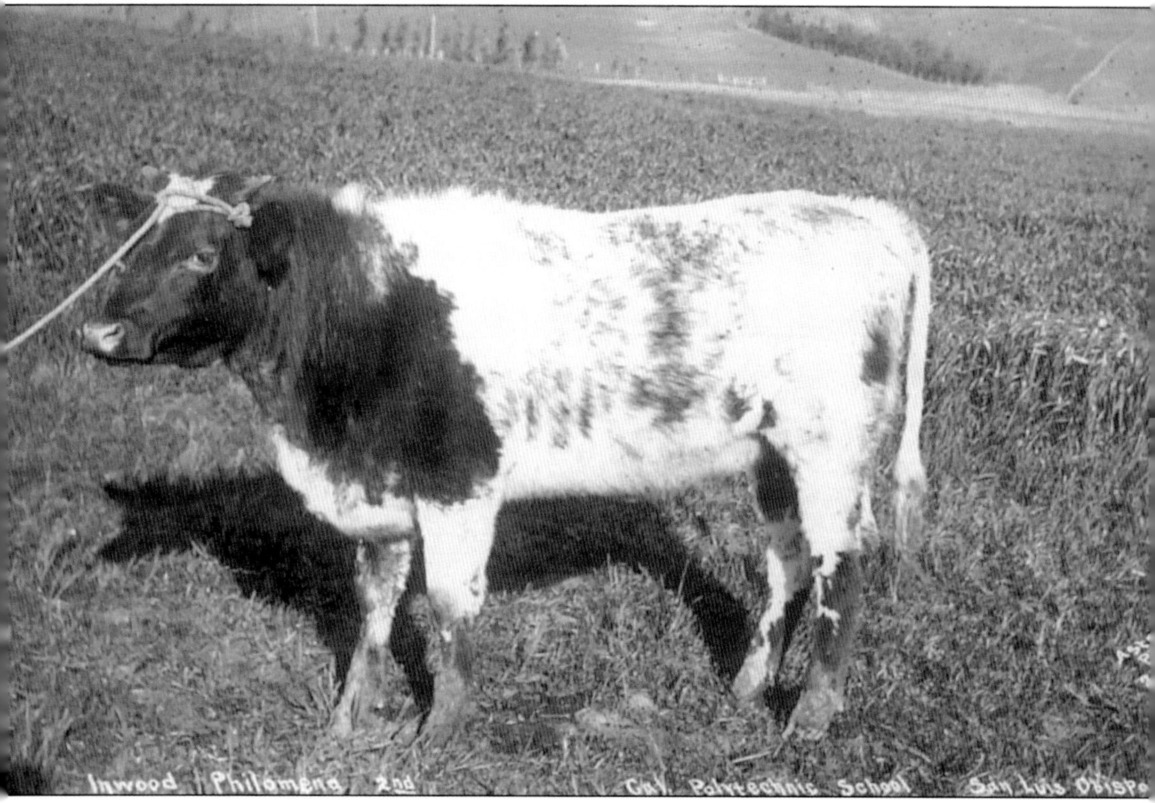

This Northern Shorthorn was the prize calf at Cal Poly the year prior to this picture. The Dairy Shorthorn not only produces good beef steers but the cows yield useful butcher carcasses at the end of their milking life. This is one of the oldest of the British breeds, which adapted quite well to the coastal rolling hills of San Luis Obispo.

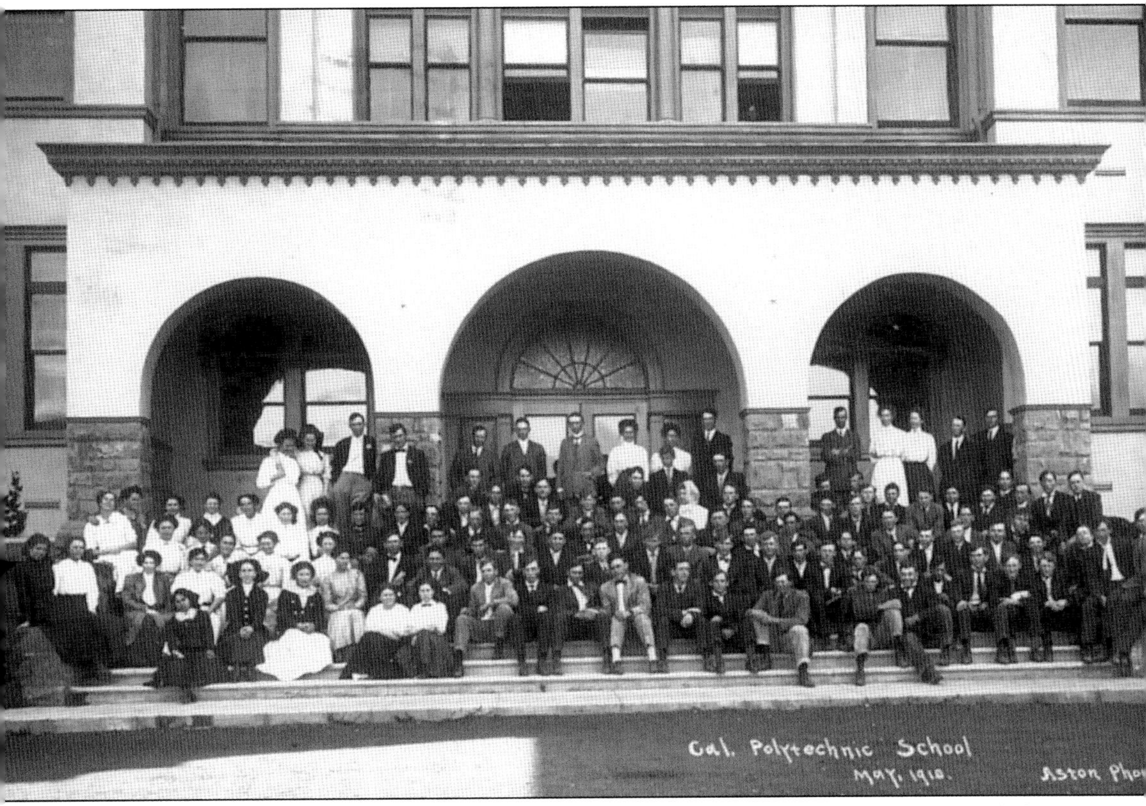

The end of the school year at Cal Poly, 1910, and the final class photo of the year. Behind the students, standing, is the faculty of the school.

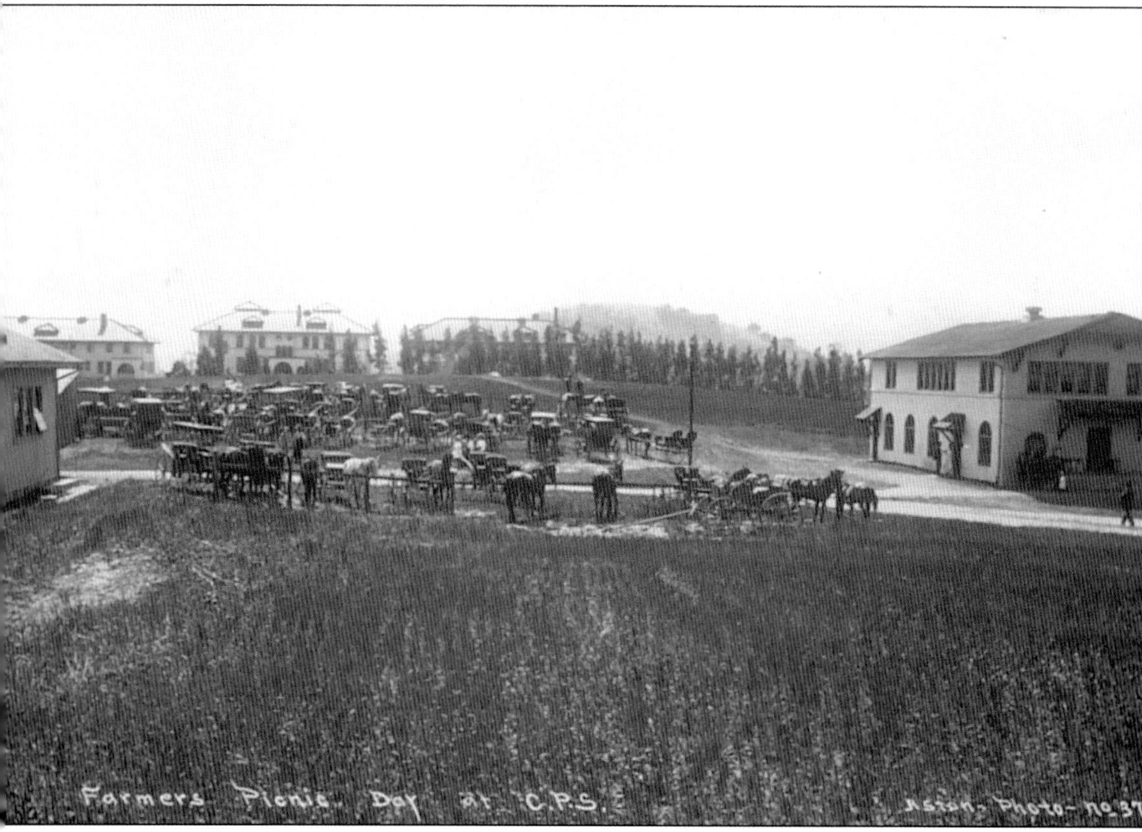

The Farmer's Picnic Day marks the beginning of the new school year, 1911.

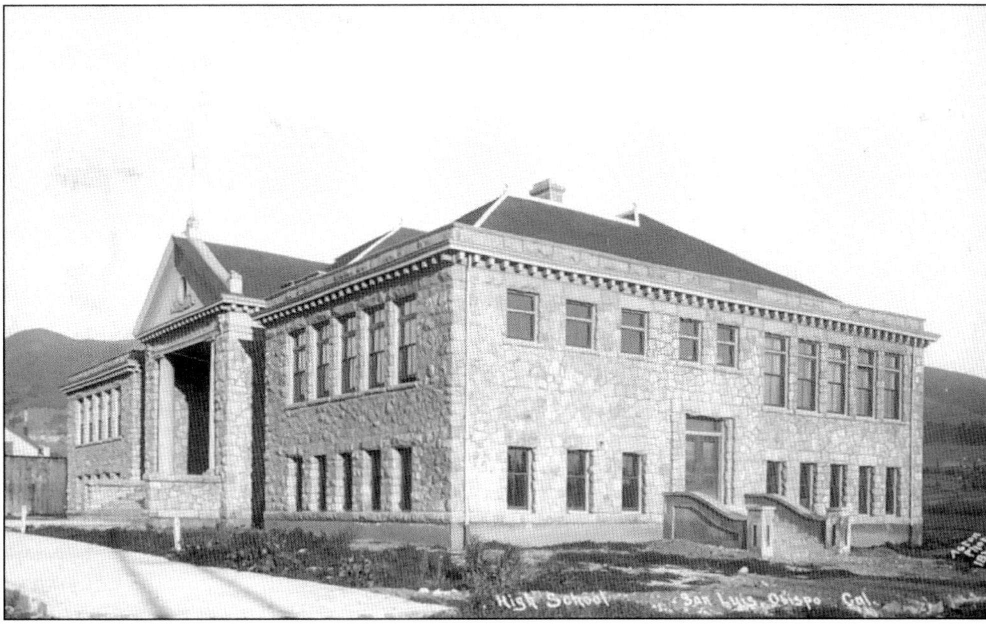

As Cal Poly became more of a Junior College, much of its high school duties were absorbed by the new high schools, built in 1908 through 1910, and 1928 respectively.

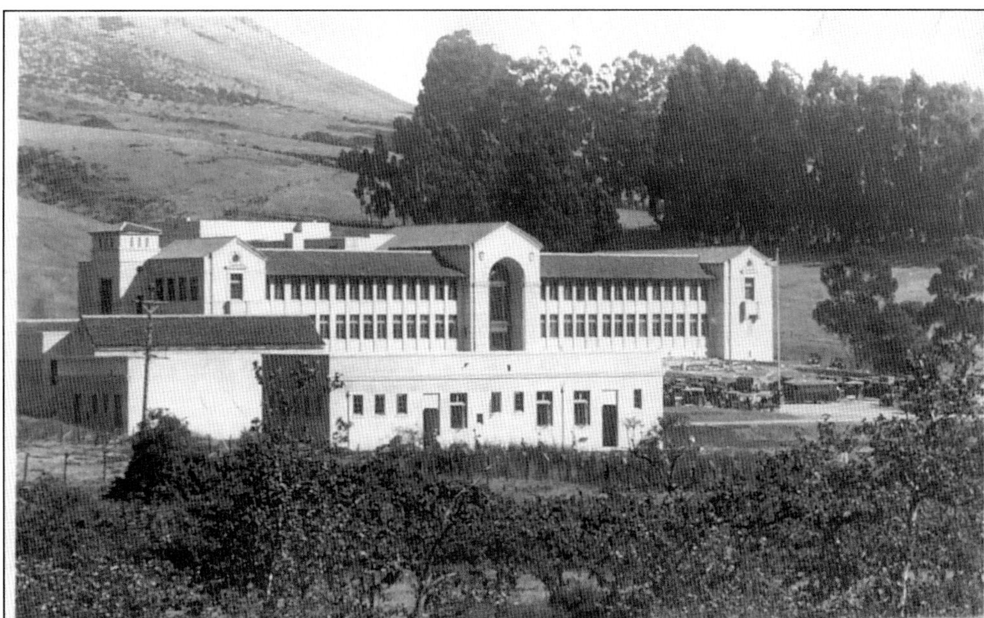

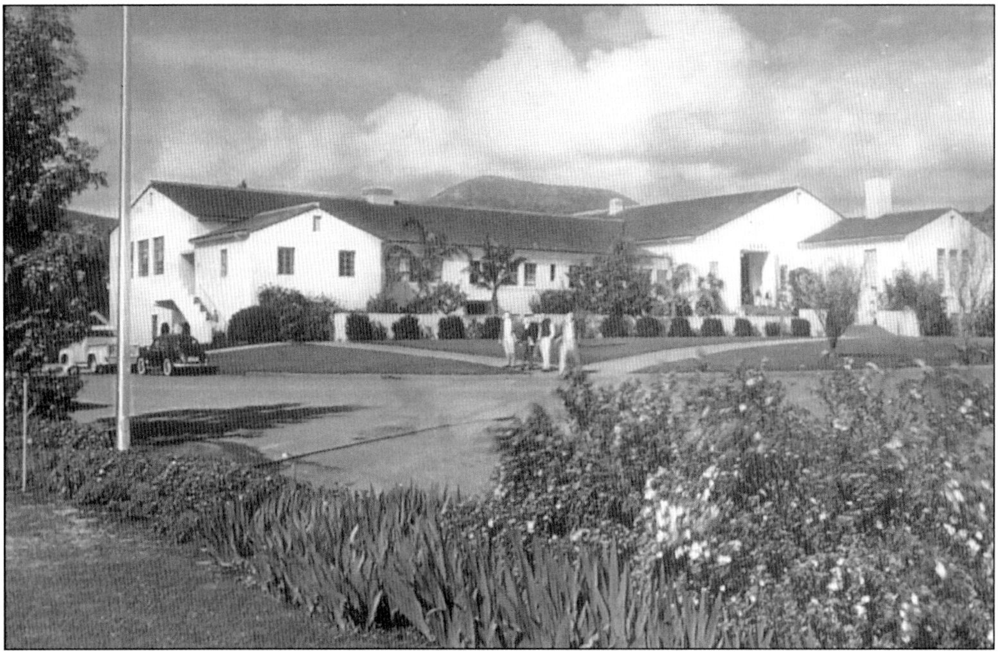

In 1956 Cal Poly officially became a coeducational state college, with an enrollment of nearly 4,000 students. Over the next 45 years Cal Poly has emerged as one of the crown jewels of the California State University System. These postcards commemorate the transformation of Cal Poly into the California State Polytechnic College, in 1956.

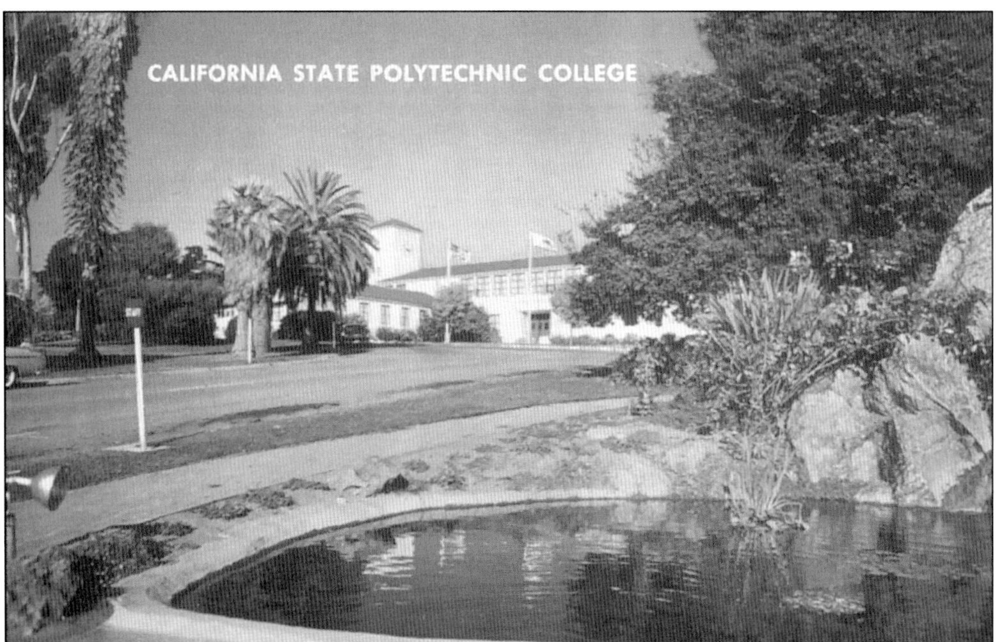